W9-BVJ-423

STANLEY KUNITZ

COLUMBIA INTRODUCTIONS TO
TWENTIETH-CENTURY
AMERICAN POETRY

JOHN UNTERECKER, GENERAL EDITOR

STANLEY KUNITZ

AN INTRODUCTION
TO THE POETRY

GREGORY ORR

COLUMBIA UNIVERSITY PRESS

NEW YORK

1985

The Andrew W. Mellon Foundation, through a special grant, has assisted the press in publishing this volume.

Library of Congress Cataloging in Publication Data

Orr, Gregory.
  Stanley Kunitz : an introduction to the poetry.

  (Columbia introductions to twentieth-century American poetry)
  Includes index.
    1. Kunitz, Stanley, 1905–   —Criticism and interpretation. I. Title. II. Series.
  PS3521.U7Z84 1985   811'.52   84-23213
  ISBN 0-231-05234-0

COLUMBIA UNIVERSITY PRESS
NEW YORK   GUILDFORD, SURREY

PRINTED IN THE UNITED STATES OF AMERICA

*Clothbound editions of Columbia University Press books are
Smyth-sewn and printed on permanent and durable acid-free paper*

COLUMBIA INTRODUCTIONS TO
TWENTIETH-CENTURY
AMERICAN POETRY

Contents

JOHN UNTERECKER

Foreword

There are three entrances into the house of poems Stanley Kunitz has built for us. Though each of them opens into the same set of rooms, it is a radically different experience to enter a house from front door, side door, or back door. No one is more aware of that than Kunitz himself, for at one time or another he has greeted his reader at each entrance.

Let us call front door *The Poems of Stanley Kunitz, 1928–1978*. The arrangement is chronological: a reverse chronology, as Kunitz points out in his Author's Note, "beginning with new poems and stepping back to my start." A reverse chronology, and a long one: fifty years of very solid accomplishment. But skimpy. On an average, three poems or translations to a year. Of our major poets, only Elizabeth Bishop matches his thrifty production.

If we take Kunitz most literally (though I suspect—for what seems to me good reason—that we should look only for approximate chronology), poem #1 of the 1978 volume, "The Knot," represents the book's most recent work and poem #146, "Vita Nuova," represents its oldest.

The experience of reading the poems in this now-to-then sequence is exhilarating. It's precisely the right way for someone unfamiliar with the poetry to begin. For in the opening section Kunitz is at the height of his power. The poems—many of them at least—seem straightforward; the syntax is on the whole uncomplicated and the voice comfortably contemporary. The man standing in the doorway is one anybody can recognize: the artist in his seventies looking back to discover the central design of his life, a man preparing for us an ordering and a summing up: a definition close to (but insistently not at) final shape.

As the reader looking at the poems for the first time makes his way through the book, the intricate complications of middle life and middle poetry gradually give way to the assurance and vanity of youth. This early poetry, a poetry geared to astonish us into admiration, is superficially far more ingenious than the late work.

And finally there is "Vita Nuova," the film run backwards to what the author contends is his starting place. This remarkable poem that is an end—and, of course, a beginning—is both brash and demanding. Young Kunitz knows that up-to-date poetry of the twenties will be dense, full of verbal pyrotechnics, and deftly allusive. He is also, however, even at the start enough of a poet to realize that allusion—though it lets us credit a tradition—ultimately has to transform to private voice. So that a phrase that starts out reminding us of early Yeats ("I will go, unburdened, on the quiet lane/ Of my eternal kind") evolves into essential Kunitz ("till shadowless/ With inner light I wear my father's face"). And if he ends his poem with an image and a technique adapted from the English Metaphysicals of the seventeenth century ("My dark will make, reflecting from your stones,/ The single beam of all my life intense"), we realize that in the context of the entire poem the Donne-like material changes into something far less metaphysical than fresh, immediate, and strange.

Front door is for a first reading, a first discovery of Kunitz. But it is of almost no value at all as a critical approach. No one is going to find a backwards-tracking commentary on the poetry of any real use at all. Here, side door and back door offer more manageable entrances. What we are after is the architect's plan for the place and some notion of the way it was assembled.

I realize, needless to say, that I'm overworking a metaphor. But there are twenty-three explicit doors in Kunitz' collected poetry, more than two dozen implicit ones (poems of keys and keyholes, lintels, bolts, stoops, transoms, sills, portals, thresholds, etc.), and nine gates. Kunitz thrusts doors at us, many of them ominous, in so aggressive a manner as to force the image into glaring significance. I want to speak a bit about that significance in a moment or two. For now, I want to look at the side door Kunitz very deliberately opened at mid-point in his career. Let's call that entrance *Selected Poems, 1928–1958*.

Selected Poems was an extraordinary volume in that it destroyed chronology. Poems from Kunitz' first two books and more than thirty new poems were deliberately commingled into a totally anti-chronological order: what Kunitz called "groups that bear some relevance to the themes, the arguments, that have preoccupied me since I began to write."

The section titles—picked up from phrases in the poems—hint those themes: "The Serpent's Word," "The Terrible Threshold," "Prince of Counterfeits," "A World to Lose," "The Coat Without a Seam." Though these section titles offer hints, they certainly fail to offer definition.

If we can judge from reviews and even from recent critical commentary, readers sensed interrelationship within sections, all right, but they had difficulty in locating the design of the whole. And with reason. To go back to my metaphor of the doorway, the side door of the 1958 *Selected Poems* opened into a house half built.

I like to think of the completed house of Kunitz' poetry as something like the house I grew up in on Anderson Place in

Buffalo, New York. (Yes, there are almost as many houses in Kunitz' poetry as there are doors—nineteen of them. If we go on to count houses as homes, the list comes to thirty. And that excludes a whole village of cabins and log cabins, huts, inhabited caves, earth-lodges, prisons, cages, tents, mansions, managers, and nests.)

The house I grew up in had three floors (Kunitz has a poem of that title) and seventeen rooms (four of them in the basement and four in the attic). Kunitz poetry has no basement at all and only nine explicit rooms, but there are several chambers, a number of closets and halls and a vividly memorable attic.

The side door of the house I grew up in opened off the driveway onto a tiny landing halfway between the first floor and the basement. Obviously it had once been a servants' entrance and the "back" stairway that the side door led to—in my mind, a secret stair since it was the only entrance to basement and attic—was criminally narrow; we used it only to get up to the attic and, much more often, down to the washroom, the coal cellar, the cold cellar, and the "playroom" my grandfather had floored for Helen and me.

I have no notion if any of the houses Kunitz literally inhabited had a side door—probably not. But if any had a side door, it would—like ours—have offered a unique entry both to the foundations and to the architectural spine of the house: the secret, hidden stairway, blocked off by doors from prying eyes of visitors on first and second floors. Metaphorically, it is the inevitable way in toward "themes" and "arguments" that are the preoccupation of a lifetime, precisely the right place for a critic to start his work. The underpinnings of the whole building, with proper insight, should be in plain view: supporting pillars and beams, imagery and ideas, themes and arguments.

The only limitation, indeed, to *Selected Poems, 1928–1958* as an essential doorway to Kunitz' poems is that it is a midpoint volume, an unfinished Collected Works. What has been needed is for a strong critical mind to apprehend the organizational structure of the 1958 *Selected Poems* and extend it to the chronologically arranged 1978 collected poems. And this Gregory Orr has brilliantly done in the perceptive opening chapter that follows this foreword. What that chapter reveals is the structural coherence of Kunitz' work: the interrelationship between biographical, psychological, and philosophical forces that produce a body of poetry stronger and more satisfying even than the dozen individual poems every reader is likely to find remarkable or than such powerful late units as *The Testing Tree* and *The Layers.*

I stress Orr's accomplishment in this chapter because it is tempting to skim generalization in favor of line-by-line analysis of particular poems: "Don't bother me with abstractions, give me the straight word on 'The Magic Curtain.' " But in Kunitz' collected poems, the straight word is contingent on our apprehension of the syntax of the whole volume. Until we see the architectural plan, we can have no real sense of the function of beams and bearing walls, let alone floorboards and nails. What Orr has done for us is to uncover the essential patterns that were hinted in *Selected Poems* and then in part disguised by the reverse chronology of the collected poems of 1978.

Once those patterns—those themes and arguments—are clearly seen, then Orr can treat the individual volumes historically, starting with Kunitz' first book and working forward to *The Layers.* And the wise reader will follow along with him to come finally to that figure in the front door looking back toward genesis.

I had said I wanted to speak a bit more about the house with many doorways that Kunitz builds for us, because it seems to me that dominant (sometimes obsessive) imagery can tell us a great deal about a poet. Everybody nowadays knows about Yeats' birds and trees. They are inescapable once you've spotted them, as inescapable as the stars that impressed Yeats himself in reading through Shelley's poetry or the multitude of forges an observant reader sees in Blake's collected poems, the water imagery in Elizabeth Bishop's, the alternate imagery of tame and wild nature in the poems of Kunitz' friend Theodore Roethke.

Imagery of this sort not only links poem to poem but can set a barely audible tonality that manipulates our response even though some manipulators may themselves not realize quite what they are manipulating. (Elizabeth Bishop once told me, for example, that she had no consciousness of the omnipresence of water imagery in her poetry until an aunt, rather late in Bishop's career, remarked on it.) There is no question, however, that so self-conscious a poet as Stanley Kunitz knows what he is doing and why.

Gregory Orr discusses some of the thematic roles of house imagery throughout his book and, in his opening chapter, linking it—as does Kunitz—to a significant tree-of-life pattern that moves through a number of poems. (Someone, incidentally, should write a really comprehensive article on the ways Kunitz and Roethke share both imagery of enclosure [houses, rooms, walls, halls, doors, windows, etc.] and imagery of field, forest, pond, and garden—for altogether different ends.) Here, however, I want to look at doors and a body of associated imagery for tonality alone: the feeling that is gradually built up in the reader, whether the persona of Kunitz' poetry is looking in or looking out, whether he is spied on or is spying. And already I've anticipated a pattern: Kunitz' doors are less for going in or coming out than for discoveries—sometimes terrorizing ones.

Let us look at a few of these ominous exits and entrances chronologically, starting from the back of the 1978 volume and working forward to page one.

"Master and Mistress" (p. 233), toward the end of Kunitz' book, *Intellectual Things*, begins with a confrontation of ghosts:

a ghostlike speaker and a figure we will in later poems come to
recognize as his suicide father: "As if I were composed of dust
and air,/ The shape confronting me upon the stair/ . . . Moved
through my middle flesh. I turned around,/ Shaken, and it was
marching without sound/ Beyond the door." The crucial door in
that poem, however, is not the one through which the ghost
leaves the house but rather the doorway directly into the speaker's heart: "The ghost/ Knocked on my ribs, demanding . . . /
'Shall I be fed?' " But though he is offered both body and blood,
ambiguously the ghost rebuffs the speaker, pointing out that already flesh and heart have been "given."

If other exits and entrances in *Intellectual Things* are not
quite so ominous, they are certainly ominous enough. In "Ben-
ediction" (p. 229), we are warned to "Admonish from [our] door/
The hypocrite and liar." In "Deciduous Branch," (p. 200) the
persona is kept awake "hearing the drip/ Upon my sill; thinking,
the sun/ Has not been promised." In "Poem" (p. 198), he records a dream of his birth-burial, a rebirth to a mother's rejection, and a consequent self-burial: "Softly grieving, ironic at the
gates of horn,/ I took my baffled head and buried it under the
corn." "For the Word Is Flesh" (p. 190) returns to the dead father for subject matter and ends with another birth/death en-
tranceway: "Let sons learn from their lipless fathers how/ Man
enters hell without a golden bough."

Kunitz' first book establishes the image of the ominous door.
His second moves it into prominence. The last two stanzas of
the last poem of *Passport to the War*, "Open the Gates" (p. 184),
demands that we acknowledge its significance:

> Here at the monumental door,
> Carved with the curious legend of my youth,
> I brandish the great bone of my death,
> Beat once therewith and beat no more.

The hinges groan: a rush of forms
Shivers my name, wrenched out of me.
I stand on the terrible threshold, and I see
The end and the beginning in each other's arms.

In *Passport to the War* almost every exit and entrance is "terrible":

Inside, a hundred doors by which to leave;
Outside, you never can come in again.
("The Harsh Judgment," p. 165)

Of those that stood in my doorway, self-accused,
Besmeared with failure in the swamps of trade,
One put a gun in his examiner's hand,
Making the judgment loud; another squats
Upon the asylum floor and plays with toys,
Like the spiral of a soul balanced on a stone,
Or a new gadget for slicing off the thumb;
The rest whirl in the torment of our time.
("Night Letter," pp. 160–61)

I said to the watcher at the gate,
"They also kill who wait."
("The Signal from the House,"
p. 156)

You are of nature's bright unlucky brood,
Born of the drop of talent in your blood
Wherewith the gates of mystery are oiled.
Mortals will touch you and your taste be spoiled,

Witches in metals test you. I observe
Defeat, taking short cuts from nerve to nerve,
Climb through the narrow transom of your will;
And I weep, for having made you vulnerable.
("The Tutored Child," p. 155)

> I think of Pavlov and his dogs
> And the motto carved on the broad lintel of his brain:
> "Sequence, consequence, and again consequence."
> ("Reflection by a Mailbox," p. 152)

Even in such poems as "The Hemorrhage" (p. 163) where "our banished king" returns from exile to our dread, his progress is toward terrible thresholds: "Escaping, crawling down/ Ditches where papers blow,/ Smearing the sills of the town." Or in "The Old Clothes Man" (p. 168) where a house seems so totally sealed that "history stagnates," still the inhabitant must face the horror of a terrible and unexpected opening in:

> There is an ooze
> Of souls too virulent to die
>
> Contagious on the baffling walls.
> You sit and watch the ceiling crack;
> Horror sifts through and softly falls
> From worlds beyond the zodiac.

By the time Kunitz reorganized his poems thematically for 1958s *Selected Poems*, he was himself well aware of the structural use to which he was putting dominant images, but ironically there was at least a hint in the interspersed new poems of a shifting tonality. The "feel" of *Selected Poems* was, almost entirely as a consequence of the new work, considerably less dark than that of the first two books.

It is not until the 1978 volume, however, when for the first time the new poems of the 1958 collection are isolated as a group under the title *This Garland, Danger*, that chronology lets us observe the shift in process.

There is not, needless to say, an abrupt transformation. Almost all doors still possess and will continue to possess more threat than promise:

Who enters by my door
Is drowned, burned, stung, and starred.
                    ("Hermetic Poem," p. 132)

A shameless keyhold god
Keeps spying on my worst . . .
                    ("Revolving Meditation," p. 143)

Citizens, close
Your doors; be warned; a man has lost
His dog, suspected to be mad . . .
. . . .
"Rover!" I call my fourfoot home,
Whose only language is a growl;
Dig up old bones, but he won't come
That chose the world: it is more foul.
                    ("Rover," p. 131)

The thing that eats the heart comes wild with years.
It died last night, or was it wounds before,
But somehow crawls around, inflamed with need,
Jingling its medals at the fang-scratched door.

We were not unprepared: with lamp and book
We sought the wisdom of another age
Until we heard the action of the bolt.
                    ("The Thing That Eats the Heart," p. 12)

Already the iron door of the north
Clangs open: birds, leaves, snows
Order their populations forth,
And a cruel wind blows.
                    ("End of Summer," p. 119)

But something new really does intrude. Although the iron
door of the north does clang open, admitting its cruel wind, the
poem itself is a poem of the seasons—and no one can forget that
winter finally ends; spring does begin. In "Foreign Affairs" (p. 108)

a poem about domestic quarrels, a slammed door ends up ajar
enough to acknowledge the possibility of reconciliation:

> Our exit through the slammed and final door
> Is twenty times rehearsed, but when we face
> The imminence of cataclysmic rupture,
> A lesser pride goes down upon its knees.

And the opening poem of *This Garland, Danger,* "The Science
of the Night" (pp. 97–98)—though similarly concerned with the
separate worlds of lovers—pleads, "Bring me the mornings of
the milky ways/ Down to my threshold in your drowsy eyes." A
doorway, for the first time in Kunitz's work, is a place for communion.

As if to reaffirm the changing tonality of these new poems,
"The Summing-up" (p. 140), an eight-line key poem toward the
end of this group, begins "When young I scribbled, boasting,
on my wall,/ No Love, No Property, No Wages" but ends

> Now in my prime, disburdened of my gear,
> My trophies ransomed, broken, lost,
> I carve again on the lintel of the year
> My sign: *Mobility*—and damn the cost!

Mobility linked to knowledge (often knowledge of the inev-
itability of pain) is to be characteristic of the new tonality that
informs the imagery of Kunitz' middle and old age. That in *The
Testing Tree* (1971) is still caught up in loss and anguish, but
now loss is frequently seen as a necessary prelude to enlightenment.

In the great title poem to the volume (brilliantly treated by
Orr, whose marvelously sane, marvelously insightful reading of
the text seems to me a model of critical excellence), the threshold image once more appears—at first as a half-surreal vision in

a recollection of childhood's lonely wanderings through forest-bordered fields:

> Around the bend
>   that tried to loop me home
>   dawdling came natural
> across a nettled field
> . . . .
>   and a stringy old lilac
>   more than two stories tall
> blazing with mildew
>   remembered a door in the
>   long teeth of the woods.

Though the lilac remembers the door in the woods, Kunitz remembers that once he owned "the key" to a trail "where flickering presences" of Indian ghosts gave him "right of passage." The trail in turn brings him to the testing tree itself, an "inexhaustible oak." In a sudden invocation to his father, he throws three stones that if thrown true enough can bring him love, poetry, and eternal life. One way to read the poem is as a series of transformations; in this, the last of them, the speaker is caught up in a recurring dream of his mother "in her bridal gown/ under the burning lilac." Behind her, the house is in ruins. She wears an owl's face and makes barking noises:

> Her minatory finger points.
>   I pass through the cardboard doorway
>   askew in the field
> and peer down a well
>   where an albino walrus huffs.
>   He has the gentlest eyes.

The doorway is still ominous in this poetry, but the omen comes close to revelation. For though the lilac that had first re-

membered the door "in the teeth of the woods" is now burning
and the house in ruins, and though Kunitz' owl-faced mother
has appeared under the burning lilac in her wedding gown, the
"cardboard doorway" she points to permits Kunitz for the first
time a direct, though dream-disguised, communion with the
drowned father whom in life he had never known: "He has the
gentlest eyes."

Similar threshold revelations seem promised in other poems
in *The Testing Tree*. In "The Artist" (p. 84), a memorial poem
on the suicide of Kunitz' friend Mark Rothko, Kunitz describes
paintings that grow darker each year: "They filled the walls, they
filled the room." Finally,

> he took a knife in his hand
> and slashed an exit for himself
> between the frames of his tall scenery.
> Through the holes of his tattered universe
> the first innocence and the light
> came pouring in.

In "The Illumination" (pp. 45–46), as Kunitz sits in a hotel
room cataloguing his mistakes and his failures ("a history of
shame"), Dante, "laureled and gaunt," steps through the hall
doorway:

> "I know neither the time
> nor the way
> nor the number on the door . . .
> but this must be my room,
> I was here before."
> And he held up in his hand
> the key,
> which blinded me.

And in "Journal for My Daughter" (pp. 39–44), though

Kunitz remembers the split wall of divorce ("In the crack/ of a divided house/ grew the resentment-weed"), his more valued memory is of standing in the hall outside his daughter's room, a "white-headed" prowler-protector; and later, like Coleridge, carrying his child outdoors to watch her first eclipse. ("Your far-off voice/ . . . said it was a leaf/ sliding over the light.")

Even the memory of his mother's appearances in doorways seem less threatening in these poems than before. At her worst, "mother" is now reduced to "a crack of light/ and a gray eye peeping" ("Three Floors," p. 47) or an even more innocuous voice from a hallway: " 'Be sure,' said mother briskly at the door,/ 'that you get Sonny off to school/ on time. And see that he combs his hair.' " ("The Magic Curtain," p. 66)

Only rarely in this late poetry are there moments when, as in "King of the River" (p. 53), "the doors of the senses close/ on the child within" or in "River Road" (p. 64) a memory of a failed marriage calls up a house in which Kunitz "never dared open the attic door."

By 1978 and the publication of the new poetry of the Collected Poems under the general title *The Layers*, the tonality of imagery of exits and entrances has been almost totally transformed. Even a nightmare of a death-summons ("Why does my racing heart/ shuffle down the hall for the hundredth time/ to answer the night-bell?") transforms the call to "a gentle, insistent ring" as Kunitz realizes that he is "not ready yet/ and nobody stands on the stoop." The two gates in his long and wonderful poem "Words for the Unknown Makers," a sequence of commemorative lyrics dedicated to the women responsible for creating an exhibition of eighteenth- and nineteenth-century folk art, open out not toward terror but a heavenly reunion:

> Mourn, too, for the nameless painter of the scene
> who, like them all, was born to walk a while

beside the brook whose source is common tears,
till suddenly it's time to unlatch the narrow gate
and pass through the church that is not made with walls
and seek another home, a different sky.

("Sacred to the Memory," p. 9)

Bless them and greet them as they pass from their long obscurity, through the gate that separates us from our history, a moving rainbow-cloud of witnesses in a rising hub-bub, jubilantly
turning to greet one another, this tumult of sisters. (A Blessing
of Women," p. 14)

A door slam in "Route Six" transforms into an apology: "Let's
jump into the car, honey,/ and head straight for the Cape,/ where
the cock on our housetop crows/ that the weather's fair" (p. 33).
Even the troubling parents, the lost father and the angry mother,
when from their graves they "slip through narrow crevices" into
their son's sleeping mind, "my cave of phantoms," though "unwelcome guests" are "not/ unloved" ("The Unquiet Ones," p. 31).

The last-first door of *The Layers* is that in "The Knot,"
(p. 1) "Scored in the lintel" of Kunitz' door is a cross-grained
knot that "keeps bleeding through/ into the world we share."
No matter how much he tries to seal it in, it comes "with a rush
of resin" back to life. Focusing on it, the last lines of the poem
become a hymn to being itself:

> Obstinate bud,
> sticky with life,
> mad for the rain again,
> it racks itself with shoots
> that crackle overhead,
> dividing as they grow.
> Let be! Let be!
> I shake my wings
> and fly into its boughs.

What does all of this prove? Not much, I suppose. That resonant, transforming imagery can be a shaping force within a body of poetry. Or perhaps that the coherence of a major artist is a half-conscious/half-accidental thing: something vaguely struggled for and realized completely only after the event, a matter of luck and genius.

I've praised Gregory Orr for this fine book. But I cannot praise too highly his own moving, spare poetry or not feel shudders of guilt that the five years he put into this volume I asked him to write might have been responsible for his creating fewer of the luminous poems that make him one of the half-dozen most eloquent poets of his generation. My consolation is that the insights of this work are a poet's insights into a very complex, very powerful older poet and that in opening up for us the rich poetry of Stanley Kunitz, Orr helps us understand the structure of poetry itself—not just Kunitz' poetry or Orr's own but poetry, that strange mix of technique, compassion, grief, memory, and the memory of language's compelling force: an amalgam shaped from and helping us move toward significant life.

Acknowledgments

Will Come to Order" (first appeared in *The Nation*); "She Wept, She Railed" (first appeared in the *Partisan Review*); "The Way Down" (first appeared in *Hudson Review*); © 1958 by Stanley Kunitz: "Revolving Meditation."

© 1962 by Stanley Kunitz: "After the Last Dynasty" (first appeared in *Poetry*); © 1966 by Stanley Kunitz: "River Road" (first appeared in the *New York Review*); © 1968 by Stanley Kunitz: "The Testing Tree" (first appeared in the *New York Review*); © 1969 by Stanley Kunitz: "The Flight of Apollo" (first appeared in the *New York Times*); "Robin Redbreast" (first appeared in *Poetry*); "The Game" (first appeared in *Poetry*).

© 1970 by Stanley Kunitz: "Journal for My Daughter" (first appeared in *New American Review #9*); "Around Pastor Bonhoeffer" (first appeared in the *Atlantic Monthly*); "King of the River" (first appeared in the *Atlantic Monthly*); © 1971 by Stanley Kunitz: "The Illumination" "The Magic Curtain" (first appeared in the *New Yorker*); "The Bottom of the Glass"; "The Portrait"; "An Old Cracked Tune"; © 1974 by Stanley Kunitz: "Words for the Unknown Makers: A Garland of"; © 1978 by Stanley Kunitz: "Quinnapoxet" "The Catch" (first appeared in the *Atlantic Monthly*); "The Quarrel" (first appeared in the *Atlantic Monthly*); © 1979 by Stanley Kunitz: "The Knot" (first appeared in *Salmagundi*); "The Lincoln Relics" (first appeared in the *New Yorker*); "The Layers" (first appeared in *American Poetry Review*).

Excerpt from "Open House" copyright 1941 by Theodore Roethke. From *The Collected Poems of Theodore Roethke*. Reprinted by permission of Doubleday & Company, Inc.

Excerpt from Sylvia Plath's "Words" © 1965 by Ted Hughes. From *Ariel*. Reprinted by permission of Harper and Row, Inc.

Chronology

1905   July 29, born in Worcester, Massachusetts, one of three children (two sisters) of Solomon Z. Kunitz and Yetta (Jasspon) Kunitz, both immigrants; father commits suicide before son's birth.

1918   Mother remarries; stepfather dies in 1919.

1920   Moves out of house to room at YMCA; works as butcher's assistant, then cub reporter for *Worcester Telegram*, a job he retains through college summer vacations.

1922   Enters Harvard; majors in English, minors in Philosophy.

1926   B.A., Harvard University, *summa cum laude*.

1927   M.A., Harvard University; wishes to pursue further studies but is informed "Our Anglo-Saxon students would resent being taught English literature by a Jew"; returns to *Worcester Telegram*, heads Sunday section—interviews Robert Goddard, covers Sacco–Vanzetti trial; later travels to New York with Vanzetti's letters in vain attempt to find publisher for them; ends up working for H. W. Wilson Co., reference publisher.

1928   Founds and edits *Wilson Library Bulletin* and initiates *Authors Biographical Series*.

1929   Travels in Europe, living briefly in France and Italy.

1930   Publishes *Intellectual Things*, first collection of poetry; marries Helen Pearce; moves to Wormwood Hill, Mansfield Center, Connecticut.

1933   Edits *Living Authors: A Book of Biographies*, for H. W. Wilson. Edits, with Howard Haycraft and Wilbur Hadden, *Authors Today and Yesterday: A Companion Volume to Living Authors.*

1934   Edits, with Howard Haycraft, *The Junior Book of Authors.*

1935   Moves to New Hope, Pennsylvania; meets Theodore Roethke.

1936   Edits, with Howard Haycraft, *British Authors of the Nineteenth Century.*

1937   Divorced from Helen Pearce.

1938   Edits, with Howard Haycraft, *American Authors, 1600–1900.*

1939   Marries Eleanor Evans.

1941   Receives Oscar Blumenthal Prize, *Poetry* magazine.

1942   Edits, with Howard Haycraft, *Twentieth-Century Authors.*

1943–1945   Drafted as conscientious objector; through misunderstandings and mistrust, undergoes three consecutive sessions of basic training; a sideline effort editing a camp newspaper leads to Air Transport Command, Gravely Point, Washington, where he is in charge of Information and Education; refuses commission and ends war as staff sergeant.

1944   Publishes *Passport to the War*, second book of poetry.

1945   Awarded John Simon Guggenheim Memorial fellowship.

1946–1949   First teaching position, replacing Theodore Roethke at Bennington College, Bennington, Vermont.

1949–1953   Directs poetry workshops at Potsdam, New York, Summer Workshop in the Creative Arts.

1950   Birth of daughter, Gretchen.

1950–1957   Directs poetry workshops at the New School for Social Research, New York City.

1952	Edits, with Howard Haycraft, *British Authors Before 1800.*
1953–1954	Receives Amy Lowell Traveling Fellowship; lives in Italy and France.
1955	Edits, with Vineta Colby, *Twentieth-Century Authors: First Supplement.*
1955–1956	Appointed poet-in-residence, University of Washington, Seattle.
1956	Receives Levinson Prize, *Poetry* magazine.
1956–1957	Appointed poet-in-residence, Queens College, New York City.
1957	Receives *Saturday Review* award.
1958	Divorced from Eleanor Evans; marries Elise Asher, painter; beginning of close friendships with painters, especially Mark Rothko and, later, Philip Guston; receives Harriet Monroe Award, University of Chicago; publishes *Selected Poems,* third book of poetry; receives Fellowship Award, Academy of American Poets.
1958–1959	Receives Ford Foundation grant; appointed poet-in-residence, Brandeis University.
1959	Awarded Pulitzer Prize for *Selected Poems;* receives National Institute of Arts and Letters award.
1961	Receives Honorary Doctor of Letters degree, Clark University, Worcester, Massachusetts.
1963	Appointed lecturer at Columbia University School of General Studies; since 1967, adjunct professor of writing, School of the Arts, Columbia University. Selected one of 250 members of the National Institute of Arts and Letters.
1964	Edits *Poems of John Keats* for Scribners.
1965	Receives Brandeis University Medal of Achievement.
1967	Translates, with others, *Antiworlds and the Fifth Ace,* by Andrei Voznesensky; edits, with Vineta Colby, *European Authors, 1000–1900.*

1968   Recives Fellowship Award, Academy of American Poets; helps organize and serves as member of staff of writing division of the Fine Arts Work Center, Provincetown, Massachusetts.

1969–1977   Edits Yale Series of Younger Poets, Yale University Press; appointed Fellow, Yale University.

1970   Elected Chancellor, Academy of American Poets.

1971   Publishes *The Testing-Tree*, fourth book of poetry.

1973   Publishes *Poems of Anna Akhmatova*, translated with Max Hayward.

1974–1976   Appointed twenty-third Consultant in Poetry to the Library of Congress; translates, with others, *Story Under Full Sail* by Andrei Voznesensky.

1975   Publishes *A Kind of Order, A Kind of Folly: Essays and Conversations*, a collection of prose; elected to fifty-member American Academy of Arts and Letters, succeeding to the chair held by John Crowe Ransom.

1976   Lectures and reads on a tour of the West Coast of Africa.

1978   Edits and acts as cotranslator of *Orchard Lamps*, poems by Ukranian poet Ivan Drach.

1979   Publishes *The Poems of Stanley Kunitz, 1928–1978*, sixth book of poetry.

1980   Receives Lenore Marshall Prize from Poetry Society of America. Lectures and reads on tour of Israel and Egypt; guest of honor, three-day symposium, *The Poet in Society*, University of Virginia.

1981   Reads Phi Beta Kappa poem at Harvard University.

1983   A chapbook of poems, *The Wellfleet Whale and Companion Poems*, published by Sheep Meadow Press; Poet of Honor, Poetry Day, Chicago.

STANLEY KUNITZ

Unless otherwise indicated, all quotations from poems are from *The Poems of Stanley Kunitz, 1928–1978*. Page numbers and titles of poems are inserted in the text or immediately following the quoted passages. Quotations from Kunitz' collection of essays, *A Kind of Order, A Kind of Folly*, are cited briefly as *Order/Folly*.

Life Into Legend

When Stanley Kunitz' magnificent fourth book of poems, *The Testing-Tree*, was published in 1971, it was hailed by Robert Lowell on the front page of the *New York Times Book Review*. As Kunitz' books make their appearance, it seems inevitable that he will be generally accorded that status which he has long since earned in the eyes of fellow poets—that of a major poet of the dramatic lyric. Yet the immediate chorus of praise and the excitement in the literary world that greeted *The Testing-Tree*'s appearance was followed by the relative critical neglect that has persistently haunted Kunitz' achievement as a poet.

Kunitz writes sparingly—on the average his books have appeared at fourteen-year intervals. In his words, he writes "only those poems that *must* be written, that force themselves into being." As a result, the transitional poems often don't get written, and each poem can represent, or appear to represent, a new departure. But transitional poems are dear to the hearts of critics and readers alike; they are often the bridges between major poems that allow us to perceive more quickly the patterns of concern and theme.

Curiously, we demand of a major poet not simply great poems but a great vision. In terms of the dramatic lyric, this great vision involves the sense of a distinct personality encountering, those particular mysteries of existence that most compel its energy and utterance. Paradoxically, the very excellence and integrity of Kunitz' individual poems have had the effect of obscuring the larger vision and continuity that guarantee his status as a major poet. The appearance of his collected volume, *The Poems of Stanley Kunitz, 1928–1978*, gives us the perspective we need to see the pattern and wholeness of Kunitz' oeuvre. The themes of identity and of the self's quest for autonomy and intensity of being emerge as the principle constellations in which each fine poem is a separate star.

In this Introduction I will be moving rapidly across the body of Kunitz' work, seeking those thematic and stylistic continuities that make his poetry more complex and coherent than that of many lyric poets. In identifying and emphasizing these underlying structures, I will be quoting only briefly from individual poems. Finally, it is these individual poems, their integrity and intensity, that determine Kunitz' stature as a poet.

The necessarily theoretical nature of this chapter will result in a temporary neglect of the individual poems, which will, I hope, be remedied by the subsequent chapters where we will move chronologically through Kunitz' books, examining individual poems in some depth.

A Few Assertions

Kunitz is a poet of the dramatic lyric who strives to dramatize the themes and contradictions of his life. He distrusts the didactic impulse in poetry—the impulse to summarize, interpret, or otherwise comment upon the dramas he presents. Keats is perhaps Kunitz' favorite poet, yet in his introduction to his edition of *The Poems of Keats,* Kunitz does not hesitate to chide him for a lapse into didacticism:

> No matter how you read, " 'Beauty is truth, truth beauty'—that is all / Ye know on earth, and all ye need to know," the lines have a thematic and didactic smack to them. Keats has a finer aesthetic perception in one of his letters when he refers to the reality of aethereal things, and names them: "such as existences of Sun Moon & Stars and passages of Shakespeare," or when, on another occasion, he asserts, "The Imagination may be compared to Adams' dream—he awoke and found it truth." (*Order/Folly,* p. 69)

Kunitz would approve of Yeats' remark that we cannot know the truth, we can only embody it. He might further add that we can dramatize the truth as an encounter, a "drama in a nutshell" ("Revolving Meditation," p. 143). Kunitz speaks of the poet's need to "polarize his contradictions." These contradictions are polarized in order to enact a dramatic encounter whose events *are* its meaning.

Kunitz is a poet of irrational or nonrational intelligence, although he is aware of irrationality's dangers:

> Irrationality may well be the safest of all disguises for the modern artist—the Mask, or Persona, that permits him the greatest freedom of expression with a certain degree of immunity; though there is a danger, to be sure, that the Mask may eventually usurp the Face. (*Order/Folly,* p. 7)

The irrational or nonrational intelligence that structures his poems takes many forms, but the alchemical ambition that marshals these forms remains consistent: to convert life into legend.

That which is to be alchemized is the self as much as the life. Through the transformation of self into language he wants to "test existence at its highest pitch—what does it feel like to be totally one's self" (*Order/Folly*, p. 17). Such a transformation also has aspects of the heroic quest; Kunitz speaks of "submitting to the ordeal of walking through the fires of selfhood into a world of archetypal forms" (*Order/Folly*, p. 13). It is the poem itself that enacts that transformative ordeal. The enterprise is the same as that of Keats when Keats speaks of this world as a "vale of soul-making."

When Kunitz proposes "converting life into legend" as a formula for his poetic enterprise, he is in part making an assertion about the lyric poet's awareness of larger structures and principles of continuity in his work. That notion of the lyric which sees each poem as an epiphanic moment crystallized in language yet isolated from all other such moments does not appeal to Kunitz. The word "legend" in the formula emphasizes a consistent narrating thread that runs through the individual poems.

"Legend" is Kunitz' attempt to make of the lyric poet's enterprise an open-ended quest whose themes, goals, and events become representative human dramas. Kunitz' legends are based in private experience; yet, translated and dramatized, they acquire universality: the quest for love, for authenticity and autonomy, for intensity of being.

The concept of the "key image" provides a second structural continuity to Kunitz' work. Basically, the key image has its source in the poet's childhood and manifests itself again and again in the poetry. Its recurrence elevates it to the status of a symbol in the poet's personal mythology and at the same time provides at the image level the continuity which legend provides at the narrative level.

The third factor of continuity in Kunitz' poetry is the self, the dramatized "I" who is the protagonist of the poems. This self is the central and centralizing persona of the dramatic lyric. The self quests, seeks meaning. Sometimes the self journeys through a horizontal landscape emblematic of the life lived inside time. At other times, the self responds to the transcendental impulse so powerful in the lyric and seems to spiral above a crucial incident or event, held by the event's centripetal power yet striving to rise up to view it from a different perspective.

These two selves, the journeying self and the spiraling self, are both valid for Kunitz. The spiraling self acknowledges the power of recurring themes in our lives and the necessity to confront them again and again. The spiraling self is most appropriately linked to the recurring key images. The journeying self acknowledges another truth: that we convey our past with us as we enter a future whose events we cannot predict. The journeying self is appropriately linked to the narrative thrust of the legends.

These continuities of narrative, image, and self are necessary in order to overcome a critical bias that seeks to minimize the scope and ambition present in the work of a major lyric imagination. Perhaps the most demeaning manifestation of this bias is the belief that the lyric poet's highest ambition is to appear in an anthology. It is necessary to propose a countertruth: to assert that in some cases, as with Kunitz' work, it is possible to say that *all* a lyric poet's poems are one poem, that the work as a whole partakes of the same impulse toward unity and coherence that shapes language and event into the individual poem.

The Legends and the Quest

Kunitz has frequently spoken of the theme of the son's quest for the father, which is indeed a central part of his work. But in fact, his work focuses on several distinct quests or legends, each having its unique narrative thrust. These legends are linked to each other in various ways, and they also have a common motive: the quest for identity.

When we speak of a quest for identity that originates in lived experience and that involves a son's search for his father, we have entered the territory of psychology. In the lived life, identity is determined largely in terms of family relationships, and it is here that the other legends emerge.

A retrospective reading of Kunitz' poetry reveals three figures who are primary poles of his imaginative existence: father, mother, and beloved. These three figures imply an "I" whose identity emerges in relation to them. The first two relationships are father–son and mother–son. From these two, a further relationship emerges: that of man (grown son) and beloved.[1]

Kunitz will dramatize the primary concerns of his life and work in terms of legends based on these three primary relationships.

The first legend I will call the "father legend." The two female figures represent a more complex interaction. Until very late in the work, the powerful figure of the mother is liable to appear in the same poem as the beloved. This fact has great significance and constitutes a legend of its own: the mother/beloved legend. There are also numerous poems in which the lover/beloved appears without the mother, and when it seems appropriate I will refer to them as one of two variations of this legend: the beloved legend or the beloved/muse legend.

In the early poetry, the figure of the beloved is idealized and frequently related to the courtly love tradition in a way that the contemporary reader may find archaic. But equally, the later

---

1. Having proposed a psychological model for the underlying structure of Kunitz' work, it is necessary to say that we need not adopt any particular theory of identity development through the interaction of family members. By the time Kunitz left high school for college in 1922, he had already read Freud. In his essays and interviews, Kunitz rarely mentions psychological figures or theories, although when Jung's name was brought up by an interviewer, Kunitz mentioned being favorably impressed by an essay on individuation.

Kunitz of *The Testing-Tree* presents some of the most fully realized, dignified, and convincing figures of women in poetry
written by men. What remains constant and consistent throughout is Kunitz' belief that love has the power to transform us—a
power he embodies in the figure of the beloved.

Besides the father legend and the mother/beloved legend,
there is a third major legend of identity that emerges most
strongly in Kunitz' later work. But, if the other legends have
their origins in psychology, the third legend seems rooted in
metaphysics. I will call it the "legend of being" or the "quest for
being itself." This third legend tends to make its appearance in
early poems as a final transformation of the father legend. It exists in such later poems as "King of the River," "The Layers,"
and "The Knot" as an autonomous legend that is the triumphant
and culminating expression of Kunitz' imagination.

The Sources

Certain key facts and figures from his youth provide the basic material for Kunitz' alchemical transformation of life into legend. In a 1971 interview with Selden Rodman, Kunitz presents
the bare bones of the life situation that so affected his work. His
immigrant parents were from grain merchant families who lived
in Luthuanian Russia, though he was never to learn for sure the
real birthplace of his father:

> Perhaps my father, who killed himself six weeks before I was born,
> came from East Prussia: I've never known much about him be-
> cause my mother made it a forbidden subject. Why he killed
> himself wasn't clear. The dress manufacturing business they'd
> started together was going bankrupt; but there must have been
> another woman, too, or mother wouldn't have made the subject
> taboo. Not even his name could be mentioned. Mother was a great

seamstress—and business woman—so after the double catastrophe she opened a little dry goods store and for years worked day and night to pay off the debts—though she wasn't obliged to legally.

I was farmed out, or in the hands of nursemaids . . . I was lonely and fatherless, but my father *had* left a library—fairly substantial sets of Dickens, Thackeray, Tolstoi and the like. . . .

My two sisters died young. Mother was just forty when I was born. When I was eight, she married again. My stepfather taught me most of what I know about love and gentleness. He was an Old World scholar, of no practical help to my mother, but she revered his learning and the sweetness of his character. She anticipated the modern liberated woman, being perfectly capable of managing by herself what had developed into a flourishing business, based on her dress designs—I can still see the loft with its cutting tables and long rows of girls bent over their electric sewing machines. Mother never trusted anybody else to repair the machines when they were out of order. But she was always tired at the end of the day. When my stepfather died suddenly in my fourteenth year, my world was shattered. It didn't leave me with much sense of family. . . .

What finally destroyed her was that she couldn't bear to fire anyone. So she went bankrupt again in the Depression, and that was the end of her business career. She had fought for money and power, and she had failed—for which she could not forgive herself. She died, alert and intransigent, in the early Fifties at the age of eighty-six.[2]

The directness and clarity of this presentation only become available to Kunitz late in his life. The overriding theme of Kunitz' work is identity—the struggle to discover and dramatize "what furies made him man" ("Goose Pond," p. 120). These forces find their locus in his childhood circumstances. Throughout Kunitz' long career, these primary family figures (father, mother, son)

---

2. Selden Rodman, *Tongues of Fallen Angels* (New York: New Directions, 1974), 99. 96–98.

and the dramatic situations they enact are what draw out his deepest emotional and imaginative responses.

The Mother and the Beloved

Although the quest for the father is often spoken of as the major thematic thrust of Kunitz' work, the motive and priority must be sought in the mother–son relationship. The figure that emerges from Rodman's biographical interview is of a remarkably powerful, competent, and unyielding mother. In order to locate the quest for identity at one of its origins, we must comprehend the situation of a boy who is left fundamentally alone with a powerful mother. His biological father is mysteriously absent, and there is a taboo against his very name. In order to establish his autonomy and identity, Kunitz must break out of the orbit created by his mother's gravitational power. When the legend concerning the mother–son relationship does make one of its infrequent appearances in the early poems, the figure of the mother is consistently seen as powerfully destructive of or inhibiting the son's quest for autonomy. She is also, in the early poems, repeatedly linked to the beloved, especially in poems of failed love as "Poem" *(Intellectual Things)* or "The Signal from the House" *(Selected Poems):*

> I cried to the mourner on the stair,
> "Mother, I hate you for those tears."
> (p. 156)

In terms of the quest for identity, the beloved is a goal, the mother is an obstacle to that goal.

Freud, in his essay, "A Prevalent Form of Degradation in Erotic Life," talks about the role of the mother at that time in a young man's life when he chooses a love object in the world. Freud contends that the mother is always the actual first love object and that the beloved is a surrogate. He maintains that at this point the young man separates love into two components: a "tender," idealizing impulse and a "sensuous," sexual impulse. These two components cannot be reunited into the figure of the mother lest incest-fear incapacitate the young man.

What happens in a great deal of Kunitz' work *is* strongly related to the mother, but the effect is different from that suggested by Freud's model. In Freud's essay, the mother is a rock against which the young man's libido flows and separates into two streams ("tender" and "sensuous") which cannot be reunited. In early Kunitz, it is as if the libido is never given any expression in the external world. In an early poem, "So Intricately Is This World Resolved," Kunitz proposes that the man cannot or must not act in the world of sexual impulse, that love not only cannot be consummated but cannot be acted upon:

> O lover,
> Lift no destroying hand; let fortune pass
> Unchallenged, beauty sleep; dare not to cover
> Her mouth with kisses by the garden wall,
> Lest, cracking in bright air, a planet fall.
> (p. 228)

In many of the poems of *Intellectual Things*, the libidinal energy thus frustrated of expression animates an inner world, an interior landscape, and creates a condition of erotic solipsism. In these poems, language itself becomes charged with the energy and actions of sexual event, but the arena is interior to the self: in "Mens Creatrix," the brain becomes a "mental womb" which will be "cleaved" by a "rhythmic Spike of Light" (p. 202).

While language and mental events become charged with sexual energy, the figure of the beloved in the early love poems becomes or remains an idealized figure from literary tradition rather than a recognizably flesh-and-blood creature. She is "love's incarnate form" or "a dove-soft nimble girl" and acts in an interiorized landscape that in no way corresponds to the external world. The result in the early work is twofold: a love poetry in which the object is idealized in such a way as to transcend any human particularity; and a poetry about poetry itself—or about mental processes—which is charged with sensual intensity.

In terms of the quest for identity, Kunitz must struggle to overcome his own inhibitions and emotional contradictions and his mother's prohibitions in relation to the beloved. One movement in this theme is from the interior, enclosed world of *Intellectual Things* (1930) outward toward a recognizable external landscape and a recognizable, if tortured, relationship between self and other in *Passport to the War* (1944).

On the psychological level, the mother/beloved legend culminates and is resolved in "The Magic Curtain" (*The Testing-Tree*, 1971). As in "Poem," and "The Signal from the House," the mother and the beloved are both present in the same poem and the same drama, but here they are present so that the boy can choose the beloved (a governess) in a way that affirms a tender, sensuous love and also affirms his identity as distinct from the mother's:

> "I'll never forgive her," mother said,
> but as for me, I do and do and do.
> ("The Magic Curtain," p. 68)

The beloved triumphs over the mother (at a human level); love triumphs over negations; forgiveness over "never forgiving."

On the metaphysical level, the mother/beloved legend culminates and is resolved in "A Spark of Laurel," where the powerful and erotic female figure that has dominated many of the poems in *Selected Poems* is recognized as reconciling mother and beloved (ideal and passionate love) and her ambiguous identity is seen as the very source of poetry: the muse, who is " 'Mother and mistress, one' " ("A Spark of Laurel," final lines, p. 147).

The Father and the Spirit Father

"To find the father is to find oneself."
(Interview, 1978)[3]

If, in the early work of *Intellectual Things* and *Passport to the War*, the beloved is a goal toward which the speaker/self moves with great intensity, then the other main goal is the father. In the figure of the father we are dealing with a fusion of the biological father, whose suicide before Kunitz' birth made his name taboo, and the gentle and loving stepfather who died suddenly when Kunitz was fourteen. The term "father" in any discussion of Kunitz' work should be understood to mean the fusion of the *pain* of the beloved stepfather's sudden death with the *imagery* and *mystery* of the biological father's suicide. In all Kunitz' poems the father is dead, but this fact in no way undercuts his reality; in fact, it heightens his reality at the psychological level. In Kunitz' memory, as we have seen, both fathers are associated with books or scholarship, and they are characterized in the poems as being loving and yet mysteriously absent or elusive. They are also, and this point is critical, perceived as being actual or potential allies in Kunitz' quest for identity and his related effort to break free of the power of the maternal. The father

3. "The Poetry Miscellany," *Salmagundi* (1978), 8:30.

is a goal of the identity quest in much the same way that the
beloved is:

> And I will go, unburdened, on the quiet lane
> Of my eternal kind, till shadowless
> With inner light I wear my father's face.
>> ("Vita Nuova," p. 236)

Jung, in his essay "Freud and Jung—Contrasts," criticizes
Freud for his overemphasis on the child's relation to the parents; he sees it finally as an entangling, sterile relationship from
which Freud offers no means of escape, no avenue for growth.
Jung claims to see in the universal cultural phenomenon of initiation rites, a human impulse toward rebirth and as such a release from "the boring and sterile family drama." Such a rebirth
is a movement beyond the biological toward the spiritual. Such
a reborn person sees that the Spirit is Father and Nature is
Mother.

Behind the biological father stands the Spirit Father, behind the biological mother stands the Nature Mother. Throughout the poems of son and father, Kunitz' Spirit Father is ambiguous (he is helper and haunter, guide and ghost), but he is Spirit
from the outset and the goal of the son's quest.

Perhaps Kunitz so quickly identifies father with Spirit because his biological father is absent and therefore transparent.[4]
Not so the figure of the mother. As Freudian biological mother,
she is an opaque and powerful figure standing between young

---

4. As Schiller says in his description of the elegiac mode in poetry: "The
content of poetic lamentation can therefore never be an external object, it must
always be only an ideal, inner one; even if it grieves over some loss in actuality,
it must first be transformed into an ideal loss" (*The Naive and Sentimental in
Poetry*).

Kunitz and the beloved. As Jung's Nature Mother she is associated with the decay that overtook the father. This decay is linked
with vegetation; the mother "buries" humans like seeds:

> In the year of my mother's blood, when I was born,
> She buried my innocent head in a field, because the earth
>
> Was sleepy with the winter. And I spoke the corn
> > ("Poem," p. 198)

Frequently, as in the following poem, animal ("carrion") and
vegetative ("a pod") nature overlap in the recurring image of a
ripening that is merely prelude to a bursting and rotting:

> Anonymous sweet carrion,
> Blind mammal floating on the stream
> Of depthless sound, completely one
> In the cinnamon-dark of no dream—
> A pod of silence, bursting when the sun
>
> Clings to the forehead,
> > ("Prophecy on Lethe," p. 209)

In "Organic Bloom" the human brain is seen as a grotesque water
lily:

> Enormous floats the brain's organic bloom
> Till, bursting like a fruit, it scatters doom.
> > (p. 234)

In the poems of *Intellectual Things*, Kunitz sees the relationship of spirit to nature as a war, a struggle in which the father
is always threatened with "a second perishing" ("For the Word
Is Flesh"). What will free Kunitz' poetry from this struggle is a
twofold imaginative transformation: the embracing of nature as
a *cyclical* (death—decay—rebirth) rather than linear (death and

then decay) process; and the location of the Spirit Father *in* nature rather than *against* it:

> O father in the wood,
> Mad father of us all,
> King of our antlered wills
> ("The Way Down," p.
> 137)

Although Kunitz seeks and even pursues the figure of the
father, he also needs to confront him in order to be free of a
father "whose indomitable love / Kept me in chains" ("Father
and Son," p. 157). In the early poems of *Intellectual Things*, the
Spirit Father either succumbs to decay or represents a transcendence of physical conditions which fails to accommodate the
central phenomenon of death. When he is at last located in cyclical nature in "The Way Down" (*Selected Poems*),

> Where the fleshed root stirs,
> Marvelous horned strong game,
> Brine-scaled, dun-caked with mould,
> Dynastic thunder-bison, Asian-crude,
> Bedded in moss and slime,
> Wake
>
> (p. 136)

then indeed, as Heraclitus says (and the poem's title indicates),
"The way down and the way up are one and the same."

This reconciliation of Spirit and Nature represents a major
advance in Kunitz' quest for identity. The Nature of *Selected
Poems* and after is a Nature whose cyclical renewals offer hope,
and the father, who represents great positive power and potential guidance for the son, is identified with this new conception
of Nature. Kunitz' abiding love of the natural world links with

his idealization of the father. In later Kunitz, Nature is Father Nature—its renewals are expressed in the phallic imagery of male potency.

The Third Legend

The first two major legends of Kunitz' poetry (the father legend and the mother/beloved legend) can be understood and appreciated at a psychological level without being confined or reduced to that level. The poems of these legends depict the way a strong male identity is formed through imaginative inter-action with the figures of father, mother, and beloved. But the third legend goes beyond the issue of individual identity, shift-ing from psychology to metaphysics, from identity to being. The third legend could be called the legend of being itself, or "the quest of being for yet more intense being"—for the secret of its own mystery, which is understood as a journey that has no goal and finds its meaning in the journey itself.

The third legend can be understood also as the human ad-venture—the absurd heroics of human grandeur—the journey for the journey's sake, but at the highest level of risk and inten-sity. One of Kunitz' favorite metaphors for this is the journey into space. Perhaps this metaphor gripped him first when, as a cub reporter for the *Worcester Telegram*, he was sent to inter-view Robert Goddard, the father of modern rocketry, who was sending aloft curious missiles from pastures near Clark Univer-sity. Young Kunitz heard him say, "In your lifetime, man will walk on the moon," and he never got over the grandeur of God-dard's imagination. "The Flight of Apollo" is the best embodi-ment of this version of the quest for its own sake. It is a hymn to the quest, but also an exploration of its motives—"Earth was my home, but even there I was a stranger. . . . Think of me as nostalgic, afraid, exalted"(p. 48).

At the core of the legend of being is the fact of our mortality and our awareness of it. Perhaps it is this that places the emphasis on journey and process rather than on any goal. Kunitz himself best expresses the fundamental dynamic of the legend of being: "The hard and inescapable phenomenon to be faced is that we are living and dying at once. My commitment is to report the dialogue" (*Order/Folly*, p. 123).

The supreme poem of this third legend is "King of the River," where Kunitz seeks a nonhuman creature to commune with: a salmon. This creature is noble (he is king of the river), and he represents the ultimate metaphysical paradox of consciousness itself, beyond all individual identity, but *within* mortality where "'The only music is time, / the only dance is love' " (p. 54).

The legend of being emphasizes process, movement, metamorphosis. Its characteristic images are those of the journey and of transcendent phallic shapes that represent pure, renewable energy questing onward without purpose, but finding meaning in the ecstasy of the process itself. We find this transcendent phallus in the rocket ship of space exploration, but even more centrally in "The Knot" where it is the "Obstinate bud, / sticky with life" (p. 1) that becomes a tree of life, or in "King of the River" where it is the male salmon, a "Finned Ego" thrashing upriver to spawn and die.

But a relentless forward thrusting is by no means the only characteristic movement of this legend. Sometimes the journeying self is aware of two countermovements within it: one that pulls toward the past (Kunitz calls it "nostalgia") and the other that pulls the self forward (Kunitz' term is "desire"). The forward thrusting of the phallic self is present in "desire" and in

"will." But the backward motion is equally strong and has its
role to play in the journey:

> I look behind,
> as I am compelled to look
> before I can gather strength
> to proceed on my journey
>   ("The Layers," p. 35)

The title of another poem, "Revolving Meditation," brings
us from the journeying self to the spiraling self. The spiraling
self involves a revolving motion around a center. The spiral is
an emblem for the obsessive self and the obsessive theme in
Kunitz' poetry: for the poem and the self that circle or revolve
above a set of images or a subject—returning to them again and
again:

> How much I disapprove of it!
> How little I love it!
> Though, contrariwise,
> Can there be
> Anything half as dear?
>   (p. 143)

The self spirals above the image or subject, trying to transform
it, to convert life into legend, to "find the drama in a nutshell."

Love and Art

When Kunitz speaks to the child of a marriage that is ending, he describes himself as "Your father, in whom two ambitions
rave, / Like stations wrangling on the foreign wave / For spheres
of influence." Such a father "loathes the heart that blends / His

guilty love; but the quarrel never ends" ("The Tutored Child," p. 155). In a companion poem later in the same book, he addresses the child's mother, whose accusing question: "What Have You Done?" was originally the poem's title. In the second poem the "two ambitions" of "The Tutored Child" are identified and fused in the transformed heart:

> From my angry side O child,
> Tumbles this agate heart,
> Your prize, veined with the root
> Of guilty life,
> From which flow love and art.
> ("The Reckoning," p. 183)

"Love and art" are the two ways Kunitz seeks his identity. When, in the central poem, "The Testing-Tree," the boy Kunitz enacts a ritual of three stones thrown at a sacred oak tree target, the goals for which he strives are the same:

> I played my game for keeps—
>
> for love, for poetry,
>   and for eternal life—
>   after the trials of summer.
>   (p. 91)

The Key Image

The key image is the single most important element in Stanley Kunitz' work. The clearest definitions Kunitz himself provides occur in a lecture given at the Library of Congress on May 12, 1975, and printed by the Library as the essay "From Feathers to Iron":

One of my convictions is that at the center of every poetic imagination is a cluster of key images which go back to the poet's
childhood and which are usually associated with pivotal experiences, not necessarily traumatic. . . . . That cluster of key images
is the purest concentration of the self, the individuating node,
the place where the persona starts. . . . . In Keats's case, one can
learn more about his quiddity by pursuing images of fever and of
ooze than by analysing his literary sources. A critical property of
key images is that they are unalterable, being good for a lifetime.

and in a 1977 interview with *Columbia* magazine:

Interviewer: You've spoken of a poet's finding his center, could
you talk about that?
Kunitz: I'll try. You have at the center of your being a conglomeration of feelings, emotions, memories, traumas that are uniquely
yours, that nobody else on earth can duplicate. They are the clue
to your identity. If you don't track them down, lay claim to them,
bring them out into the light, they'll eventually possess you, they'll
fester, or erupt into compulsive behavior. The farther you stray
from your center, the more you will be lost. That's one of the
teachings of Lao-tzu. When you're there, at the existential core,
you'll know it. Hopkins said in one of his letters that he could
taste himself, and the taste was more distinctive than the taste of
ale or alum, or the smell of walnutleaf or camphor. You can tell
the poets who are working at their center by the distinctiveness
of their voice, their constellation of key images, their instantly
recognizable beat. (p. 5)

When Kunitz proposes such an important role for the cluster of key images, he is affirming the fact that his is a symbolic,
associative intelligence rather than a conceptual, discursive one.
For Kunitz, even at his most allusive, Christianity and Neo-pla-
tonism are sources of images for impulses and emotions, not
philosophical or religious perspectives.

In Kunitz' work, key images can be verbs (e.g., flow, throb, pulse, turn, burst) as well as nouns (e.g., wound, house, threshold, tree, heart). The meanings of these key images emerge both *intensively* in the context of the particular poem and *extensively* in their various (and sometimes metamorphosed) recurrences throughout the life's work.

Key Images Through Time: The Wound and the House

One way of understanding how a key image functions in Kunitz' work as a whole is to trace its occurrences in the poems chronologically. Although a key image may be, to use Kunitz' phrase, "good for a lifetime," it is far from static. For example, during the course of the work, the wound image, perhaps the most important of Kunitz' key images, evolves and metamorphosizes, appearing also as a hurt, a stain, a scald, or a burn.

In the early poems of *Intellectual Things*, this image cluster centered on "wound" is linked to the mortality that so haunts the volume. It makes its first, earliest appearance as "hurt" (an abstraction) and as "stain":

> The blessing in this conscious fruit, the hurt
> Which is unanswerable, fill the brow
> With early death.
> > ("Beyond Reason," p. 235)

> The shape confronting me upon the stair
> (Athlete of shadow, lighted by a stain
> On its disjunctive breast—I saw it plain—)
> > ("Master and Mistress," p. 233)

The stain of the second poem is associated with a ghost/apparition. The hurt of the first is associated with the brow. In later poems, the hurt will become less abstract, more violent and concrete, and increasingly associated with the head and brow. At the outset it is an image soiled by mortality, but it is held at a distance, abstracted and intellectualized, even resisting its own physical implications. Later, this stain of mortality will reappear as a "mudstain" the son promises to wipe from the father's corpse ("Father and Son"). In a poem called "The Pivot," the following strange image occurs:

> he leaves behind
> A faunlike head upon a tray,
> Spear buried in the mind.
>
> (p. 205)

In an early poem about the process of poetry, "Mens Creatrix," a "rhythmic Spike of Light" was said to "cleave" the brain.

Without being reductive we can assert that this pervasive set of images is linked to the father's suicide as imagined by the son. Since the suicide is the central fact of Kunitz' imaginative life, that from which all else flows, it is perhaps appropriate to skip from the first book to the fourth book and present the pivotal poem of the entire oeuvre, "The Portrait." In this poem the personal, biographical source of Kunitz' being is presented with the extraordinary simplicity and understatement characteristic of his later work (it appears in *The Testing-Tree*, published when Kunitz was 66):

> My mother never forgave my father
> for killing himself,
> especially at such an awkward time
> and in a public park,
> that spring
> when I was waiting to be born.
> She locked his name

in her deepest cabinet
and would not let him out,
though I could hear him thumping.
When I came down from the attic
with the pastel portrait in my hand
of a long-lipped stranger
with a brave moustache
and deep brown level eyes,
she ripped it into shreds
without a single word
and slapped me hard.
In my sixty-fourth year
I can feel my cheek
still burning.

(p. 86)

"The Portrait" is the first poem to mention the father's death as a suicide. When we consider that children turn to their parents, the source of their being, for answers to their identity, the implications of a father who kills himself while the son is in the womb are indeed disturbing. This self-willed contradiction of life by one's own life-source is sufficient (when fused with the beloved stepfather's sudden death) to send Kunitz' life down a curious path. He must seek the father; he must confront this contradiction of life at his life's source, a contradiction whose image is the wound.

Among other significant information about Kunitz' life, "The Portrait" tells us that his father committed suicide in a public park and that all mention of the father and the event were prohibited by Kunitz' mother. This leads us to a crucial speculation: that the young Kunitz must *imagine* the method of suicide and that he imagines it as a revolver shot to the head (though drowning is not impossible and ponds and lakes are also key images associated with the father's death). Looking backward from

"The Portrait," we can recognize that the plot of an earlier poem, "The Hemorrhage," closely parallels the actual circumstances of the father's suicide and that the wound is the centralizing image:

> The people made a ring
> Around the man in the park.
> He was our banished king
> Of blames and staunchless flows,
> Exhibitor of the dark
> Abominable rose;
>
> Our chief, returned at last
> From exile, with the grim
> Stamina of the lost,
> To show his sovereign hurt.
> (p. 163)

The hurt, the hemorrhage, the "staunchless" flow are powerful images both for the source of Kunitz' trauma and the power of that trauma to persist and constantly threaten his own being.

Without attempting to define or confine the meaning of the key image of wound, we can assert the following: it is connected to mortality; it is frequently located at the forehead or brow; it is connected to the father; and ultimately it becomes a link between father and son: a badge of shared suffering that each wears, a legacy from father to son that unites them. This last aspect of the image is seen in embryonic form in the orange/nail image of "Father and Son," becomes a legacy in the burning cheek of the final lines of "The Portrait," and achieves its final role as an emblem of communion in the very late poem "Quinnapoxet," where the son signals to the father's ghost in the poem's final image:

> I touched my forehead
> with my swollen thumb

and splayed my fingers out—
in deaf-mute country
the sign for father.

(p. 5)

In "Quinnapoxet" the speaker dreams a wound (a "gashed" and swollen thumb) and then sees the apparition of his two parents approaching. Like "The Portrait," it is a poem of the family triad, one where we see very clearly the negating power of the mother over Kunitz' sense of self:

"Why don't you write?" she cried
from the folds of her veil.
"We never hear from you."
I had nothing to say to her.

(pp. 4–5)

Here, the mother is imagined as a barrier between son and father (now that death is no longer the barrier, death having been imaginatively overcome in "The Way Down"). The son signals to the father with his wound: wound to wound, they commune. The "swollen thumb" has to do with a phallic life-force, a life-force hurt into being, yet potent.

"Quinnapoxet" is the culmination of the father legend— Kunitz has gone as far as he can go in psychological terms and in the context of son–mother–father. In "The Knot," the father legend (symbolized by the "bleeding" knot wound) yields to the legend of pure being (symbolized by the phallic tree of life). The metamorphosis (or regeneration) of wound into phallus is that point at which we pass from psychology to metaphysics, from a hymn to the father to a hymn in praise of pure being and its power to renew itself and us with it.

A less spectacular, but equally important set of key images that relate to the legend of pure being is that of "house" or "home." House/home represents the backward motion of being (nostalgia) just as the phallic rocketship, tree of life, and "Finned Ego" of the salmon represent its forward motion (desire).

How does the image of house/home relate to nostalgia? By investigating the image of house/home we uncover the power of context in determining the meaning of a key image. Considered without a specific dramatic context, one might well assume that house/home had positive meanings related to security, domestic intimacy, and belongingness. But in Kunitz' poetry these positive qualities are constantly undercut in such a way as to establish a fundamental aspect of his vision: that security and stability in the physical and emotional or social worlds are illusions.

He establishes and undermines the positive aspects of the image at the same time. The most revealing instance of this is in "Father and Son." In this poem the son has pursued the father's ghost across a dream landscape, hoping at last to catch him and confront him with his needs for guidance in the world. The pursuing son anguishes over the opening words to this crucial encounter:

> How should I tell him my fable and the fears,
> How bridge the chasm in a causal tone,
> Saying, "The house, the stucco one you built,
> We lost."
>
> (p. 157)

The father, whose presence would give stability to a son's identity, had the power to "build a house"—to create a surrounding stability and security. The house that the father built his survivors have lost.

Here we see the essence of Kunitz' dilemma in the father legend: he is in awe of a father he never knew. He feels a son's intense need for fathering and guidance. One image of the father's mythic power is the house he built, and when the son looks back into the past, he does so with *longing*. He wants, impossibly, the dead father to return—" 'Father,' I cried, 'Return! You know / The way.' " As long as Kunitz associates the house with the lost father, he sees it in the distant past.

In the poem that immediately precedes "Father and Son," we see the image of the house connected to the mother/beloved legend, and thus the image acquires other meanings. In this poem, "The Signal from the House," the house is associated negatively with both the mother and the beloved, people who "were too much with" the speaker and therefore "secretly against" him. He seeks to abandon them and the house in order to embark on a journey and to escape "the old life." The signal of the title calls him back "like cry of conscience" to what he knows to be his destruction. If the house was built by the father, it is inhabited by the mother. The son, in order to grow, must leave the house and embark on his journey; if he actually yields to the backward, nostalgic pull of the house, he accedes to his own self-destruction.

Although the house/home image is strongly linked with the past and pastness, it most truly belongs with poems of the legend of being, where homelessness is connected to desolation and solitude as a condition of being. At the mythic level this is the story of our eviction from Eden, our first home. In "Robin Redbreast," where one of the poem's primary strategies is to identify the bird's situation and the speaker's, we see Kunitz making connections between Eden, the self's desolation and insecurity, and the house image:

> It was the dingiest bird
> you ever saw, all the color
> washed from him, as if
> he had been standing in the rain,
> friendless and stiff and cold,

> since Eden went wrong.
> In the house marked For Sale,
> where nobody made a sound,
> in the room where I lived
> with an empty page . . .
>
> (p. 56)

In another poem of the legend of being, "The Flight of Apollo," the poem's primary movement is the outward journeying of adventurous desire, but the opening lines establish Kunitz' special sense of home as a precondition of the quest—"Earth was my home, but even there I was a stranger" says the astronaut, and later "think of me as nostalgic, afraid, exalted." The astronaut's journey is one of the purest forms of the legend of being, and its source is a home that is not a home.

When Kunitz dramatizes the legend of being as a male salmon, the "King" of the river journeying upriver to spawn and die, house/home becomes "kingdom," and the poem's final paradox again concerns home and homelessness as a state of being:

> he is not broken but endures,
> limber and firm
> in the state of his shining,
> forever inheriting his salt kingdom,
> from which he is banished
> forever.
>
> ("King of the River," p. 54)

In one sense this "salt kingdom" is the ocean he is journeying away from, upriver, and up fish ladders over dams. Earlier in the same poem, through the image of a ladder, Kunitz links the salt kingdom/home *behind* the salmon to nostalgia:

> If the heart were pure enough,
> but it is not pure,

you would admit
that nothing compels you
any more, nothing
at all abides,
but nostalgia and desire,
the two-way ladder
between heaven and hell.

(pp. 53–54)

We have here the fundamental dynamic of the legend of being.
A backward urge toward "house/home" that is called "nostalgia"
and is either illusory or, if acted upon, dangerous. And a forward urge called "desire" whose movement is the journey and
whose image is often phallic as in the "Finned Ego" of the male
salmon. Desire in the legend is not desire for some object or
goal, but is simply an index of the intensity of being itself: " '*What
do I want of my life?* / *More! More!*' " ("Journal for my Daughter," p. 42).

The overriding image is of the self's journey, but the backward glance of nostalgia that I have discussed earlier is as much
a condition of being as the restless forward journey into the unknown.

We can speculate that for a key image to work successfully
in a body of poetry, it must be rooted in personal experience.
Among literary modes of thought, the key image (a variant of
symbol) has a peculiar power of verticality: it can function with
equal authority at different levels of being or reference. Kunitz
demonstrates his awareness of these different levels of being or
reference that the key image has simultaneous access to when
he remarks apropos of the key image "pond" in his work, "As
far as I am concerned, the pond in Quinnapoxet, Poe's 'dank tarn
of Auber,' and the mere in which Beowulf fights for his life with

Grendel and the water-hag are one and the same" (*Order/Folly*, p. 125). Similarly, if we glance briefly to the side and recall Kunitz' ambition of "converting life into legend" (life and legend being two parallel levels of being), we can see that the image of the wound functions in one context (say, "The Portrait") at the literal level of the lived life, and in another context it functions at a universal, legendary level as the wound of mortality and human suffering.

The Spiral and the Journey: Two Forms of Self

The central and centralizing figure of all lyric poetry is the dramatized self. In trying to understand the nature of the dramatized self in Kunitz' work and how it functions, we gradually become aware that there are two distinct concepts of the self and that they are ultimately complimentary. Like the wave and particle theories of light, neither of which alone explains the phenomenon of light, both concepts of self are needed by Kunitz in order to let him tell his whole story.

The first is the concept of the spiraling self. The spiraling self represents our human impulse to return again and again to a particular issue. The spiraling self circles over this recurrent issue with a funneling motion that goes either higher (wider arcs) or lower (narrower), depending on whether the self is trying to rise above the issue or approach it more closely. Whether the self is ascending or descending, its purpose is the same: to arrive at a different level of being from which to view the same issue. To understand an old problem at a different level of being is to arrive at a new understanding of the problem.

The spiraling self acknowledges also the centripetal power of certain themes, images, or events (sometimes traumas) in human life: certain moments we return to again and again seeking release, transcendence, transformation, clarity. These powerful moments are none other than Kunitz' key images and are dominated by the powerful figures that often stand behind them: mother, father, beloved.

When we spoke earlier about the figures of Spirit and Nature behind the father and mother, we might also have spoken in terms of the spiraling self. The Spirit Father is at the same position on the spiral as the biological father, only on a higher level of being. When I say "higher" or "lower," I am not speaking evaluatively; lower simply means closer to the key image and its source in lived experience. Higher speaks about the self's impulse to deal with an event at the level of archetype or myth or by means of substitution and displacement—an impulse still anchored to its source in the world of experience.

The second self is the journeying self. If the spiraling self has a vertical impulse around a central key image, then the journeying self has a linear, horizontal movement. Here meaning concentrates in the figure of the self, the "I," as it journeys through the landscape of the poem. This self has a history in terms of pastness ("nostalgia" is its emotional coloring) and an impulse toward the onward journey (which it understands as "desire"). This self has an urgent, linear sense of time and of mortality. The journeying self is the one most adapted to the legend of being as it unfolds in the later poems, but often, as in "The Layers," both "selves" function together to create the fullest story.

The Constellation and the Spiraling Self

When Kunitz speaks about key images that recur throughout a poet's work, one might easily arrive at the notion of obsession. One could argue that the history of important lyric po-

etry from, say, Sappho or Petrarch on is a history of obsessed
poets whose obsessions are thematically profound. But there are
certain negative connotations to the word obsession which should
be confronted, connotations of narrowness and spiritual stasis or
fatalism. These negative connotations might seem appropriate to
a poet such as Sylvia Plath whose vision of the world might image the cluster of key images as a kind of interiorized astrological fatalism as in the final lines of her poem "Words":

> While
> From the bottom of the pool, fixed stars
> Govern a life.
>> (from *Ariel*)

But Stanley Kunitz' poetry is a poetry of survival, questing,
and renewal through imagination. If Kunitz' poetry errs in its
view of things, it errs deliberately on the side of the heroic:

> I am your man on the moon, a speck of
> megalomania, restless for the leap toward
> island universes pulsing beyond where the
> constellations set.
>> ("The Flight of Apollo," p. 48)

The question becomes: how does the concept of a cluster of
key images accommodate itself to movement and growth? The
answer is: through the spiraling self. The spiraling self can be
imagined as a funneling movement above a still center composed of the cluster of key images: a funneling movement above
a constellated stillness of images. If the key image can represent
the grim fixity of fate, then the spiraling self is motion, movement, possibility circling above fixity and seeking to transform
it.

We find real warrant for the notion of a dynamic spiral in the work itself:

> The spiral verb that weaves
> Through the crystal of our lives,
> Of myth and water made
> And incoherent blood . . .
>   ("A Spark of Laurel," p. 146)

We see the spiral motion self-consciously present in the poem title, "Revolving Meditation," whose opening lines enact the ambivalence of the spiraling self toward its own obsessions:

> How much I disapprove of it!
> How little I love it!
> Though, contrariwise,
> Can there be
> Anything half as dear?
>   (p. 143)

and whose later lines show the marriage of free will and compulsion that characterize the self that has yielded to the power of recurring images in order to unlock the mystery of their meaning:

> Preferring to hear, as I
> Am forced to hear . . .
>   (p. 145)

In this poem, Kunitz revolves around trauma seeking a way out, seeking a way to make the *circle* of endless repetition into a *spiral* of higher levels of consciousness (life become legend). In "Night Letter," we encounter "the spiral of a soul balanced on a stone" (p. 161).

In a late poem, "The Illumination," Dante appears to Kunitz, in a vision, standing in a spiral-like "cone of light" (p. 45). When the bewildered Dante speaks he says, "I was here before," and thus touches on a central truth of the spiraling self: the need to repeat a significant act or image in order to reach its meaning. Dante himself is both a spirit guide to Kunitz (a precursor poet who converted life into legend in his "Vita Nuova") and a Spirit Father: Kunitz' own, long-sought father at a higher level of being. Dante's "cone of light" and his return tell us about the spiraling self and its desire to transform.

If we were to inquire what image is at the center of Kunitz' funnel of self at its narrowest, we might follow another image of the spiral:

> The gestures made is woven in the sleeve,
> The spiral echo sinks into the grain.
>   ("The Harsh Judgment," p. 165)

The image here is of the knot in wood. It is a variant of the wound/mortality image in Kunitz: one that is heavily fated and static in this context. Kunitz' late poem "The Knot" enacts a triumph of renewal and affirmation over this fatal image that is both the father's death wound and all human mortality. Here the knot of "trauma" is not fixed and unalterable, for out of the very wound itself, renewal and regeneration occur:

> I hear it come
> with a rush of resin
> out of the trauma
> of its lopping-off.
> Obstinate bud,
> sticky with life.
>   (p. 1)

The spiraling self encounters a phenomenon again and again—hoping to transform it. The wisdom of *repetition* in regard to hard things is a lesson the natural world teaches in the late poem, "The Mulch":

> A man with a leaf in his head
> watches an indefatigable gull
> dropping a piss-clam on the rocks
> to break it open.
> Repeat. Repeat.
>
> (p. 55)

Later in the same poem we hear:

> "Try! Try!" clicks the beetle in his wrist

We are involved not only in the repetition of actions but the repetition of words—a favorite stylistic device in Kunitz. This phrasal repetition that occurs throughout Kunitz' work is closely linked to incantation and the magical use of language as a means of transformation:

> Ha! Once again I heard
> The transubstantial word
> That is not mine to speak
> Unless I break, I break.
> ("A Spark of Laurel," p. 146)

The Journeying Self

There is a second, equally central version of the self in Kunitz' work, one that complements the spiraling self but discloses its own meanings and possibilities. The journeying self might be the one Kunitz is referring to when he speaks of the strategy of certain modern artists: "A few dare to submit them-selves to the ordeal of walking through the fires of selfhood into a world of archetypal forms" (*Order/Folly*, p. 13). This version of the self emphasizes process, movement—images of journey that are linear as opposed to spiraling.

We encounter the journeying self at the very outset. In a poem from the first book, the speaker feels the need to leave a house and, in the final lines, embark on a journey:

> And I shall go
> By silent lanes and leave you timeless here.
> ("In a Strange House," p. 232)

The final poem of this book, "Vita Nuova," echoes these lines— "And I will go, unburdened, on the quiet lane / Of my eternal kind." "Vita Nuova" takes its title from Dante's poem of spiri-tual rebirth after loss. It establishes the quest as a central struc-tural device of individual poems as well as a theme for the work as a whole.

In "Vita Nuova" the journey is specifically concerned with the father. Later, the journey becomes an image for a meta-physical gesture:

> But I fly towards Possibility,
> In the extravagantly gay
> Surprise of a journey,
> Careless that I am bound
> To the flaming wheel of my bones
> ("Revolving Meditation," p. 145)

In the image of the flaming wheel, fate (the spiral flattened to the closed repetition of circle) impinges on the freedom and op-timism of the journey metaphor.

Journey in Kunitz is related to quest—to the heroic self encountering the basic conditions of its personal destiny (as in "The Approach to Thebes," where an omniscient Oedipus journeys to the city) or the impersonal hugeness of the universe, as in "The Flight of Apollo," where the astronaut speaks:

> Earth was my home, but even there I was a stranger. This mineral crust. I walk like a swimmer. What titanic bombardments in those old astral wars! I know what I know: I shall never escape from strangeness or complete my journey. Think of me as nostalgic, afraid, exalted. I am your man on the moon, a speck of megalomania, restless for the leap toward island universes pulsing beyond where the constellations set. (p. 48)

The ultimate imperative of the journey is courage:

> It is necessary to go
> through dark and deeper dark
> and not to turn.
> ("The Testing-Tree," p. 92)

The journey is recognized in later Kunitz poetry as the appropriate governing metaphor for the legend of being: it is the truest story of our consciousness. The salmon on his journey upriver to spawn and die is an image of ourselves, our creature selves. He is pulled forward by desire, pulled backward in imagination by nostalgia, but he *exists* "in the state of his shining"—that is: in the active intensity of the journey itself. There is no rest, and no goal. Finally, even death is regarded as "the threshold of the last great mystery"—a mere marker the heroic journeyer will pass and pass beyond:

> no doubt the next chapter
> in my book of transformations
> is already written.
> I am not done with my changes.
> ("The Layers," p. 36)

"The Layers" is no doubt the penultimate poem of the journey. It begins:

> I have walked through many lives,
> some of them my own,
> and I am not who I was,
> though some principle of being
> abides, from which I struggle
> not to stray.
>
> (p. 35)

In the midst of this poem celebrating the journey of self, we find a precise image of the spiral (here partly repudiated by the ambiguous adjective "scavenger") and the static constellation of key images which the spiral moves above:

> and the slow fires trailing
> from the abandoned camp-sites,
> over which scavenger angels
> wheel on heavy wings.
>
> (p. 35)

The dominant journey image returns:

> Yet I turn, I turn,
> exulting somewhat,
> with my will intact to go
> wherever I need to go,
> and every stone on the road
> precious to me.
>
> (pp. 35–36)

This journey has purpose, if only in its own courageous acceptance of the process itself, and is contrasted with a purposeless and meaningless form of journey in which "I roamed through wreckage."

Kunitz has always arranged the sequence of his poems within a book with the utmost care. It is therefore significant that the first poem in a very late book is a major poem of the vertically rising spiraling self ("The Knot") and the final poem is metaphorically governed by the journeying self ("The Layers").

Because the journey takes place inside history and time, it has an implied beginning and end. Kunitz tends to focus his poems in mid-journey, even when the end is foreknown as in "The Approach to Thebes." Why? At one level Kunitz is deeply fatalistic—"the verdict's bitten on the brazen gates," Oedipus says of his future ("The Approach to Thebes," p. 112). It is possible to say that death ends all journeys—and against the tension of that fate, Kunitz protests with the power of imagination to transform or the self itself to metamorphose. Out of the great negation comes the heroic affirmation of being:

> Let be! Let be!
> I shake my wings
> and fly into its boughs.
> ("The Knot," p. 1)

The human self journeys from beginning to end. But because of imagination, we are both more and less than human: we can descend to the creature self or fly upward as the angel/bird/winged demon of the final lines of "The Knot." In other words, the vertical nature of the spiraling self is not simply linked to trauma's recurrence but also to the way the imagining self eludes its fate in time.

Survival and Self

In Kunitz' work the questing self is a self determined to survive against the odds of "the hurt / Which is unanswerable [and] fill[s] the brow / with early death" ("Beyond Reason"). The themes of identity and a surviving self merge in later Kunitz:

> My name is Solomon Levi,
> the desert is my home,
> my mother's breast was thorny,
> and father I had none.
>
> The sands whispered, *Be separate,*
> the stones taught me, *Be hard.*
> I dance, for the joy of surviving,
> on the edge of the road.
> ("An Old Cracked Tune," p. 87)

In this poem's persona we recapitulate the characteristics of the parental dynamic in Kunitz' imaginative life: the rejecting mother, the almost mythically absent father, and the psychic consequences for the son's identity—the ambiguous lessons of isolation and "hardness." But the final resolution is again one of affirmation: the sheer act of survival becomes a joy and a motive for being.

In the later work, intensity of being and intensity of desire fuse and become the animating force of the surviving self, as seen in "Journal for My Daughter," where Kunitz depicts himself as a "white-haired prowler" haunting his daughter's dreams and life:

> the folded message in his hands
> is stiff with dirt and wine-stains,
> older than the Dead Sea Scrolls.
> Daughter, read:

> *What do I want of my life?*
> *More! More!*
>
> (p. 42)

Or in the climactic incantation of "The Knot" where the repeated exclamation exists paradoxically as both a plea for the life force to desist and an affirmation of that very life force in all its intensity: "Let be! Let be!"

For Kunitz the quest for identity involves encounters with such painful aspects of the human condition as suffering, trauma, fear, loss, rejection, and mortality: those aspects of the human condition that most threaten the self and its search for meaning. These aspects are encountered in the arena of the dramatic lyric and a representative struggle ensues, out of which the self emerges as the human embodiment of being. A touchstone for the self's encounter with negating forces might be a statement by Paul Tillich, which Kunitz quotes in his 1977 *Columbia* magazine interview: "the self-affirmation of a being is stronger the more non-being it can take into itself" (p. 5).

The Private and the Personal in Lyric Poetry

When Baudelaire speaks of the poet as a kind of "public dreamer," he is describing both the nature of a kind of lyric poem and the curious burdens it puts on the poet and the facts of the poet's life. If the dream is a model for the process and the product of a certain kind of lyric imagination, then how is the lyric poem to be reconciled to a higher order than the self? Kunitz has endorsed Gerard Manley Hopkins' statement that he desires a poetry which retains "the taste of self," and his own program, the "conversion of life into legend," is a precise statement of such a poet's task in expanding the implications of lyric poetry without denying the central, centralizing reality of the self.

A major lyric poet such as Baudelaire, Rilke, or Yeats gambles on his ability to dramatize the personal issues of the life in such a way that we as readers gain access to them and yet they retain the tension and intensity of private crisis. An important audience aspect of this endeavor is *curiosity:* we want to know about other lives; we want to hear stories about other lives. The power of curiosity can operate in the poet's favor almost as a magical spell when the story is presented in compelling language as in Coleridge's "The Rime of the Ancient Mariner":

> He holds him with his glittering eye—
> The Wedding-Guest stood still,
> And listens like a three years' child:
> The Mariner hath his will.
>
> The Wedding-Guest sat on a stone:
> He cannot choose but hear.

The other aspect, which rests with the poet, is his ability to exteriorize the drama of the life and give it aesthetic structure. It is a test of the power of this kind of lyric poet's imagination—whether or not he can dramatize the private tensions, crises, images, and events of his life in such a way as to make them meaningful and accessible to others.

Yeats succeeded in assimilating facts and events of another person's life into the ongoing themes of his poetry: Maude Gonne is a dramatis persona in his work and undergoes even further imaginative transformation to appear as Helen of Troy. In Baudelaire we see mythological structures and references, but we also see a version of "warring opposites" or "polarized contradictions" (the ideal and the real world; the dream and the reality of "The Double Room" of *Paris Spleen*), a strategy that also appears in early Kunitz. One of the main functions of literary allusion (e.g., the Neoplatonic and Christian references in early Kunitz) is as a storehouse of publicly accessible images that can mediate between the poet's private world and the public world of the reader.

Privacy ultimately translates as failure in lyric poetry. The poem must be rooted deeply in the personal, and yet some level of universality of human experience must be posited and located, either consciously or unconsciously, by the poet in the work. The poem must go from the level of life to the level of legend.

In one of Kunitz' rare commentaries on a poem of his own ("Father and Son"), we have a lucid statement of the connection between life and legend (i.e., poem) that is central to his ethos as a poet:

> I do not propose to launch into a full-scale autobiography here, but I am ready to say that all the essential details of the poem are true, as true as dreams are, with their characteristic fusions, substitutions, and dislocations. (*Order/Folly*, p. 124.)

We have here the meeting of outer and inner reality, life and legend. We also have the dream as a model for the transformation process (what Kunitz calls "conversion"). The process is complex, involving fusion, substitutions, and dislocations: the powerful processes of the associative imagination that are central to Kunitz' art. These processes are irrational but intelligent; as Freud believes, dreaming is that mode of thought employed by the mind when it is asleep.

To say that such a poet is egocentric or narcissistic is to miss the point and the purpose of such poetry. The "I" of such a poem is also a transformed "I," a dramatized figure whose movement through the language of the poem is a representative human quest for meaning in a particular set of circumstances. Such a poet cannot escape the power of certain events in his life, but he can transform, through imagination, these events in such a way that they crystallize and constitute meaning.

One may be, as Auden says of Yeats, "hurt into poetry"— but poetry is hurt transformed. Kunitz is hurt into his quest, and the quest discloses level upon level of meaning as it spirals outwards from its source in pain. Lines of Yeats on the power of imagination and self-transformation seem relevant here:

> *The friends that have it I do wrong*
> *When ever I remake a song,*
> *Should know what issue is at stake:*
> *It is myself that I remake.*[5]

The dramatic lyric poet knows that the "I" of the poems is not limited by the conditions of the "I" of the life: the poet's quest is to remake the "I" into that form of meaning known as the poem. The self, the "I" of the poems, is the figure that enacts the drama, but the poet's belief is in imagination (which transforms) and in poetry itself. What poetry accomplishes is the embodiment of the transformed life beyond oblivion and change, in the crystallized permanence of form and the eternal present of its telling.

The dramatized lyric I am describing consists of at least three parts: *the life,* those subjective and objective facts to which the

5. William Butler Yeats, *The Collected Works in Verse and Prose of William Butler Yeats* (Stratford-on-Avon: 1908), vol. 2, unpaged proem. This is the only appearance of this poem previous to the Variorum Edition.

poet is compelled to be faithful; *the legend,* that level of the human story that is shared and is in some way universal or archetypal; and *conversion,* the dynamic process that transforms life into legend and which poets are prone to call imagination. Life and legend, when successfully functioning in a poem, are parallel levels of being. A curious thing about the dramatic lyric is that we do not find it satisfying or compelling if it takes place entirely on the level of legend; it must have what Hopkins called "the taste of self."

In connection with conversion, a quotation from Kunitz serves to emphasize the lyric poet's faith in the power of magical language (here the key image) and his personal yet universally comprehensible motive: "It's curious how certain images out of the life—not necessarily the most spectacular—keep flashing signals from the depths, as if to say: 'Come down to me—and be reborn!' " (*Order/Folly,* p. 305.)

Kunitz' poems often ponder or enact the process of transformation and are consciously concerned with spiritual renewal through transforming imagination. Such a poem will sometimes contain the dross (the "litter") in order to transform it at poem's end, as in "Revolving Meditation" or "My Surgeons," both from *Selected Poems.* Keats' notion, expressed in a letter of May, 1819, that this world is not a "vale of tears," as religion misconceives it to be, but "a vale of soul-making" speaks directly to the poet's self-appointed task of self-transformation and spiritual growth through imagination.

Form and the Dramatic Lyric: Story, Symbol, and Self

A poet whom I respect a great deal once announced to me that "all personal tragedy is in fact metaphysical tragedy." I responded that to me the converse seemed true: "All metaphysi-

cal tragedy is in fact personal tragedy." The two of us represented two profoundly differing temperaments; his abstracted the
tragic encounters of his personal life; mine personalized phenomena which, tragic or not, are part of the human condition. I
thought at the time that these temperaments could not be reconciled, could not coexist in one consciousness or one poetry.

Kunitz, in his best work, resolves themes on both a personal, psychological level and a metaphysical level, and with equal
authority. When the legend of the beloved and mother is followed forward through Kunitz' work, it culminates psychologically in "The Magic Curtain"—where the beloved replaces the
mother and love and forgiveness replace angry intransigence. At
the metaphysical level, it resolves itself in "A Spark of Laurel,"
where "mother and mistress" are recognized as one, and identified as the source of tragic (fatal) poetry: siren and Clytemnes-
tra: the dark, compelling muse.

If "The Magic Curtain" resolves itself as *story* (the human,
linear level), then "A Spark of Laurel" resolves itself as *symbol*
(the transcendent, vertical gesture). Story and symbol are the
two central forms of meaning available to poetry structured by
nonrational intelligence.

When Tolstoy remarks that "all happy families resemble one
another," he is acknowledging the necessary and experienced link
between disharmony and story. Where there is no disharmony,
no discrete centers of energy, there can be no interesting story.
The *drama* of the dramatic lyric necessitates conflict and contraries. When in "The Marriage of Heaven and Hell" Blake says,
"Without Contraries is no progression. Attraction and Repul-
sion, Reason and Energy, Love and Hate, are necessary to Human Existence," we might add that they are necessary to human story as well. At the formal level, the contraries of story
polarize language: make it tense, intensify it. Without the ten-

sion-creating quality of disharmonious story, language would simply dribble down the page.

In Kunitz' poetry, the drama can be an interior drama such as the primordial conflict of heart–mind, or some other polarity such as memory versus oblivion. When it is external, it might be that most ancient of dramas: he–she. The main point is that a fundamental structure of the dramatic lyric is that of a story in which two centers of energy (often two characters, sometimes a character and a landscape or object) enact a drama that polarizes and intensifies language while the story moves through time (down the page) toward some resolution of its conflict. A lyric poet who fails to discover or posit this essential underlying framework of contraries may be forced to exaggerate the sensuous, nondiscursive aspects of language (e.g., "The Lost Son" of Roethke or many of the poems of Hart Crane).

We often speak of a poet's gifts, certain innate talents that discipline and experience can develop but cannot substitute for. Among the most frequently mentioned are a "good ear" (i.e., a sensitivity in hearing and employing sounds), a gift for metaphors, and a feel for compelling rhythms. I would assert that, in the case of the dramatic lyric, a gift for formal unity should be included in the list of talents or gifts the ideal poet is blessed with. If we acknowledge the existence of organic form as Coleridge defines it, we must account for it as an innate predisposition and possession of the poet's consciousness, not just of the individual poems the poet produces.

In the dramatic lyric, the gift for formal unity is inextricably tied up with the self. The self is that central, centralizing force that constellates all the elements of language and experience into that peculiar form of meaning called the poem. The image I would use for this "self" and its role is derived from chemistry: it is possible under certain conditions to create a supersaturated chemical solution in which molecules are held in suspension and do not precipitate out. When a piece of string is lowered into a beaker of this liquid, the molecules cling to and crystallize around the string. That string is the self lowered into the supersaturated solution of the unconscious: language clings to it in forms as absolute and precise as the internal structure of each crystal, yet as seemingly random as the attachment of one crystal cluster to the next along the string.

The self is a given quality of consciousness, a gift. The lyric poet possesses it and *must* possess it in order to create lyric poetry that has the unity and wholeness we require of all art. Like all gifts and talents, it is possessed in greater degree by some poets than by others; some lack it almost entirely and strive to compensate for it through learned skills.

Keeping in mind one of Kunitz' definitions of the key image ("You have at the center of your being a conglomeration of feelings, emotions, memories, traumas that are uniquely yours, that nobody else on earth can replicate. They are the clue to your identity"), we can say that for a lyric poet the self means having access to a lifetime's key images, images which form the structures of consciousness and the structures of poems.

It is difficult to say exactly where and how this self exists in the life of the poet. It is certainly not the ordinary ego-I of the poet's daily existence. Perhaps we can locate and ponder it best by studying the transformed "I" that enacts the drama of the poem, because it is there—in the poem—that we see the self as the active, formative, form-giving principle of the lyric. Even when the "I" is not overtly present in the poem, the self is present: each word is its footprint in the snow of the page. To return to the earlier image—even when the self is not manifest, it must be there *within* the language of the poem, just as the string is present within its sheath of crystals.

CHAPTER 1

Intellectual Things

"In my youth," Kunitz told Robert Boyers, "I suppose I rather willed myself on being a hermetic poet."[1] No more precise or lucid comment could be made about the youthful work of *Intellectual Things*. The almost archaic usage of "I . . . willed myself" gives proper emphasis to the active role of will in the early work. Kunitz also acknowledges his desire for hermeticism—a clue to the difficulty of the early poems.

The poems in this book survive because of their intelligence and intensity. They are highly allusive, fusing and mingling images and themes derived from religion (primarily Christianity), metaphysics (primarily Plato and the Neoplatonists), the English literary tradition (primarily Shakespeare and the Metaphysicals), and Kunitz' own obscure legends.

At this stage, Kunitz sees poetry as a noble, occult calling; one in which the high mysteries of art, metaphysics, and religion may reveal themselves to the man who steeps himself in secret, sacred knowledge. The poem itself is frequently a journey/quest.

The title of the first book is taken from William Blake's "The Grey Monk":

---

1. Interview, *Salmagundi*, (1973), nos. 22–23, p. 71.

> For a tear is an intellectual thing
> and a sigh is the sword of an angel king

Blake's lines signal both a metaphysical ambition and a stylistic strategy in early Kunitz' work—by an act of imagination Blake insists on the identity of the abstract and the physical, intellect and feeling. If we say that the Kunitz of *Intellectual Things* is a metaphysical poet, we are in danger of saying only half the truth. In the best of the poems, he does not illustrate metaphysical dilemmas by referring to physical things, but fuses the metaphysical and the visceral.

Kunitz' own personal legends are, at best, known only partly to the poems of this book; they show up more as subthemes than themes. The third poem in the volume, "For the Word Is Flesh," presents the quest for the father in terms that are simultaneously straightforward and obscure. The poem's title is essential early Kunitz: a phrase which, when played off against the poem's content, enacts an entire drama within itself. Nowhere can we better see the intensity with which Kunitz attempts to fuse the metaphysical and the physical. A first, unironic reading of the title appears to affirm the mystical incarnation of the Logos and carries with it strong suggestions of the magical power of language and of poetry. Its immediate source might be the New Testament:

> For the Word was made flesh, and dwelt among us, and we beheld his glory, the glory as of the only begotten son of the Father full of grace and truth. John 1:14

This affirmative reading, in which the power of Logos infuses the human body, will encounter an ironic, reversed reading in which the power of fleshly decay and death infect the Logos. These "contraries" (to use Blake's phrase) appear at first to be reconciled in the declarative nature of the title, but beneath we see a struggle enacted.

"For the Word Is Flesh" opens with a tone of mingled invocation and beseeching and addresses the dead father directly, with a warning and a demand:

> O ruined father dead, long sweetly rotten
> Under the dial, the time-dissolving urn,
> Beware a second perishing, forgotten,
> Heap fallen leaves of memory to burn
> On the slippery rock, the black eroding heart,
> Before the wedged frost splits it clean apart.
>
> (p. 190)

The syntax of the complex first sentence (the entire stanza) demands that a long-dead father be active enough to "heap fallen leaves of memory to burn" or else risk a "second perishing." This ambiguous existence of the dead father is central to Kunitz' poetry in general and this verbal formula ("ruined father . . . heap fallen leaves") establishes it in all its strangeness. The stanza asserts that a fire of memory could halt a natural process (frost) that threatens the integrity of a "slippery rock" and by extension such possibly stone objects as the "time-dissolving urn." Death, a first perishing, has already triumphed, but a second perishing still threatens.

The second stanza further focuses the poem on the relationship of the living to the dead: "What shall the quick commemorate?" The relationship is tied to memory and to words:

> what deeds
> Ephemeral, what dazzling words that flare
> Like rockets from the mouth to burst in air?

Sons and fathers, the living and the dead, are poles of energy in this poem. Language is that thing which might mediate between these poles: words that commemorate. The final verb of the first stanza, "splits," is the destructive consequence of frost, and the final verb of the second stanza, "burst," is related through the pun on rockets as "fireworks" to the preventive and preservative power of "fire" in stanza 1. Nonetheless, "burst" partakes of ephemerality; it like the entire stanza, is a hope extended and withdrawn.

Stanza 3 shifts strategy and subject, proposing in an anecdotal manner the possibility that souls survive death:

> Of hypochondriacs that gnawed their seasons
> In search of proofs, Lessius found twenty-two
> Fine arguments, Tolet gave sixty reasons
> Why souls survive . . .

But this detached approach of reason and argument is seen as an evasion, as irrelevant both to the dead father and to the son who rejects such a possibility. The personal urgency surges up as the sentence continues into the fourth stanza where the "factual spikes" and agony of the crucified Christ overwhelm the consoling Platonic fantasy of Er:

> And what are they to you?
> And, father, what to me, who cannot blur
> The mirrored brain with fantasies of Er,
>
> Remembering such factual spikes as pierce
> The supplicating palms, and by the sea
> Remembering the eyes, I hear the fierce
> Wild cry of Jesus on the holy tree,
> Yet have of you no syllable to keep,
> Only the deep rock crumbling in the deep.

It is not merely the physical factuality of the spikes and eyes that compel the speaker's allegiance. The "fierce wild cry of Jesus" is a buried allusion to the primacy and anguish of human relationship, something unacknowledged in Plato. Just as the poem's title derives from John, the fierce wild cry must be that of the Gospels of Matthew and Mark: "Eloi, Eloi, lama sabach thani?"—"My God, My God, why hast thou forsaken me?" This is the anguished cry of the Son to the Father. It is typical of this densely allusive poem, which seems to want to hide as much as it wants to reveal, that the reader must introduce the content of the "fierce wild cry" into the context of the poem in order to unlock more of the poem's meaning and structure. (And this is what Kunitz means when he says that he "rather willed himself on being a hermetic poet.")

In one sense the story of Jesus represents the "word made flesh"—an abstract principle (here seemingly one of suffering and supplication) incarnated in the physical and factual world. The speaker "remembers" Jesus because of literature, because deeds and words were recorded. The story of Jesus represents "the flesh made word"—the power of language to commemorate deeds and words in such a way as to transcend death and oblivion.

It is this awareness of how time-transcending literature is dependent on ephemeral deeds and words that brings the son/speaker back to his father. He has "no syllable" of his father's to keep, nothing to build upon, nothing tangible except "the deep rock crumbling in the deep." We have come full circle to the imagery of stanza 1: the final image of the "deep rock crumbling" (a kind of underwater gravestone?) telescopes all the objects in stanza 1: the garden sundial, and "time-dissolving" memorial (carved of stone) as well as "the slippery rock, the black eroding heart." If so the image of "the deep rock crumbling in the deep" represents a complete triumph of decay and oblivion, in which the only physical relic of the father succumbs to further decay and dissolution.

In a sense, the poem completes itself at the end of stanza 4. Not only the imagery but the repetition of "deep" gives a strong sense of closure to the stanza's final line. There is a marked shift from stanza 4 to stanza 5, enough to make it seem at first a detached and detachable epilogue to the poem's drama. One indication of this shift is that the terms of the underlying relationship change. In each of the preceding stanzas the father was addressed directly (Father, Senior, your); now he is subsumed in the impersonal, generalizing category of "fathers." Likewise the speaker's personal urgency disappears into "sons." The imperative grammatical form of the stanza's two sentences completes the impersonality:

> Observe the wisdom of the Florentine
> Who, feeling death upon him, scribbled fast
> To make revision of a deathbed scene,
> Gloating that he was accurate at last.

These lines appear to be endorsing the Florentine writer's complete detachment from his own situation when encountering his imminent death. The anecdotal nature of these lines makes them stylistically parallel to stanza 3's Tolet and Lessius, who also exhibit detachment: as Tolet and Lessius are pedants of the Beyond, the Florentine is a pedant of the death scene. Where they gathered arguments to refute the completeness of death, his response is to transform the fact of his death immediately into accurate literature. Lest this seem too straightforwardly heroic a response, we have language that undercuts the dignity of the endeavor ("scribbled") and the individual himself ("gloating"). In a further sense, the anecdote of the Florentine, for all its purported "wisdom," fails to encounter one of the two basic dramatic premises of the poem: he is neither father nor son. The Florentine exists in an existential vacuum and this trivializes his literary effort, especially when compared to Jesus' "fierce wild cry on the holy tree."

The anecdote of the Florentine appears to culminate in an ironic way the poem's theme of the power of literature over personal mortality. But in fact the remarkable final couplet returns the theme of literature to the heroic sphere for a final, devastating irony at the same time that it completes the poem's other theme, that of the living son's relationship with the dead father:

> Let sons learn from their lipless fathers how
> Man enters hell without a golden bough.

"Let sons learn." This is one of the main goals of the father legend throughout Kunitz' work: the seeking of wisdom and knowledge. This is the essence of the son's beseeching: teach me. What he learns, what sons learn from the dead fathers is the absolute triumph of physical death and oblivion. *The Aeneid* is turned inside out: there is no return from death, whether or not one is Aeneas or the forsaken Jesus.

The episode in Book VI of *The Aeneid* is invoked only to be repudiated. Not only is the physical decay of the dead stressed: the "lipless" fathers communicate their morbid wisdom by their very inability to speak. Their "words" are flesh in the grimmest sense. Just as the transcendent fantasies of Er were rejected at the end of stanza 3, the mythic fantasy of *The Aeneid* is rejected in favor of the "factual" reality of physical decay.

The title's irony is now complete. The "second perishing" is inevitable. The fallen leaves of memory are doomed to rot rather than be transformed into the fire of literature. Likewise, the sons, no matter how heroic, will be forsaken, as Jesus was, and will enter death without the golden bough that assures return passage to the land of the living.

If Kunitz succeeds in imagining a successful father legend in *Intellectual Things*, as he will do in "Vita Nuova," the story will not take place on the physical plane where death and decay rule but on a transcendent plane.

Although the second of the main legends, the son–mother/beloved, plays a much smaller role in the first book, it is nevertheless present in the significant poem entitled "Poem." If the legend of the son's quest for the father is characterized by a beseeching, a seeking after guidance and wisdom, then the legend of the mother/beloved is characterized by the son's struggle to break free of the powerful maternal relationship in order to achieve a mature erotic relationship in the world. According to the version of the mother/beloved legend that appears in "Poem," the son's movement away from the mother is thwarted by her:

> In the year of my mother's blood, when I was born,
> She buried my innocent head in a field, because the earth
> Was sleepy with the winter.
>
> (p. 198)

The poem's structure is circular, the first and last lines are identical:

> O Heart! this is a dream I had, or not a dream.

What progress the poem appears to make in its linear narrative movement (from mother to beloved) is overwhelmed and encircled by this line. The dream—to the extent that it is a dream—

is concerned with a truth that emanates from the gates of horn rather than those of ivory. The son/speaker of "Poem" will undergo two deaths at the hands of the feminine, just as the father of "For the Word Is Flesh" was threatened by "a second perishing" against which the poet son struggled.

> O Heart! this is a dream I had, or not a dream.
> Lovingly, lovingly, I wept, but my tears did not rhyme.

Tears, things from the physical world, are expected to rhyme—their failure to do so is the son's first defeat. This linking of the physical world and the abstract world of formal language in a magical relationship is reminiscent of "For the Word Is Flesh" and is a recurring concern of Kunitz' work. The poem consists of fourteen couplets plus a final line that repeats the opening line. Couplets are the appropriate form for tears; and although as the poem asserts, the opening couplet does not rhyme, the following couplets rhyme alternately.

It is a mythic fable, reminiscent of a Blakean visionary poem like "For the Sexes." It is a central poem because it relates the fable of the human consciousness growing through various births, deaths, and rebirths toward adult sexuality. The child's first death comes at the hands of the mother:

> In the year of my mother's blood, when I was born,
> She buried my innocent head in a field, because the earth
>
> Was sleepy with the winter.

The child's head is like a seed, and the mother's action is in accordance with the natural seasons. The child and specifically the child's language (in which the child speaks corn and cries the clover into germination) are magically linked to vegetative renewal:

> . . . And I spoke the corn,
> And I cried the clover up, with the dewy mouth of my mirth.

That leads to a vegetative self-begetting related to the summer and its "long generation":

> That leads to a vegetative self-begetting related to the summer and its "long generation":
>
> In the honey of summer my brain conceived: a child, I flowered
> Over the maiden-stalks, drinking sweet upper light

The vegetative child is intensely related to the sun, until that relationship turns destructive:

> For I was intimate with the sun, till he devoured
> Me utterly, O Heart, his tenderest neophyte.

A second death occurs (this time at the hands of a male figure); and a second rebirth occurs. This birth, though still related by the image of mandrake and loam to vegetative nature, clearly marks a birth to a plane of being that is more humanlike:

> The cyclic hour I pulled life's bony root, slow inch
> By inch, from its loamy trap; shrilly, like a mandrake, screamed
>
> To rip the cord, suck liberal air

The second rebirth brings an awareness of a woman as object of sexual desire:

> Womanly, a shadow combed
>
> Her dark tremendous hair beyond the violet border
> Of my sleep. Strong passionate hands I had, but could not find
>
> The red position of her heart, nor the subtle order
> Of her lips and breasts, nor the breathing cities of her mind.

The images shift from the power of mouth (ll. 5–6) to "hand" as instruments of adult sexual desire. This attempt to grasp the love object is thwarted "because our sorrows did not coincide," an ominous echo of the tears that did not rhyme in line 2. This leads the speaker to a self-destructive gesture:

> I broke the spine of my pride
>
> Upon a stone

In the image of "the spine of my pride" we have an early instance of one of the central, recurring images in Kunitz' poetry: a phallic image that represents intensity of being and pride. In "Poem" these images are clearly related to the sexual theme of the poem, in their first appearance as "life's bony root" and in the allegorized image of the spine of pride.[2]

The self-destructive gesture of breaking the spine is followed by a further act, a suicide of the sexually thwarted self, which reenacts the mother's first thwarting and links the speaker to vegetation again but in a conclusive, negative way:

> Softly grieving, ironic at the gates of horn,
> I took my baffled head and buried it under the corn.

By passing through a series of small cycles of birth and death, the self has progressed up the scale of being only to be finally fatally enclosed in a larger cycle that "baffles" and defeats him. The self in early Kunitz tends to equate desire and destructive-

2. The centrality of the phallic symbol in Kunitz's work is seen in another early love poem, "Geometry of Moods." The poem's primary conceit is the Neoplatonic concentric crystal spheres of the universe, within which the speaker is "core of the world, a bead in a ball of glass." But what Kunitz adds to this traditional conceit is an aetherialized phallus at the center: "My spinal pole, tipped with a globe of light." The central image of the poem "Very Tree" is a transcendent tree beyond vegetative nature's "flowering stick / Filled with the sperm of sun," yet nevertheless sharing its shape.

ness and feels compelled to censor the erotic impulse as in the final lines of "So Intricately Is the World Resolved":

> O lover,
> Lift no destroying hand; let fortune pass
> Unchallenged, beauty sleep; dare not to cover
> Her mouth with kisses by the garden wall,
> Lest, cracking in bright air, a planet fall.
>
> (p. 228)

The image of the beloved in *Intellectual Things* tends to be idealized in such a way as to preclude any human particularity. Her attributes are more likely to be derived from literature—from Marvell and mythology—than from direct observation. When the speaker attempts to collapse the distance between the idealized beloved and himself by a gesture or deed of desire, as in "Poem," it ends disastrously. The beloved has an ambiguous identity in the early poems: idealized, she belongs to the realm of art and literature—beautiful but unsatisfying.

Consider her appearance in "Postscript":

> A man can starve upon the golden-sweet
> Impossible apples of Cezanne; a man
> Can eagerly consult a woman's head
> (Picasso's), but her slow and stupid eyes
> Drink light in vegetative apathy.
>
> (p. 211)

In that poem's concluding lines, the beloved's physical reality leaves the speaker equally "baffled" and unsatisfied:

> O darling, a man can cry out to his love
> All night and day, and still be comfortless.
> The meaning of a mouth, a breast, is plain,
> But what you mean to me is dipped in blood
> And tangled like the bright threads of a dream.

The early poems of the beloved legend cannot progress past this "bright tangle" of desire and frustration. That the "meaning" of the beloved is "dipped in blood" refers to the central mystery around which all the poems of *Intellectual Things* orbit: mortality, death, the terror of vegetative decay. The figure of the beloved in the early poems is trapped by this agony: as a physical being, an object of desire, she partakes of death and vegetative decay; as a figure idealized in such a way as to transcend the flesh that rots, she is aetherialized beyond human particularity and the deeds of desire.

Though the enormous emotional and intellectual intensity of Kunitz' early poems is frustrated in relation to the beloved, it is channeled effectively inward and focused on Kunitz' other ambition, that of art (by which Kunitz always means poetry). "Mens Creatrix" is a poem which turns its attention to the process of creation itself: the creating mind. The subject authorizes a turning away from the external world and a focusing on inner event—something which the intense self of the early poems, thwarted in its effort to reach the father or the beloved, can be grateful for. The poem begins with an aspiration toward cold, pure, emotionless thought:

> Brain, be ice,
> A frozen bowl of thought,
> Pure radius of the marble eye . . .
>
> (p. 202)

Stanza 2 represents a triumph of the "freezing" ability of brain that encloses/entombs the fever of blood and calms it, the necessary precondition for a further aspiration: the desire to "hear / The truthful pulse of beauty / Beyond this evil good." "Evil good" is the poem's term for ordinary consciousness which is divided and in conflict with itself: "brain" is threatened by "blood," cold thought by "trembling thigh." The poem's tone is one of magical invocation in which the mind is commanded to "Be fever's sepulcher, / Entomb the noise of frightened blood." By the end of stanza 2 this symbolic death has been accomplished and the "sepulcher" of stanza 2 has become, by analogical shape, the "mental womb" that now confronts a theophanic event:

> Mental womb,
> Intelligence of tight
> Precision: He comes, the sudden Lord,
> A rhythmic Spike of Light,
> To cleave you with that spike:
> Himself, His flowing Word.
>
> Strike, O Poem, Strike!

The god's form is lightning-like; his manifestation that of violent sexual assault. The mentally constructed womb/tomb is "cleaved" open by the god who is a "rhythmic Spike of Light" and a "flowing Word." A mingling of the imagery of sexuality, religion, and language is typical of *Intellectual Things,* as in the postcoital reverie of "Promise Me": "with the cross / Fallen, the breast in disrepair." Or in the resurrection of "When the Dead Arise":

> When this maggoty dumb earth
> Prounounces verbs erect and vertabrate,
> Will the sexes flow with sweet
> Wild honey of God's mirth?

In "Mens Creatrix," "rhythmic" and "flowing" represent a resurgence of the principle of motion which in stanza 2 was associated with blood and feeling—as if a resurrection had taken place, or, more accurately, a "translation" from the physical body to the "body" of the poem. The pulse in the veins has become the rhythmic pulse of language in poetry.

The language of the third stanza ("He comes, the sudden Lord") seems to echo a Greek chorus announcing, by epithet, Dionysus or some similar, violent god. It is simultaneously a supplication to the god seeking his appearance and an announcement of the imminence of that appearance. Its fusion of spike and incarnate word seems Christian (one thinks of the "factual spikes" of "For the Word Is Flesh"), but finally the tone seems closer to that of the Greek mystery cults whose initiation rituals of death and resurrection contributed to the Christian crucifixion mystery.

The poem itself is a magic ritual. The "He" of the third stanza is the sudden Lord, a rhythmic Spike of Light, Himself, his flowing Word, and the Poem. This flurry of identities is a mystery of simultaneous beings not attributes. He is the spike *and* the word which the spike causes to flow. The poem, like the god, embodies *and* enacts its mystery. Kunitz here, as elsewhere, insists on the magical properties of language in poetry.

"For the Word Is Flesh" treated the theme of poetry's power over death ironically in relation to the father quest. In "Mens Creatrix" the theme of poetry and the power of resurrection is interiorized: the object of resurrection is human consciousness, not a physical being in the world, and the poem can declare its faith with the forceful authority of Donne's "Batter my heart three-personed God."

Death is the central affront to the poet of *Intellectual Things*, and sometimes the dramatic structure of death and resurrection seems to tempt the speaker to take a quasi-Christian stance, as in these lines from "Deciduous Branch": "I brood / On a Chris-

tian thing: unless the leaves / Perish, the tree is not renewed"
(p. 200). But the dominant metaphysical stance of the book is
the quasi-Platonic transcendence exemplified by "Very Tree"
which admonishes us to "Forget the tube of bark, / Alliterative
leaves" and to reject as well the "Bright incidental bird" whose
song is the "Wild spool of the winding word." The words "alliterative" and "winding word" indicate that the external, sensual
tree of the first two stanzas of the poem is associated with language and with poetry. Such a tree is repudiated in favor of an
ideal, essential tree ("let there be / Only Tree"), for:

> Earth's absolute arithmetic
> Of being is not in the flowering stick
> Filled with the sperm of sun,
> But in a figure seen
> Behind our eyelids when we close
> Slow petals of the brain
> At evening like a rose.
>
> (p. 207)

"Very Tree" describes the process of interiorizing the essential tree, and thus escaping time ("timeless structure") and
the impure mutability of the physical world. But once the tree
is reduced to its essence ("Stripped of green root and leaf / Get-
ting no seed to sprout), once its "loveliness" or esthetic meaning
has been proclaimed ("Yet lovely, lovely / God's Very Tree"), its
purpose and human significance must still be ascertained. "Very
Tree" at first appears to be a straightforward hymn to a Platonic
principle of ideal, timeless forms, yet it is subtly undercut by
the fact that the final two stanzas are not the declarative sentence we at first think them to be, but a *question:*

> God's Very Tree
> Form of whose intense inner life
> Abstractly branches to attain
> What glory, Tree, what pain?

What does this "Very Tree" symbolize about the human spirit? Its intense inner life and the striving of its branches to reach toward something or things beyond themselves are clearly qualities affirmed by the poem. But the final qualities, "glory" and "pain," exist as terms beyond the poem. Furthermore, the final question is addressed to the Tree itself—but this ideal Tree exists precisely because it is beyond language's "winding word," and so it cannot answer. The rhetorical nature of the final question and the very terms of the question (glory and pain would seem to belong to the untranscended world of becoming) serve to undercut the Platonic theme. Though the aesthetic achievement ("lovely, lovely") is clear, the human purpose and achievement of such transcendence is questioned almost as much as it is affirmed.

"Very Tree" makes clear Kunitz' mingling or fusing of phallic sexual imagery with imagery of transcendent, potent being. Even such an apparently Platonic poem is also permeated with a sexualized Christian religious imagery—in this case the "flowering stick" that could refer either to Aaron's rod or to the apocryphal legend of Joseph's being chosen as Mary's husband through the miracle of his stick blossoming in the synagogue. Kunitz is quasi-Platonic: he longs for transcendence, for being rather than becoming. But he is likewise quasi-Christian, drawn to the glory and pain of human existence that can be centered in the drama of crucifixion on the "holy tree" and the theme of death and resurrection. Whether Kunitz adopts a Platonic or Christian stance in any given poem, the underlying impetus is the same: a fear of death and change. Death is the central mystery: the place where in Yeats' phrase "all ladders start."

If the quest for the beloved is thwarted in the early love poems so that the figure of the beloved is either an idealized abstraction from the literary tradition or a palpable creature caught in the coils of mortality and personality, then the quest for the father is thwarted in an even more decisive way: "O ruined father dead, long sweetly rotten." ("For the Word Is Flesh"). In the external, physical world the father does not even exist. Once again, the quest turns inward and is transformed. It is this central fact of the father's death that provides the overriding imaginative structure and strategy for *Intellectual Things*.

The figure of the father in the first book is of an awesome present-absence. The son seeks the father, but death and decay interpose themselves, and the son must come to terms with them and related phenomena (time, change) before he can make imaginative contact with the father. This coming to terms takes the form of warring opposites that enact a psychomachy or battle of the soul. All of these opposites are contraries that relate to the central issues of death and decay. They are experienced with an emotional intensity which seems almost peculiar until we realize that they all refer in some way to the barrier that interposes itself between young Kunitz and the father.

We might sketch out these contraries as two columns: those on the left have in common the taint of death and defeat; those on the right seem by and large to offer some release and hope:

sensuality	vs. asceticism
"corruption" (vegetative)	vs. purity (the celestial)
material	vs. abstract
emotion	vs. thought
body	vs. mind
Christ (as sufferer)	vs. Plato
seasonal deciduous	vs. evergreen
blood	vs. crystal
chaos	vs. cosmos
mutability	vs. permanence

It should be noted that the sexual polarity of male/female is not enlisted in this psychomachy. Nor do these columns represent moral categories. The psychomachy is fueled by the psychological imperatives of fear and need.

One concept may dominate an entire poem's drama (e.g., vegetative decay in "Prophecy on Lethe") only to be contradicted by its contrary in another poem (the spiritual eternity of "Vita Nuova"). Or a single poem might dramatize the conflict as in "Organic Bloom" where "the steady paradox of thought and sense" is a kind of struggle which the brain tries to contain and transform:

> The brain constructs its systems to enclose
> The steady paradox of thought and sense;
> Momentously its tissued meaning grows
> To solve and integrate experience.
>
> (p. 234)

This sonnet begins with a confident assertion of the dynamic powers of thought to encompass the implicit struggle of sense and thought and thereby "explain / Our chaos into cosmos." These dynamic powers of the brain will frequently be expressed in metaphors derived from geometry, one of Plato's favored purities.

Though the brain has the power to enclose the steady paradox, there is a counter quality of equal strength and dynamism:

> But life escapes closed reason. We explain
> Our chaos into cosmos, cell by cell,
> Only to learn of some insidious pain
> Beyond the limits of our charted hell,
> A guilt not mentioned in our prayers, a sin
> Conceived against the self. . . .

We might pause at this point to note that the key phrase, "tissued meaning," in line 3 is a fusion of the physical and mental which superficially resembles Blake's fusion of a tear as an "intellectual thing." However, the dominance of the physical and organic over the mental and conceptual is implicit in the title of Kunitz' poem and in his choice of the concrete noun, "brain," as the chief representative of dynamic ordering. If the abstract, system-making quality resides in physical tissue then the entire poem's drama ultimately falls within the orbit of the organic and mortal.

The concentric spheres of crystal that rendered lovely the Neoplatonic system in the opening of "Geometry of Moods" are here rendered sensual and therefore imbued with death and corruption: "So, vast and vaster / The plasmic circles of gray discipline / Spread outward to include each new disaster." Not until the final couplet is the brain of line 1 again intently focused upon, now entirely characterized by images from the natural world:

> Enormous floats the brain's organic bloom
> Till, bursting like a fruit, it scatters doom.

The floating organic bloom of line 13 seems a grotesque parody of a Buddhist lotus symbol. The drama between subsuming expanding systems and that which escapes them is resolved by apocalypse, a term we will encounter in the opening lines of "Vita Nuova":

> Henceforth apocalypse will get my bread
> For me. . . .

In "Organic Bloom," images from the vegetable world (bloom, fruit, the gray lotus of line 13) triumph over nonorganic ordering images (systems, charts). This triumph has in it the apocalyptic resolution one might expect from images of bloom and fruit—that which is scattered is "doom"; it is both seeds (of a fruit) and death (from the other, buried metaphor of a hand grenade or bomb), implicitly a kind of brain hemorrhage.

"Closed" and enclosing "reason" is the doomed protagonist of "Organic Bloom"; the brain at poem's end is "like a fruit" and thus fatally tainted with vegetative decay. The next poem's title announces the need to go "Beyond Reason" at the same time that it picks up the fruit image: "The blessing in this conscious fruit, the hurt / Which is unanswerable, fill the brow / With early death" (p. 235). The poem's speaker is aware of an alternative to the melancholia of the mind/brow: "the milk of love" whose source is the "Sion of the heart." The possible love relationship is expressed as an enclosing circle with the self at the center:

> But as the long eye holds the spinning bird
> Enclosed in the circumference of sight
>
> And yet the bird is infinitely free. . . .

When this imagery occurred earlier, the love relationship was actually one of struggle for dominance:

> The compass of the ego is designed
> To circumscribe intact a lesser mind
>
> With definition. . . .
>   ("Lovers Relentlessly," p. 212.)

The protagonist of the relationship in "Beyond Reason" is chastened ("I do not come intent to be your lord"). The relationship envisioned by "Lovers Relentlessly" calls for an ego that is unitary and intact. The speaker of "Beyond Reason" is far too aware of his self-division for such an enterprise; he is akin to the

"Creatures that carry in their little blood / Malignant influences."

The mechanically enclosing circles of reason alone are inadequate to cope with these internal enemies that threaten to destroy both the self and the self's impulse toward the beloved.

"Beyond Reason" 's final lines recast the dilemma of anguished self-division and propose a resolution:

> . . . If in my sleep
>
> The ape, the serpent, and the fox I find
> Shut with my soul in fortune's writhing sack,
> I tame them with the sections of my mind
> And teach my mind to love its thoughtless crack.

The struggle has moved from the vegetative level of "Organic Bloom" to the creature level. Man, like the ape, serpent, fox, and bird, is a creature. It is tempting to speculate about the significance of the animals. Do they represent vices that undermine unity of personality? An ape for man's fallen nature, a serpent for evil, a fox for cunning? If so, are they vices particularly inimical to the love relationship? Or could the animals be related to the Roman punishment for parricide that Cicero records: the murderer is placed in a leather sack with a dog, a cock, a viper, and an ape and then drowned? If this obscure reference is relevant, then we are brought again to the father's death as a central source of mystery and anguish for the son.

The only possible resolution of this dangerous conflict is a kind of dynamic tension: a fusion of metaphysical will and the charity of love. The first of the final two lines ("tame them") concerns will and dominance. Its imagery is derived from the geometrical purity of Platonic and Pythagorean metaphysics and represents a moral/philosophical resolution directed by the mind against the creatures within. The final line ("teach" rather than "tame") is directed *at* the mind (as its object) rather than the creatures and concerns an emotional and nonrational solution emanating from the heart. This solution involves the mind's coming to *accept* "its thoughtless crack" and represents a repudiation of an absolute idealism and the perfecting of consciousness by sheer dominance of thought and will. Kunitz strongly asserts both the powers of the mind/will and also the powerful, primary existence of the flaw within that must be "loved."

In the concluding three poems of *Intellectual Things*, we see a steady attempt to escape the warring opposites that are fatally permeated by mortality. The book's progression of poems has now gone "beyond reason" and is ready to embrace love entirely and enter the visionary "new life" beyond the struggles and sufferings of mortality. This movement beyond reason toward intuitive vision can still be understood as being within a quasi-Platonic framework. We have reached that point in a Platonic dialogue where discourse ends and myth and parable alone suffice to embody truth. Likewise, we have reached the point in Kunitz' book where the terminology of metaphysics must yield to the terminology of religion.

The central mystery of *Intellectual Things* is death. It thwarts the quest for the father that is the key to identity. "Vita Nuova" fuses the quest for the father with aspects of the quest for the beloved into an ultimate visionary prediction of the speaker's integrity and intensity of being.

The title is that of Dante's famous sequence. In Dante's poem the physical death of the beloved Beatrice yields a vision of the spiritual world beyond and a purpose for the author: to write worthily of her and the spiritual world she represents. It is a sequence in which loss of the beloved through physical death leads forward toward a birth or rebirth into the spiritual life. If

elegy looks backward after loss, then Dante's "Vita Nuova" becomes that response to death which looks forward and becomes
a kind of spiritual allegory.

What is striking about Kunitz' adaptation of Dante's situation is that the specific death that haunts the poems and insti-
gates the "new life" is that of the father. The father is the inspi-
ration and goal of Kunitz' quest for identity:

> till shadowless
> With inner light I wear my father's face.
>   (p. 236)

But the second legend, the quest for the beloved, likewise culminates in "Vita Nuova." The quest for the beloved on the
physical plane has been consistently thwarted in these early
poems. By book's end, there is a turning away from lover and
toward love, a turning away from the physical embodiment in
favor of the spiritual principle. The father legend with its urgent
central mystery usurps the beloved legend. "The dead would
murder action" announces the speaker of "In a Strange House"
and this assertion serves as motive for abandoning a beloved: "And
I shall go / By silent lanes and leave you timeless here." This
gesture of renunciation finds a parallel in the language of "Vita
Nuova": "And I will go, unburdened, on the quiet lane / Of my
eternal kind."

The warring opposites are very much present at the outset
of "Vita Nuova" and their struggle can be resolved only by embracing a transcendent principle (love), an identity beyond death
("my father's face"), and a vision of unity of being ("the single
beam of all my life").

The contraries that structure "Vita Nuova" are of two types.
The first concerns planes of being. We have moved from a vegetative being ("Organic Bloom") to creaturely being ("Beyond

Reason"), and in this poem we will move to a transhuman level: from a "daily self that bled" to "my eternal kind." Besides this ascending, hieratic movement of identity, there is another movement which involves consolidation: from "many selves" to "my undivided nature." These two movements of renunciation ("I abdicate my daily self") and consolidation are in the service of the poem's quest for an intense unity of being that is beyond time, change, and death.

The opening lines present us with the passionate and tortured self who is the protagonist of so many of Kunitz' poems:

> I abdicate my daily self that bled,
> As others breathe, for porridge it might sup.
> Henceforth apocalypse will get my bread
> For me.

The "daily" self concerned with the economics of sustenance ("porridge" and "bread") is out of harmony with circumstances because it is too intense: it bleeds where others simply breathe. Recognizing this disharmony, it chooses to move to a different level whose terms of being (apocalypse) are commensurate with its consciousness. Prior to this there has been an anguished, self-torturing self-censorship in order to function, in disguise, on this inferior level:

> I bit my tongue and gnawed my lip
> But now the visor of my name is up.

The anonymous and armoured knight reveals his identity and prepares to embark on his quest. Indeed the dramatic structure of the whole poem is that of a knight-errant's vow. It is deliberately high speech—the self's quest for identity and unity of being is heroic—a "noble" calling. He is also the young poet announcing his presence, his ambition, and his themes.

Stanza 2 opens with the knight's vow of allegiance, but to the principle of love rather than a specific beloved: "Giving to love my undivided nature." This "undivided nature" is contrasted with an earlier state: "I have been otherwise a part-time creature, / With many selves to fool myself with hope, / And in myself a gentler self to weep." "Part-time creature" is a phrase that humorously picks up the "workaday" economic images of stanza 1 and relates them to the theme of identity. The former "many selves" seem to be regarded with scorn, but who is the "gentler self" of line 10? It is an inner identity that has been concealed heretofore. The pun on "gentle" as "of noble birth" links it to the knight's noble identity revealed in line five, and contrasts it with the "common" or vulgar multiplicity of identities.

Structurally, the final lines in the first three stanzas are imagistically parallel and further the theme of the speaker's identity. In line 5, protective armor concealed a face and an identity. In line 10, a "gentler" self is concealed within the fierce protagonist. In line 15, this inner self (an inner light) has surfaced to become the speaker's identity and physiognomy. The movement of these three lines is from a removal of armor, to an acceptance of a gentler self within, to a fusion of identities. In the poem's final line, this interior process is imagined as so successful that it goes from a "shadowless light" (l. 15) to the focused intensity of a beacon or lighthouse beam extending out into the world (l. 20).

Stanza 3 reiterates the scornful renunciation of vulgar multiplicity and shifts the rest of the poem into a predictive future:

> Now I will peel that vision from my brain
> Of numbers wrangling in a common place

Numbers, like the "many selves" are to be repudiated in favor of unity of being. These "numbers" are not only the internal division of many selves, but are seen as identities exterior to the self, and in the context of "noble–common," they are the "others" of line 2 toward whom the spiritually awakened speaker feels superior. These numbers are also tied to economics, just as the "common place" represents the vulgarity of the marketplace. This "vision" can be peeled from the brain as if it were so much wallpaper, perhaps because it concerns the illusory, material world. Disdaining the mob of people, identities, and appearances, the speaker pursues his quest in ascetic solitude:

> And I will go, unburdened, on the quiet lane
> Of my eternal kind, till shadowless
> With inner light I wear my father's face.

The material world has been entirely transformed by the spiritual, just as the son's face has been transformed into the father's. The speaker's "shadow" (the material world seen from the perspective of the spiritual world?) has fallen away and the speaker's body will be like an urn or vase "filled with inner light." It's a lovely, fascinating image for an enlightened state that involves unity of being (rather than dispersal of being as in some forms of enlightenment). But why is one element of it the wearing of the "father's face"? Why not "a holy face" or "a crystal face" both of which would satisfy the meter? It's important to ask, because it's important to know from the outset that in Kunitz' work the word "father" is one of the irreducible elements of the mystery of being. He is one of the figures at the origin of the mystery: there is no thing behind him, no way to see through or around him to some deeper mystery. He is one of the centers of the quest of Kunitz' work: both motive and goal, both alpha and omega.

What occurs in this image in "Vita Nuova" is a leap of faith in which the questing son goes beyond the encounter with the dead father that can only end in despair: "Let sons learn from their lipless fathers how / Man enters hell without a golden bough." Vision replaces confrontation, and affirmation becomes possible. The barrier of physical death dissolves and son and father fuse in a single identity. What the religious language of hope longed for in the book's first poem ("Here, Now, and Always, man would be / Inviolate eternally; / This is his spirit's trinity," "Change"), this image asserts powerfully as a consubstantiation of father and son beyond time, change, and death. We could say that, were it not for later poems of the father legend, this image of the father's face would be in danger of becoming a private symbol, an image whose force and centrality a reader could observe without comprehending. When the full story of the father legend emerges in the later work, "Vita Nuova" becomes a perfectly realized poem.

In stanza 4, the speaker, about to depart on the quest, invokes powers to accompany him, to add their power to his in a way that will further transform him:

> Moon of the soul, accompany me now,
> Shine on the colosseums of my sense,
> Be in the tabernacles of my brow.
> My dark will make, reflecting from your stones,
> The single beam of all my life intense.

The first three lines create a curious, almost allegorical landscape that is not quite external, not quite internal. This landscape is both profane and sacred, involves both sensation and thought. These apparent contraries are brought under the unifying light of the "moon of the soul." In the final lines, the speaker's "dark" (his untransformed self?) will reflect off that same moon (the source of the "inner light" of line 15—an interior moon?) to create the final image of intense, focused, unified being. The paradox of "darkness" acting as if it had the properties of light is an imaginative jolt, and might be related to the "dark night of the soul" mystics talk about. In the bizarre compression of these final lines, it is possible to read "my dark will make" as an imperative with "will" as a noun.

The final line with its "single beam" image returns us to the theme of "undivided nature"; it is a nature not only undivided, but composed of a paradoxically focused darkness, almost as if the soul acted not as a reflector, but as a lens focusing and intensifying the rays of darkness. Intensity and unity of being, and consistency of being through time are all sought and claimed (declared for) in the final line. There is something fierce and nonhuman about the final image. We have indeed entered another world that is other than the recognizable material world the speaker has renounced. The single beam from a lighthouse; it is another analogue of the phallic images that so frequently represent intensity of being in Kunitz' work.

It is this identification with the father in the final poem of *Intellectual Things* that will make possible the unification and intensification of being that Kunitz so desperately seeks.

CHAPTER 2

Passport to the War

Fourteen years intervened between the publication of *Intellectual Things* and *Passport to the War*, which appeared in 1944 while Kunitz was serving in the Army. The new book reprinted all the poems from the long-out-of-print first book and twenty-seven new poems. *Passport to the War* is a book whose story on the personal, family level could be characterized by the key word "guilt" and whose story on the less personal level could be characterized by the word "history."

In *Passport to the War*, Kunitz' quest for unity of being is thwarted. The characteristic self-division of *Intellectual Things* was of warring opposites, opposing tendencies that existed as personified abstractions. The self-division persists, even deepens; but it is now manifested as a bewildering multiplication of personas, such as the "butcher boys" of "My Surgeons" who carve up the speaker's mind, or a cynical and sinister shopkeeper from whom the speaker seeks a mask of identity.

Unity and authenticity of being remain goals of Kunitz' quest, and unifying motives for the poems, but the quest has little or no success in this dark book. However, the father's role as a key figure in this quest does become clarified and emphasized.

Although the new poems are individual dramatic lyrics, they are arranged in such a way as to create a kind of narrative continuity. At the personal level, this narrative concerns the anguished and guilty dissolution of a love relationship. The dominant tone of this story is one of despair and guilt. Another new element in the work is the intrusion of history into the poet's life and world of emotions. The passport of the book's title could itself signal that the time has come for Kunitz to abandon his interior landscape and take his place in the external landscape of history. The psychomachy of *Intellectual Things* yields to dramas enacted in recognizable external landscapes and involving recognizable other figures, such as a child, a wife, or Hitler.

The opening poem signals this shift into the outer world, even in its title: "Reflection by a Mailbox." The overriding reality of the Second World War asserts itself. In his first book, Kunitz' poems frequently needed the imagery of nightmare and apocalyptic pronouncements to express the poet's inner experience; now the poet finds his nightmares present in the objective, external world. What was earlier experienced as the sometimes crushing personal burden of subjective intensity is now the general experience of all sensitive people experiencing events in the world. Kunitz is released into "history, that wide and mortal pang" ("Night Letter").

"Reflection by a Mailbox" begins with a reference to the external reality of Hitler's "madness" and "trauma"—a madness that surrounds the poet and yet, paradoxically, will release him from the self-obsessed subjectivity of his earlier poems:

> When I stand in the center of that man's madness,
> Deep in his trauma, as in the crater of a wound,
> My ancestors step from my American bones.
>
> (p. 151)

(One of the curious, moving elements of this poem is that it is one of the few poems where Kunitz' family are not locked in conflict with each other; like the poet himself, they are temporarily released from inner struggles by the overriding reality of Hitler.)

The awareness of Hitler's madness precipitates an imaginative journey backward through time and family:

> There's mother in a woven shawl, and that,
> No doubt, is father picking up his pack
> For the return voyage through those dreadful years
> Into the winter of the raging eye.

Kunitz journeys to Europe by retracing the circumstances that brought his parents to America. The persecution of "one generation past" (the pogroms of Central Europe and Russia) is rendered present both physically and in verb tense:

> One generation past, two days by plane away,
> My house is dispossessed, my friends dispersed,
> My teeth and pride knocked in, my people game
> For the hunters of man-skins in the warrens of Europe

His family's recent history of persecution in Europe becomes his personal link to the current horrors of Hitler's Europe:

> The impossible creatures of an hysteriac's dream
> Advancing with hatchets sunk into their skulls
> To rip the god out of the machine.

Stanza 3 begins to ponder the nature and origin of the "impossible creatures" of line 12. This vision of the "massman" ("as if a soul had been given to petroleum") who supported Hitler and did his bidding is perhaps a sinister version of the "numbers wrangling in a common place" that Kunitz distrusted and separated himself from in "Vita Nuova."

Stanza 4 is a single line, a single question: "How shall we uncreate that lawless energy?" The question is rhetorical—the furthest extent his speculative imagination of the European situation can take him.

In the next line, the poem for the first time locates itself in a recognizable physical landscape and a present moment: "Now I wait under the hemlock by the road." The internal rhyme of "I wait" with "uncreate" functions as an ironical answer to the question: the poet's stance is that of passive waiting.

Intelligent reflection and moral imagination can help him grasp the situation (stanzas 1 and 2) and ask important theoretical questions about the nature and origins of the situation (stanza 3) and a final practical question (stanza 4), but he cannot initiate action:

> Now I wait under the hemlock by the road
> For the red-haired postman with the smiling hand
> To bring me my passport to the war.
> Familiarly his car shifts into gear
> Around the curve; he coasts up to my drive; the day
> Strikes noon; I think of Pavlov and his dogs
> And the motto carved on the broad lintel of his brain:
> "Sequence, consequence, and again consequence."

I say that in stanza 5 Kunitz asserts a passivity before the objective events and begins merely to recount them (the postman's arrival), but in fact the postman's arrival triggers a last upsurge of imagination: a vision/thought of Pavlov and his dogs. As opposed to the "lawless" energy of the Nazi masses, Pavlov has a single, absolute law ("the motto carved on the broad lintel of his brain").

There is an intense ambivalence here: the insight that Pavlov has is deterministic in the extreme, mechanistic; it is a vision of man as a machine *after* the god has been taken out of it. But Kunitz does not deny or denigrate Pavlov's vision: the lintel of his brain is "broad"—even if there is only one thing carved on it. This image of lintel/threshold is one of Kunitz' key images, part of an image cluster of lintel/threshold/gates that recur in such important poems as "Open the Gates," "The Approach to Thebes," "The Testing-Tree," "King of the River," and "The Knot." A close parallel recurs in "The Summing-Up," where he carves a motto on a lintel. Usually the lintel image is associated with some powerful pronouncement or revelation—like the carving over the gates of hell in Dante's *Inferno*. So "Reflection by the Mailbox" respects the truth of Pavlov's vision, if not its antihumanistic implications.

One of its implications becomes clear in the poem as Kunitz recognizes that he is more like one of Pavlov's dogs in the famous ringing bell and salivating dog experiment than he is like Pavlov himself. In the described sequence of events of the postman's arrival (that are repeated each day and that culminate with a synaesthetic time-sound image: the sun strikes noon), Kunitz acknowledges that he himself has been dehumanized and—as he waits for his draft notification to arrive—is now a part of a predetermined series of events in the world. The poet "thinks" rather than "salivates," but his thoughts are about his powerlessness in the face of these forces larger than the individual.

The poem began with the figure of Hitler as a madman who realized his nightmare in the objective, historical world. The poem ends with another looming figure, Pavlov, who is not mad or lawless, but whose vision of the external world and his technique for changing it, while not anywhere near as menacing as Hitler's madness, has been adopted by Hitler to further those mad ends. We have in Pavlov an image of the triumph in the world of a detached mind and rationality, and in Hitler, the triumph of irrationality. Mind and passion are no longer reconcilable—each takes its own path to its own nightmarish triumph of extremity. There is no glimpse now of any such healing vision as Blake's that counseled the necessary marriage of heaven and hell, reason and energy.

Unlike many other introverted personalities, Kunitz is able to articulate the transitions from the personal to the public, perhaps because some of the tortured personal imaginings of his first book have given him a foretaste of horror and an imagery to express it. The "god" in "the machine" might well be an apotheosis of early Kunitz' images of the superiority of mind over matter and spirit over body. In any event, the deux ex machina, who delivered the judgment of the gods in Greek drama, is here ripped from his heaven by men with "hatchets sunk into their skulls," an image that partakes of the violence with which the "sudden Lord" cleaves the mind with a spike of light in "Mens Creatrix." The metaphysical dichotomies of warring opposites and the Blakean fusions of the first book are inadequate to his new experience.

In such final poems of *Intellectual Things* as "Beyond Reason," Kunitz confidently imagined reconciling the rational and irrational elements of his own consciousness. Now, he can no longer entertain such hopes or ambitions: experience has left him uncertain, paralyzed, passive, and it is this new self who appears as both speaker and "patient" in the second poem, "My Surgeons":

> My surgeons are a savage band,
> Surely their patient is ill-fated.
>
> (p. 153)

This is the private nightmare beginning to find language for itself. "Surgeons" implies that the "I" is a patient: diseased, passive, voluntarily undergoing a mutilation. If the world intruded on Kunitz' life in "Reflection," in "My Surgeons" the world intrudes on his mind, his inner life:

> Deftly they opened the brain of a child,
> And it was full of flying dreams;
> Father was prowling in a field
> With speckled tongue and a collar of flame.
> They labeled it "Polluted Streams,"
> The body floating with the same.

Nor can we have confidence in the therapeutic nature of this operation: the two surgeons are mad and represent opposite madnesses at that, denouncing their patient in communist and fascist cultural/political rhetoric. Indeed, these quasi-political surgeons triumph in an unfortunate way:

> Lastly they squeezed out of my veins
> The bright liquor of sympathy;
> I lost the touch of souls, the reins
> On white revenge, and I was free
> Of pity, a solid man of snow.

The speaker has been remade; has been drained of all tenderness—all those qualities that restrained his evil and promoted human goodness in him. The "solid man of snow" is now a worthy citizen of that grim world glimpsed in "Reflection by a Mailbox."

The fourth stanza, which recounts the dubious success of the operation, ends with a question that represents the first upsurge of the "I" in the poem. This shift is formally reinforced by its being the first and only time in the poem that succeeding lines end in full rhyme:

> Of pity, a solid man of snow.
> But in the night to whom could I go?

This questioning, this last spark of rebellion, announced a recovery of the intimate human: a desperate seeking after, not love, but the ability to love. The circumstances of the speaker (and the world) have gotten so bad that the poem convincingly demonstrates the need to believe in the possibility of love. (By breaking the syntax of the line, Kunitz makes clear that his belief is both in love and because of love.) The dignified cadence of the final line emphasizes the quiet triumph of the individual and the values (love, forgiveness) that only the individual can keep alive in a nightmare world where the raving surgeons seem to rule:

> Lie down with me, dear girl, before
> My butcher-boys begin to rave.
> "No hope for persons any more,"
> They cry, "on either side of the grave."
> Tell them I say the heart forgives
> The world. Yes, I believe. In love.

If we heard a tale of unhappy warring lovers in the early poem "Lovers Relentlessly," it was a tale told at an abstract level. In "The Tutored Child," a similar tale descends into the world of experience: a child and its parents who are not by any means in harmony with each other. Stanzas 1 and 2 present the respective fierce and quarrelsome isolations of the mother and father.

Stanza 3 turns at last to the child whose tragedy is one of entrapment.

"The Tutored Child" is best read in conjunction with "The
Reckoning"—a poem that, under its first title "What Have You
Done?" originally concluded the book. The paralyzing agony of
the relationship in "The Tutored Child" introduces a main narrative thread that structures the book and that culminates in the
guilty departure and final gift-giving of "The Reckoning." Both
poems concern guilty bequests.

These two poems, toward the book's beginning and end,
frame the love relationship that constitutes one of the book's
narrative continuities. This relationship is anguished from beginning to end; we are unable to separate its suffering from its
joy. Before we arrive at "The Reckoning" (whose subtitle is a
question, perhaps a final one), we encounter a poem entitled "The
Last Question" that epitomizes Kunitz' intense ambivalence about
the relationship:

> Touching, you bring
> Rumors of heaven and its generous spoils
> Here, even, where our hooded shadows rise
> To play the stab-scene, the end of love
>
> (p. 178)

"The Reckoning," which seems to be addressed to the child
may also be addressed to the beloved. In any event, it is a final
encounter between two parties. "The Tutored Child" addressed
the child directly. The body of "The Reckoning" is a response
to the question of the subtitle: "What have you done?" In the
context of the story of guilty love, "What have you done?" has
the sound of an accusation, but it is also a demand for a reckoning: "What have you accomplished?"

"The Reckoning" is Kunitz' attempt to explain and justify

himself, just as "The Tutored Child" attempted to explain and implicitly justify the poet to his child. What he finally offers in "The Reckoning" is not the "pity penny" of the earlier poem but something more substantial:

> Be patient with my wound:
> Too long I lay
> In the folds of my preparation,
> Sinuous in the sun,
> A golden skin,
> All pride, sores, excretion,
> Blazing with death. O child,
> From my angry side
> Tumbles this agate heart,
> Your prize, veined with the root
> Of guilty life,
> From which flow love and art.
>
> (p. 183)

"The Reckoning" represents the dream of the alchemy of imagination. It is an early imagistic statement of what Kunitz meant when late in his life he spoke of his wish to "convert life into legend" and asserted that life and art cannot be separated in his work. But the poem also shows an uneasiness, a pleading, an anxious seeking to explain and justify.

An earlier appearance of the self as reptile is also a vehicle for the self-accusation characteristic of this book:

> Whose bonecase (melted down)
> Shimmers with scaly wit.
> What have I not permitted?
> ("The Illusionist")

The word "coils" occurs in both "The Reckoning":

> Your question comes with coils
> Like years behind,
> Which I am crawling from.

and in an earlier poem in the book:

> Twisting my coils, this dangling life of mine
> ("Night Letter")

"Coils" reveals an image complex of anxious, self-conscious ambivalence that fuses reptile and puppet. Directed first at the beloved ("Your question comes with coils"), it has overtones of entrapment. The image alternates between hope ("I am crawling from" the snake's shed skin) and helpless despair ("dangling life"). But if Hamlet's "when we have shuffled off this mortal coil" was meant to partake of the transformation of caterpillar to butterfly, Kunitz' snake and puppet coils are nowhere near as sanguine.

Certain themes and situations recur from poem to poem in *Passport to the War:* life and art, the breakup of a love relationship, the impinging nightmare of a warring world, a self tortured from within and without. The parallels between "The Tutored Child" and "The Reckoning" illuminate some of these themes. Kunitz in the former poem describes himself as "your father, in whom two ambitions rave," and a little later, as a man who "loathes the heart that blends / His guilty love." He articulates precisely what those "two ambitions" are in the latter poem: love and art. These are the two "flowings" (a key image-verb for Kunitz) that have been fused in the final, ambiguously affirmative images of the latter poem:

> this agate heart,
> Your prize, veined with the root
> Of guilty life,
> From which flow love and art.

This transformed heart reconciles the previously warring entities of love and art by way of its own paradoxical qualities. It is mineral—beyond all change and suffering—yet its "veins" permit it to still participate in the world of movement—the rhythmical "flow" of language in a poem, blood in a body.

The image also works a personal salvation by subsuming the book's personal autobiographical theme (the "guilty love" of "The Tutored Child") and transforming it beyond suffering so that we now have a speaker who might, in a poem late in the book, say:

> On the anvil of love my flesh has been hammered out.
> Indifferent, in the indifferent air,
> I circulate and suck the star-space in.
>
> ("How Long Is the Night?")

But unlike the speaker in "How Long Is the Night?" who can say "No one is dear to me now," the anguished but coping speaker of "The Reckoning" presents his transformed heart as a gift. This gift-giving returns the poet to the world of human relationship, even if only in a magical and tragic way. Such a gift-giving encounter, and all that it implies about the relationship between life and art, also seems to overcome the guilt about selfishness that has dominated several poems in *Passport to the War*.

Returning to a chronological reading of *Passport to the War*, we find in "A Signal from the House" a tallying up of Kunitz' situation in couplets.

Perhaps this is the appropriate time to recall that "house" is a word/image that is part of the cluster of key images that defines Kunitz' art and consciousness. Among other things, "house" represents that space within which the family drama takes place. As such, it becomes a reference point by which one can locate a character's situation and define the drama of a poem. For example, in "The Signal from the House," the speaker has left a house and is being signaled to return to it (in what he feels is a doomful way) by the signal of the title. In the following poem, a central poem of the ouevre, "Father and Son," one of the first things the son wants to say to the dead father is " 'The house, the stucco one you built, / We lost.' " In later poems, the dramatic situation will have Kunitz living alone in a house "marked 'For Sale' " as if to image the personal isolation of the speaker and the provisional nature of our stay on earth, even in that most solid-seeming of things: our dwelling place.

Kunitz' imagination structures experience partly by the recurrence from poem to poem of a word like "house" until it has the history and multifaceted, accumulated meanings of a symbol. But, like his mentor Blake, who moved by "contraries," Kunitz' imagination sets up another term to contrast or conflict with the original key image. In the case of "house," the opposing term is frequently "journey." If "house" implies stability and intimacy, it can also imply stasis and spiritual and emotional stagnation; by contrast, "journey" implies movement and quest. The journey is the solitary quest of the individual for the ultimate meaning of his life, as first put forward in "Vita Nuova":

> And I will go, unburdened, on the quiet lane
> Of my eternal kind

Such a journey is implied at the end of "The Signal from the House" and enacted in "Father and Son."

"The Signal from the House" is the major poem of the mother/beloved legend in this book. Like its predecessor, "Poem," in *Intellectual Things*, it asserts the psychological connections between son, mother, and love object. Unlike the protagonist of the earlier poem, the speaker survives his encounters with the figures who threaten his existence, but this survival demands he repudiate the figures.

Formally, the poem is a series of couplets, the first four dealing with encounters with three figures. Of the three figures, the identity of the first is elusive:

> I said to the watcher at the gate,
> "They also kill who wait."
>
> (p. 156)

The figure's meaning can only be deduced from the speaker's compressed parody of the final line of Milton's sonnet, "When I Consider How My Light is Spent": "They also serve who only stand and wait." It is the watching and waiting—the implicit stasis—that strike the poet/speaker as inimical to his being.

The second figure is described, identified, and responded to:

> I cried to the mourner on the stair,
> "Mother, I hate you for those tears."

The secret of Kunitz' mother as the "unforgiving" mourner of Kunitz' suicide-father is locked in the still-to-be-written central poem "The Portrait," but these lines, with their triangle of crucial words (mourner, mother, hate), provide a shorthand for the son–mother relationship and the son's motive for his behavior.

The third encounter—with the beloved—is not so quickly dealt with and takes two couplets to encompass:

> To mistress of the ruined hall,
> The keeper of the sacred heart,
>
> I brought the mind's indifference
> And the heavy marble of my face

The mistress/beloved guards the emblem of the emotional life, but the syntactical and visual parallels of lines 5 and 6 (mistress/keeper; ruined hall/sacred heart) insist on the deteriorated state of her role. To his encounter with her, the speaker brings detachment and a lack of affect. Beginning in line 9, we learn the motive for these multiple repudiations:

> For these who were too much with me
> Were secretly against me:
>
> Hostages to the old life,
> Expecting to be ransomed daily
>
> And for the same fond reason
> From the deep prison of their person.

The echo of "prison" and "person" in line 14 powerfully reinforces the poem's theme of the self's isolation.

The strongest hold these figures have on the self is moral— it is guilt, the "cry of conscience" that signals the speaker to return to this house and its three occupants. But these figures cannot be rescued, and the message of their signal is that the speaker too must be destroyed:

> Their lantern shining in the window
> Had signaled me, like cry of conscience.
>
> Insisting that I must be broken
> Upon the wheel of the unforsaken.

The imagery of "The Signal from the House" is archaic, emblematically medieval, but its message is far from knightly gallantry. The repudiation of relationship in order that the self embark on a journey, as I have already noted, occurs in "Vita Nuova."

> And I will go, unburdened, on the quiet lane
> Of my eternal kind

But "The Signal from the House" dramatizes the realities of that repudiation—gives psychological reality to "Vita Nuova" 's blithe prediction of an "unburdened" quester. According to "The Signal from the House," not to repudiate and flee is to make the unforsaken other (watcher, mother, mistress) into an instrument of self-torture.

"The Signal from the House" represents *Passport to the War*'s main statement of the mother/beloved legend: it is a statement of repudiation of relationship (though not without anguish). The poem takes place at night—with the speaker witnessing the plaintive and tempting signal, but too aware of its ultimate implications to return. Where then, does the "unburdened" speaker go? Freed from the mother/beloved legend, he can embark on the central quest that "Vita Nuova" envisioned: the search for the lost father. Thus, it is no accident that the speaker turns his back on a house in one poem, only to begin a night journey in pursuit of the father in the next.

"Father and Son" is the earliest full and intimate treatment of the "quest for the father" theme in Kunitz' work, a theme which is probably the deepest and most central in all his work. Kunitz' main theme is the self's quest for identity. What gives this quest its special power is that Kunitz is perhaps the first poet in the twentieth century concisely to link the quest for identity to the insights (at first Freudian, later Jungian) of twentieth-century depth psychology. The mother/beloved legend or the son's quest for the father are imaginative adaptations and dramatizations of major Freudian insights into how the individual sense of identity develops through the interplay of primary family relationships. Although family interactions have frequently been dramatized and pondered in prose, Stanley Kunitz is among the very first poets to bring the personal intensity

of the dramatic lyric to bear on the theme of how the self develops in relation to parental figures. Prior to Kunitz' "Father
and Son" (published in 1942), who in the history of poetry in
English has written a poem in which a son addresses his father,
seeking from this source (it seems so natural and obvious to us)
values and guidance: "teach me how to work and keep me kind"?

"Father and Son" begins its quest as a journey that starts
calmly enough ("follow" occurs twice as the first verb for the
journey), but soon escalates to an active pursuit ("raced").

> Now in the suburbs and the falling light
> I followed him, and now down sandy road
> Whiter than bone-dust, through the sweet
> Curdle of fields, where the plums
> Dropped with their load of ripeness, one by one.
> Mile after mile I followed, with skimming feet,
> After the secret master of my blood,
> Him, steeped in the odor of ponds, whose indomitable love
> Kept me in chains. Strode years; stretched into bird;
> Raced through the sleeping country where I was young,
> The silence unrolling before me as I came,
> The night nailed like an orange to my brow.
>
> (p. 157)

The figure of the father has great power over the son. "The secret master of my blood" represents an overwhelming dominance the source of which is genetic and thus inescapable. This
primary relationship is regarded by the son with great ambivalence, and the image for it ("whose indomitable love / Kept me
in chains" [note the ironic line break]) partakes of the imprisonment metaphors of the preceding poem, "The Signal from the
House." The pursuit intensifies with a dreamlike transformation
that occurs to the speaker as sudden, graceful music: "Strode
years; stretched into bird" and continues across a landscape that
is now time as well as space:

> Raced through the sleeping country where I was young,
> The silence unrolling before me as I came,
> The night nailed like an orange to my brow.

"The night nailed like an orange to my brow" that ends this stanza has been the subject of considerable critical discussion, some readers feeling it an image of pain centered on the violent intensity of the full dream-moon that illuminates this journey. When Kunitz himself discusses it (in Anthony Ostroff's *The Poet as Artist and Critic*) his remarks are both illuminating and limiting:

> Nobody, alas, seems to like my line, "The night nailed like an orange to my brow," but I have lived with it too long to think of changing a word. What is so outlandish about it? Throughout the poem the moon, though never named, is fiercely burning . . . shining in the bone-dust and the mist, reflected at the last in "the white ignorant hollow" of the father's face. Most of us must have known breathless nights, so heavy and close that the moon has walked with us. To suffer this night of the moon so intensely is to be impaled by it. To one who says flatly, "Oranges are not nailed," my flat answer is, "In this poem they are." The reader cannot be expected to know that when I was six years old, running barefoot, I stepped on a nail that protruded—God knows how—through a rotten peach and hobbled home with that impossible fruit hammered to my flesh.

He continues, "Nail and fruit, then, have a long history of association in my mind, and the image that eventually sealed their connection has nothing to do with ornament or fancy, but is an emanation of my felt truth."[1] When Kunitz describes the origin

---

1. Anthony Ostroff, *The Contemporary Poet As Artist and Critic*, 4th ed. (Boston: Little, Brown, 1964), p. 78.

of this image in childhood experience we dead-end in the opacity of private experience; yet when we compare the image to similar images of wounding in his other poems, we are brought closer to it as an "emanation of felt truth." There is the spike of light that cleaves the creator's head in "Mens Creatrix." In being linked to the brow, the violence is connected to "the stain / Of life upon my crested brain." Once again, we recognize a variant of the key image of the wound. It is one more of the many woundings experienced by the speaker of Kunitz' poems. Finally, and here its secret role in this particular poem is evident, its violence and the placement of the wound are linked in Kunitz' imagination to the father whom he imagines as having died of a self-inflicted wound. In a poem called "The Hemorrhage," he imagines a man bleeding to death in a park, a man who is also "our banished king." The father's dual identity, both man and banished king, parallels the dual story of many of Kunitz' poems of this period, including "The Hemorrhage" and "Father and Son." The poems seek simultaneously to occupy the literal and mythic levels in their narratives. "Wound" and its variants of violence are either linked almost invariably to the figure of the father or, as in the nailed orange image of "Father and Son," serve as a link between the suffering of the son and that of the father. The wound is perhaps the most central of Kunitz' key images, representing both mortality and suffering, but also, and more important, it is an image capable of communicating some of the deepest meanings of the father–son theme in Kunitz' work.

When we have recognized the central, recurring wound image and its connection to the dead father and its role as a link between dead father and seeking son, we are on the verge of yet another thematic linking up of key images. The wound is linked to the father and, by extension, is a badge of mortality; but when it is linked to the son it becomes connected to Kunitz' quest for a poetry that transforms suffering into beauty:

> The urgent letter that I try to write
> Night after night to you to whom I turn,
> The staunchless word, my language of the wound,
> Begins to stain the page.
>
> ("Night Letter")

The pulsing of blood from a wound becomes the contained rhythmic flow of language in a poem. The main constituent of this link between blood and language is the verb "flow":

> From which flow love and art.
> ("The Reckoning")

It is repeatedly linked to the father:

> Father, the darkness of the self goes out
> And spreads contagion on the flowing air.
> ("The Guilty Man")

or the ennobled father surrogate:

> He was our banished king
> Of blames and staunchless flows
> ("The Hemorrhage")

It is the "flowing word" of "Mens Creatrix"—an art the ultimate source of which is the personal agony of the wound. Many lyric poets have sensed a parallel between the rhythmic pulse of their blood and language in a poem, but it is of the essence of Kunitz' art that the threshold that transforms blood to ink is not tongue or mouth, but wound:

> And Agamemnon's thigh
> Opened at length to cry:
> This laurel-sparking rhyme
> ("A Spark of Laurel")

The culminating, emblematic image of the night nailed like an orange to the son's brow focuses the poem's story of the preceding lines on the intensity with which the son is experiencing the pursuit. The opening lines of the second stanza of "Father and Son" complete the focal shift from landscape to subjective experience within the son's brow (the urgent confusion of thought and feeling that takes place in the son's mind) as he articulates the encounter:

> How should I tell him my fable and the fears

"Fable and fears" are the essence of Kunitz' work: fable—narrative coherence that is either given to the self or achieved by the self (it's called "the curious legend of my youth" in "Open the Gates")—and "the fears," the anarchic emotional assaults that constantly threaten the narrative coherence in his poems. The typical successful Kunitz poem struggles to subdue these assaults into the coherence of fable (e.g., "Vita Nuova") or to dramatize the struggle between the fable and the fears.

The next line, with its ironic sound echo of "chasm" and "casual," introduces the son's fantasy of how he will attempt to tell his fable and fears, when and if he actually overtakes the fleeing father:

> How bridge the chasm in a casual tone,
> Saying, "The house, the stucco one you built,
> We lost"

What the father's power has accomplished: the building of a house, the establishment of the intimate stability of the family dwelling, has been lost with the father's death or absence. The family itself has dispersed in "strange" ways, and the son's "fable" continues to unfold in terms of the key image of house or dwelling:

> I lived on a hill that had too many rooms:
> Light we could make, but not enough of warmth,
> And when the light failed, I climbed under the hill.

Within these three lines we have two major literary allusions—
the first a reference to the Gospels ("In My Father's house are
many mansions") that, in Kunitz' ironic version, highlights the
son's inadequacy relative to the father. Where the Gospel's pronouncement is an affirmation of God the Father's hospitality, his
loving acceptance, in Kunitz' reworking the multiple rooms become excess and the effect of a single person in a many-roomed
house is one of loneliness and desolation. In the next line, we
have gone from solitude ("I lived") to relationship ("Light we could
make") and then to the relationship's failure for lack of emotional warmth.

In the following line, the speaker moves "under the hill,"
enacts a kind of ritual self-burial that is also a distant echo of
Blake's image of "the lost Traveller's Dream under the Hill" from
"To the Accuser who is the God of this World," the epilogue of
"For the Sexes: The Gates of Paradise." Significantly, the allusions to both Blake and the Bible are used by Kunitz to communicate a deep forlornness and both have as the source of their
authority a relationship of the speaker to a more powerful authority (Jesus to God the Father; Blake to "The God of This
World," who is in fact the Accuser). These three lines establish
the son's situation as one of anguished inadequacy somehow derived from the father's absence. Although it is possible to take
the line about heat and light literally (a house too large, with
adequate lights, but difficult to heat), its tone and the surrounding allusions threaten to take this section of the poem to too
contrived an archetypical and symbolic level. The final two lines
of the stanza serve to undercut the literary tone of the preceding lines and insist that this metaphysical anguish is anchored in
the mundane world:

> The papers are delivered every day;
> I am alone and never shed a tear.

The speaker's affectless solitude subsequent to a tortured relationship is a recurring motif in *Passport to the War*. The speaker asserts ironically in "My Surgeons" that he has become "a solid man of snow" and in "How Long Is the Night" that "No one is dear to me now" and that he would "walk between the world's great wounds, unpitying."

The third stanza returns us to the story of the pursuit, which has in fact reached its final event. At this point, the son actually does address the father aloud for the first time in the poem:

> At the water's edge, where the smothering ferns lifted
> Their arms, "Father!" I cried. "Return! You know
> The way."

There is a shift in the content of what the son now wishes to say to the father: he no longer seeks to explain his situation, but instead focuses on his need for the father and his sense of the father's omniscience. The tone is now one of beseeching and pleading. This transition is imaged physically in the ferns. The sense of the oppressive, smothering quality of the son's life in stanza 2 is thrown off in the active reaching and pleading gesture of "lifted / Their arms." We know (the ferns tell us) that both figures have stopped and that the son has raised his arms in appeal to the figure of his father. They are at the water's edge— perhaps the same place that the father's figure emerged from earlier, since he is "steeped in the odor of ponds." In fact, the pond is a threshold between the world of the living and the underworld of the dead (as in "Goose Pond" or the reservoir in "Quinnapoxet"). The father's ghost figure pauses at this threshold as the son mixes promise with prayer. The "promise" bespeaks the intensity of the son's need for the father, even as it mocks itself, considering that it entails the absurd human belief that by wiping away the stains of physical death, we can return the beloved dead to life:

> "I'll wipe the mudstains from your clothes:
> No trace, I promise, will remain"

The son is Blake's "lost Traveller"; the father "knows the way." This is one of the central themes of the father/son legend in Kunitz' work. In terms of Kunitz' quest for identity, the message is clear: though the speaker is an adult, he is, because of his fatherlessness, paradoxically condemned to remain a child—he is forever in thrall to the father as "secret master." But the speaker believes that if he can reestablish the father–son bond that death has disrupted, he can "return" to the start of his identity and, with the father's "instruction," grow into an adult whose emotional life is rich and whose values are humane. His plea to the father for instruction contains a program that returns him to the thwarted beginnings of his life and sequentially recapitulates growth from "child" to "brother" to adult "friend."

> "Instruct
> Your son, whirling between two wars,
> In the Gemara of your gentleness,
> For I would be a child to those who mourn
> And brother to the foundlings of the field
> And friend of innocence and all bright eyes.
> O teach me how to work and keep me kind."

A parallel recapitulation from "mourn" to "foundlings" concerns Kunitz' personal history of grief and "orphanhood." It is the death-disrupted bond of father and son, the speaker asserts, that has brought about his desolation: his inability to act effectively or to feel compassion.

The stanza end concludes the son's direct plea to the father. It is a plea full of anguished hopefulness. There is a pause, what one wants to call a "terrible pause," before the poem's final two lines. It is the only gesture that the father's figure makes toward the son; it consists of a "turning" that satisfies perfectly Aristotle's definition of tragic reversal (as the advent of new information that alters the drama's direction):

> Among the turtles and the lilies he turned to me
> The white ignorant hollow of his face.

All the son's expectations, all his confidence in the father's capacity to aid him are repudiated by the final face-to-face moment in which the son stares into the vacant ghost-skull of his father. It seems significant that the father is "among" the lilies and the turtles: that is, the father's figure has already entered the pond, perhaps only the head imaged on the water like a ghostly version of the full moon reflected on the pond's surface. Though Kunitz in Ostroff's book himself rejected any allusion to biblical turtles (doves) and lilies (of the field not pond [but only three lines before we've heard of "foundlings of the field"]), the paralleling or narrative fusing of religious allusion and literal fact is consistent with the rest of the poem.

In terms of the father–son theme, it is extremely significant that the poem's final word is "face," that the dramatic reversal of the speaker's aspirations are located in the father's face. The most positive and confident prediction of a father–son bond as the fulfillment of Kunitz' quest also centered on the face: "Till shadowless/ With inner light I wear my father's face" ("Vita Nuova"). The son does, in a sense, wear the father's face. "Father and Son" tragically fulfills the prediction: the son's ignorance and desolation are, in the poem's final gesture, seen to mirror the father's ignorance at the same moment that the discovery of the father's ignorance appears to cut off the son's last, best hope for wisdom and guidance.

We could almost say that the poem's final event happens after the poem: the father disappears beneath the pond's surface. Again—as in "For the Word Is Flesh"—a terrible knowledge has been communicated between fathers and sons on a threshold to the underworld ("Let sons learn from their lipless father how / Man enters hell without a golden bough"). Here, in this far more personal and anguished poem, the father has the power to return to earth briefly (in dream) but has no knowledge to impart, except the "liplessness"—the triumph of physical decay over all the son's human aspiration.

The poem "Night Letter" links the two main positive figures in Kunitz' work: the beloved and the dead father. The dramatic content of the poem is that of a letter written out of a night solitude and addressed to an absent beloved ("Postscript" is an earlier parallel to this poem in *Intellectual Things*). The poem is an anguished examination of self and century that in a letter-within-a-letter addresses the father's ghost (" 'Pardon,' I plead, clutching the fragile sleeve / Of my poor father's ghost returned to howl / His wrongs"). But though such a linking of the two figures appears a positive imaginative act, the poem's situation (a late night letter) dramatizes the speaker's impenetrable passive solitude, his inability to act. He is paralyzed between a guilty past associated with his father and an almost hopeless future connected with the beloved.

"The Guilty Man" provides a peripheral but interesting glimpse into the relationship between Kunitz and Theodore Roethke, which at the time of the poem's publication in 1934 was intense both personally and artistically. Both poets were haunted by powerful fathers, were prey to an obscure yet powerful sense of guilt that they sought to express in lyrics too "personal" for the taste of the times. That they found each other is an anecdote in their respective literary biographies—that their early literary relationship was one in which Roethke more or less apprenticed himself to Kunitz is less well known. At the time, Roethke showed all his work to Kunitz for comments and when Kunitz' image of defiant vulnerability from "The Guilty Man,"

> Touch me: my folds and my defenses fall;
> I stand within myself, myself my shield
> (p. 180)

was adopted by Roethke for his poem "Open House":

> I'm naked to the bone,
> With nakedness my shield.
> Myself is what I wear:
> I keep the spirit spare. . . .

Kunitz was quick to point out the borrowing in a letter. It is an index of Roethke's early indebtedness to Kunitz' thematic territory and style that, rather than relinquish the image, he let it—in 1941—appear as the title poem of his first book, three years before "The Guilty Man" first appeared in book form.[2]

2. Perhaps the quality of the relationship between Kunitz and Roethke is best expressed by a letter at one remove from the immediate exchange. The sequence is as follows: Roethke sent Kunitz the poem that later appeared as "Open House" for criticism. Kunitz pointed out that the image of nakedness and shielding was, perhaps subliminally, borrowed from his (Kunitz') own "The Guilty Man" that had appeared in a magazine in September 1934. Roethke responded with great embarrassment and self-accusation, to which Kunitz replied as follows: "Dear Ted: Don't be a damned fool. *The poem is your own.* Nobody else wrote it or could have written it. Furthermore, it's a good poem—the best new one

We come now to an extremely interesting and puzzling fact concerning the poem "The Guilty Man." In the three books in which "The Guilty Man" appears, the last few lines occur in three different versions. Poets are prone to revise their work when they gather it in retrospective collections, but Kunitz is unusual in that he makes almost no changes at all when he gathers his poems first into *Selected Poems* and then into *The Poems of Stanley Kunitz, 1928–1978*. It is therefore significant that this poem's conclusion seemed to him to call for repeated revisions. Since these revisions occur only in the final stanza, I will first discuss the poem as it originally appeared in *Passport to the War*, and then the subsequent two revisions. Finally, I want to consider how the revisions affect the poem's meanings.

"The Guilty Man" opens with a witty confidence:

> The years of my life were odd that now are even.
> Think! to be young, amused, and not a fool:
> Playing the world's game—think!—with world's own rules,

I've read in months, I think. I do want you to publish it and to forget about this nonsensical "fake" business. Now I curse myself for having mentioned the matter at all. I did it, believe me, in no accusing spirit and wholly without malice, as one might dissect a moth to find, among its pulp and sap, the buried engine of its tropic life.

"As for the passage in question, I believe I got the idea and some of the phraseology from a paragraph in Thoreau. Rilke expressed the same sentiment, variously, at least a dozen times. I could not, therefore, lay claim to either the substance or the expression. All of us take what we can from the mother speech, who is herself a bitch.

"You persecute yourself too much. The poet's only fidelity is to the poem. One must know what one is doing, but one must not use that knowledge against oneself. That is the death of the will.

Stanley
November 1935"
(Theodore Roethke Archive
University of Washington)

that unravels in its very saying:

> And nothing lost, I think, I think . . . but years.

The repeated verb "think" changes meaning in the course of the opening four lines, so that its first appearance adds to the opening tone of flippant nostalgia ("Think!" as "Just imagine!") and its later appearance ("I think, I think") betrays an underlying uncertainty beneath the brashness. With the repetition of "years" the first four lines have come full circle to the opening noun; but the speaker's mood and preoccupation have spiraled downward, and the theme of time has become burdened with guilt and uncertainty. The next lines announce an incipient self-division within the speaker and indicate that emotion (heart) rather than thought is about to gain control of the poem's language:

> Heart against mouth is singing out of tune.

This self-division intensifies until there is a kind of "return of the repressed" expressed in corporeal terms:

> Night's whisperings and blanks betrayed; this is
> The end of lies: my bones are angry with me.

The stanza ends with a declaration that a long-delayed self-confrontation is about to take place ("this is / The end of lies").

The second stanza dramatizes this self-confrontation as the son's confession to his father:

> Father, the darkness of the self goes out
> And spreads contagion on the flowing air.
> I walk obscurely in a cloud of dark:
> Yea, when I kneeled, the dark kneeled down with me.
> Touch me: my folds and my defenses fall;
> I stand within myself, myself my shield.

Abandoning lies and pretense, the speaker addresses the father from the true depths of his ignorance and self-hate and reveals how they infect his whole life. This is not a "dark" that can be focused into a single, intense beam, like that encountered in the final line of "Vita Nuova"; this dark obscures and clouds. The image of the cloud, and the religious gestures and diction ("Yea, when I kneeled") call to mind the fourteenth-century Christian mystical text, *The Cloud of Unknowing*, with its counsel to embrace our self-ignorance and obscurity and await God's illuminating grace. Again, we have the figure of Kunitz' dead father assuming the status of a Spirit Father and being vaguely associated with an omniscient Christian Father God who is addressed in prayers and pleading.

If the primary way Kunitz elevates this son's confession to the father is through biblical echoes, the second is through the archaic martial imagery of chivalry ("myself my shield"). Yet how great an emotional distance from the proud chivalric predictions of "Vita Nuova" ("the visor of my name is up") to the self-doubt and obscure paralysis of "the darkness of the self goes out / And spreads contagion on the flowing air." This loss of confidence and purpose itself becomes a subject of the poems.

In "The Fitting of the Mask" (a poem that is a marvelous Audenesque blending of Kunitz' personal themes and the impinging world of contemporary events), the "visor" lifted to reveal the true self in "Vita Nuova" has become a "mask" that the haunted speaker vainly wishes to purchase and believe in, a mask of:

> . . . the youth, the undefeated
> Whose falcon-heart, winged with the golden shout
> Of morning, sweeps windward from his native city,
> Crying his father's grief, his mother's doubt.
>
> (p. 180)

In Kunitz' continuing search for a way to dramatize the archetypical nature of his themes (son and father; son–mother/beloved), he still has recourse to the ennobling imagery of the chivalric quest, but irony and self-doubt—as in "The Guilty Man"—have undermined its original meanings.

The son's confession of disease and dis-ease in stanza 2 of "The Guilty Man" is therefore part of a descent that must precede an ascent: it is the path of spiritual darkness. The "folds" perhaps represent a buried image of a serpent: the convolutions of an introverted, self-torturing self, not unrelated to the serpent self of "The Reckoning." When the speaker kneels down, the next phrase is "Touch me," which will echo two lines later with the first words of the third stanza, "Teach me," the son's typical plea to the father. The speaker announces to the father: "Touch me: my folds and my defenses fall" and that he stands within himself, himself his shield. According to this paradox, by being defenseless he comes to have a shield. The movement is from the amorphousness of the cloud surrounding the "I" to the clarity of shield and body—all achieved through the transformative touch of the father. In "The Last Question" a similar transformative power inhered in the beloved's hands: "Touching, you bring / Rumors of heaven."

In the first two lines of the final stanza of "The Guilty Man," the "I" of the poem wants the father to teach "my reasons," which I take to be motives, my reasons for doing what I do. It is important that these reasons must be linked to language, to articulation: "I would know their names." His next plea: "Cry scandal, drive my secrets out" is an equally curious situation: the guilty man asks his father to reveal his (the guilty man's/son's) secrets. The implication of course is that the father, and the father especially, *knows* this scandal, knows these secrets the guilty son both conceals and experiences as concealed from himself (a paradox, like the "cloud of dark" in stanza 2). But this second plea is syntactically and logically linked to the next line and thus provides us with evidence about the speaker's motives for his plea if not information about the actual "secrets" and "scandals":

> Cry scandal, drive my secrets out, because
> I hate the good-enough that spoils the world.

The speaker is tormented by guilt and is also an absolutist, a hater of compromise. We should not have much difficulty recognizing the quasi-Platonic idealist of *Intellectual Things* here, but even closer to the poem's event we have the speaker of "Invocation" talking about his task:

> Yet, Circler, one incendiary vein
>
> I have defended, purified, to slake
> You

This rage to purity is extremely powerful, this idealism that hates the "good-enough" can set the speaker at odds with the whole race, as when he says to the child of "The Tutored Child," "mortals will touch you and your taste be spoiled."

As the first version of "The Guilty Man" continues we see that "virtuous men" who turn the conscience kind" (i.e., counsel forgiveness, or self-forgiveness) are "traitors." One senses here that the speaker's idealism verges on the pathological and that it possesses him, he does not possess it. He cannot be released by a conscience turned kind: by forgiveness or self-forgiveness. (Kunitz' old literary mentor, William Blake, had counseled "mutual forgiveness of each sin.") He wants to be left alone ("depart from me") with the father who is the only figure who can aid the speaker in his drive toward a pure articulation of his guilt. He ends the poem with an absolute statement that is a paradox of hopelessness:

None may forgive us for the ancient wrongs.

Clearly the speaker has taken upon himself an ancestral guilt, a guilt somehow connected with the distant past (ancient wrongs). One is reminded less of Christian original sin than of certain Greek notions of pollution and guilt that infected families and blood kin for whole generations beyond the original crime.

These grim and unalterable curses or pollutions (explored by E. R. Dodds in *The Greeks and the Irrational*) dominated the so-called Dark Ages of Greece and were still present in the legends of the House of Atreus that Aeschylus dramatized. We will see later, in such critical poems as "The Portrait" and "The Magic Curtain" (both from *The Testing Tree*), that "forgiveness" is the pivotal word in the human drama of Kunitz's work—it is the key to love. In the meantime, we can only note that "forgiveness" cannot be given by anyone. As already noted, in "Night Letter" the son had pleaded with his father's ghost for some form of forgiveness:

> "Pardon," I plead, clutching the fragile sleeve
> Of my poor father's ghost returned to howl
> His wrongs . . .

The original version of "The Guilty Man" asserts that such pardon cannot come from the father; that all the father can do is teach "reasons, cry scandal, and drive [the son's] secrets out [into the open]." These words are cryptic and yet their final meaning seems to be that, since he cannot have forgiveness, he wants the father's help in revealing all his secrets so that even the falling might have a kind of "perfection" in their purity: they will be themselves rather than being hidden in stanza 2-'s octopus-cloud of dark.

In *Selected Poems*, the first public revision of the final stanza, we see a complete change of the final line from "None may forgive us for the ancient wrongs" to "The souls of numbers kiss the perfect stars." This version of the final line is a completely nonhuman, transcendent resolution. Rather than a revision, it seems to be a reversion to the mode of *Intellectual Things*, a Pythagorean-Platonic notion that in no way illuminates the dilemma of the speaker or resolves it, except by an implicit defeat. If we compare this final line to the end of the poem that precedes it in the volume, "How Long Is the Night?" we see in the latter an urge toward the nonhuman as a release from suffering:

> I would [like to] abandon this loose bag of bones
> And walk between the world's great wounds, unpitying.

The final gesture of walking among the world's great wounds, while it is mysterious (trying to visualize the wounds in the proportion suggested by the poem, we feel them to be large and isolated like stars or planets) is a gesture that grows out of the action and actor of the preceding lines and feels of a piece with the rest of the poem. When we encounter the *Selected Poems* version of the final line in "The Guilty Man" we are surprised and unprepared. Trying to orient ourselves and make sense of the line in relation to the rest of the poem, we might turn to an implied contrast of terms: "perfect stars" as opposed to "spoils the world"; the celestial as opposed to the mundane. It is as though the poem suddenly and relentlessly transcends all human terms (except perhaps the gesture "kiss," but that has a chilling feel in this context) as if to say, the spoiled and compromised human/mundane world can have nothing to do with this kind of transhuman and pure world.

What we cannot quite get straight is where this statement places the speaker. It appears to withhold from him all possible

celestial grace and hope in much the same way as the earlier
final line ("None may forgive us for the ancient wrongs") did in
its own way. The speaker of the poem *does* reject the "virtuous
men" with their compromise and forgiveness, and therefore implicitly identifies himself with the rightness, the justice of the
final judgment that seems to have no place at all for the human.
But if it has no place for him, it does satisfy his craving for purity, for transcendence, if only by its existence; it doesn't exist
in relation to him (since he is a muddled human). Nevertheless,
it seems important to Kunitz that this purer world exist as a real
idea (and here we see his Platonism persisting). To be forgiven,
to consort with the "virtuous men" would somehow confirm the
speaker's fallenness, a soiledness he cannot reconcile himself to.
In Kunitz' poetry of dramatized crisis and struggle, the tension
between a sense of human fallenness and guilt and the reality of
a transcendent purer world is an enduring one. As late as *The
Layers* (1978) the poem "What of the Night?" begins in self-
loathing and rises to an auditory "vision" of the "high, inhuman
chord" of the music of the spheres.

   The third and final version of the last stanza of "The Guilty
Man," the one that appears on page 180 of *The Poems of Stanley
Kunitz, 1928–1978* is:

> Teach me my reasons, I would know their names,
> Cry scandal, drive my secrets out, because
> I hate the excellence that spoils the world.
> So quit me now, you honorable men
> Whose treason is to turn the conscience kind.
> And do not turn until you hear a child.

This final version is the most affirmative ending—there is the
possibility of reconciliation with those kind-conscienced traitors.
The speaker gives a condition ("do not turn *until*") under which
he would be willing to see them again. That condition is the cry

of a child. For the first time, a *human* figure is present, and it symbolizes hope, some possibility in human form, but existing, as children often do, as an image of potentiality and future. There is also a vague biblical echo of the prophecy: "And a little child shall lead them." Although the biblical echo and even its tone seem to indicate the persistence of a desire for a form of magical release, the line also points us back to the poem's beginning: to the possibilities of youth (the first three lines of the poem) and release *into* the human not *from* the human.

Passport, a carefully structured book, draws to its close. In its original appearance the last poem was "The Reckoning," preceded by "Open the Gates." In *The Poems of Stanley Kunitz,* the order is reversed. Without belaboring the significance of this change, I would say that to end the book on "The Reckoning" emphasized the personal human drama that the book had explored: the end of a marriage or love relationship, and the theme of guilt and of "love and art." By contrast, the poem "Open the Gates" is a marvelous poem of transcendent, visionary solitude. The speaker is a fellow spirit of the speaker of "How Long Is the Night?" He has left the human world far behind and has set out on his fierce and personal quest. "Open the Gates" reads in full:

> Within the city of the burning cloud,
> Dragging my life behind me in a sack,
> Naked I prowl, scourged by the black
> Temptation of the blood grown proud.
>
> Here at the monumental door,
> Carved with the curious legend of my youth,
> I brandish the great bone of my death,
> Beat once therewith and beat no more.

The hinges groan: a rush of forms
Shivers my name, wrenched out of me.
I stand on the terrible threshold, and I see
The end and the beginning in each other's arms.

(p. 184)

As was the case with the quest-journey of "How Long Is the Night" where the speaker circulated among "the star-space," this poem also puts us above the earth in some transcendent landscape: "the city of the burning cloud." In "The Guilty Man" the speaker moved within another cloud, a "cloud of dark"; but this cloud is burning and large: it has an architecture that is grand ("the monumental door"). When the speaker says he drags "[his] life behind [him] in a sack," we recall "fortune's writhing sack" from "Beyond Reason" and especially his self-characterization in "How Long Is the Night?" as a "loose bag of bones." The image of life as a dragged sack also resonates with the other images of the burden of the past ("Your question comes with coils / Like years behind / which I am crawling from," "The Reckoning").

Stanza 1 presents us with the speaker on a quest within a visionary world. From the outset the poem has a tone of clarity and authority that alerts us to the fundamental existential importance of the quest. The speaker is vulnerable, yet fierce ("naked I prowl"), and mysteriously tormented:

scourged by the black
Temptation of the blood grown proud.

I take this torment to be a version of the self-torment so frequently encountered in Kunitz' work, as if one is driven (scourged) and seduced forward (temptation) at the same time by "blood grown proud." This proud blood may well be a kind of hubris of the sort that characterizes a Greek tragic hero. It may also re-

late to the images of nobility and spiritual superiority we encounter elsewhere in Kunitz, as if the speaker himself were aware
of some destructive melancholic element in his pride. Last, and
most significant, the image of the "temptation of the blood grown
proud" is an image of phallic sexuality. As such, it is one of the
recurring symbols of intensity of being that occur throughout
Kunitz' work. In the context of "Open the Gates," the phallic
intensity returns with the image of the "great bone of my death."
When the speaker slams this bone against the great door, we
realize that the gesture and the poem's dramatic situation (forced
entrance to the stronghold) make Kunitz' poem first cousin to
the violent, spiritualized sexuality of Donne's "Batter my heart,
three-personed God." The sexual imagery that begins with the
blood grown proud culminates in the sexual embrace witnessed
in the final line.

Given line 7 ("I brandish the great bone of my death") we
might well assume that the city the speaker has entered is some
mysterious version of the Heavenly City and that he has arrived
there after his death on earth. In an earlier cryptic poem ("Single Vision") Kunitz has shown himself capable of fierce post-
mortem purpose: "stripping all / The tender blanket from my
bone, / [I will] Rise like a skeleton in the sun." In "Open the
Gates" this post-death encounter yields a vision of the end and
the beginning in each other's arms. As a poem about the search
for the origins of identity dramatized as an encounter between
"the end" and "the beginning," "Open the Gates" shares a pattern with the later poem, "Goose Pond" (1956), where a drowned
boy rises up through a pond and walks out "Until, along that
marshy brink, / The springy trails devoid of plan, / He meets his
childhood beating back / To find what furies made him man."

Such a quest animates the speaker of "Open the Gates," who
pauses before the "monumental door / Carved with the curious
legend of [his] youth." These lines form a pure cluster of key

images (door/threshold, carved) as they impinge on the central, "curious" legend of his origins. Given Kunitz' assertion that a poet's cluster of key images defines, as if by constellation, the essence of his being, it is clear that these lines are crucial, both to the poem and the work as a whole.

Door as a key image represents a borderline situation: closed, it conceals something, prevents entrance; open, it allows entrance into a new situation and also reveals whatever is occurring beyond its threshold. Again and again in Kunitz' work we see doors, thresholds, and lintels appearing at crucial points in a poem's drama. A brief tracing of the threshold/lintel/gates image cluster will disclose some of its primary implications. It is important to bear in mind that one of the primary dramas in Kunitz' work concerns the sense of identity in the dynamic struggle of the family triad (son–mother–[dead/absent] father). The first occurrence of gates is in "Poem," a poem we have already examined in relation to the mother and beloved figures:

> Softly grieving, ironic at the gates of horn,
> I took my baffled head and buried it under the corn.

As we might expect from the Kunitz of *Intellectual Things*, it appears first as literary allusion.

In the next book, its appearance is only slightly less stylized—as portal or peristyle in "No Word":

> Through portal and through peristyle
> Her phantom glides, whose secret mouth,
> The absence of whose flagrant smile,
> Hangs on my chimney like a wreath of cloud.

In the recurring dream that is a central drama of "The Testing-Tree," Kunitz' mother directs him with "minatory finger" to pass through a "cardboard doorway." With these three examples be-

fore us, we can make a series of assertions about the image cluster, about its associations and meanings in Kunitz' work.
Gate/threshold/doorway is consistently related to the feminine
and its power; often a female figure is present in the poem when
it occurs, whereas the father (the dominant other figure in Kunitz' imagination) is not present in relation to the image, even when
we might reasonably expect him to be as in "For the Word Is
Flesh," which ends: "Let sons learn from their lipless fathers how
/ Man enters hell without a golden bough." We have "enters"
hell, but no entrance.

We can make the easy (and not inaccurate) link of the
threshold to the female body: the entrance/exit from the mother's womb and the vagina of "secret mouth" in "No Word."[3]

The threshold situation is also related to *revelation* as in
"Open the Gates" where we have a powerful fusion of Apocalypse (the opening of Revelation: "I am Alpha and Omega, the
first and the last") with Freud's Primal Scene:

> Here at the monumental door,
> Carved with the curious legend of my youth
> . . . .
> I stand on the terrible threshold, and I see
> The end and the beginning in each other's arms.

Knowing as we do, the "curious legend" of Kunitz' youth, we
can understand that his beginning, his engendering by a Spirit

---

3. In this context, and keeping in mind the basic quest in Kunitz for the
absent father and a mature masculine identity, it is interesting to consider how
the wound/stain key image is consistently associated with the father and the
masculine. By easy symbolic association, one might expect wound/stain to be
another image connected to the vagina and thus the feminine power (as it is only
once in "the golden wound that does not heal" of "She Wept, She Railed"). What
we *do* have throughout Kunitz' work is a struggle for a masculine identity that
at its most affirmative takes the form of phallic identity and the tree of life: we
could almost describe the origin of the father–wound link as a father-phallus-
lopped-off because traumatically absent and yet magically capable of regeneration (as in "The Knot").

Father or a dead father, *is* his end, that his destiny and his identity are somehow tied up with the mysterious and shocking circumstances of his origin (in a biological, metaphysical, and psychological sense).

The third quality of the gate/threshold cluster is also present in "Open the Gates," the quality of *fatality:* that destiny is determined at the source of being in an inexorable way. This is often linked to a powerful verb: "Carved with the curious legend," "carved on the broad lintel of his brain" (referring to Pavlov and his deterministic theories of behavior in the final image of "Reflection by a Mailbox"), or "The verdict's *bitten* on the brazen gates," i.e., etched with acid (from "The Approach to Thebes," Kunitz' version of self as Oedipus; my italics).

Such powerful pronouncements carved on lintels might have their literary origin in Dante's entrance to hell, or, when the image is of a narrative carved into large gates, we might look to the carved doors in Book VI of *The Aeneid*—the same book that refers to the golden bough and Aeneas' descent to the underworld to find his father.

When we place together the three conceptual aspects of the gate/threshold image: feminine power, revelation, and fatality, we begin to see the familiar story of Kunitz' imaginative life: a quest toward the father (toward identity) that is impelled by a traumatic force at its origins: a father's absence, a fatality (in both senses) that propels him outward away from birth/mother at the same time that it curses him with a "curious," life-denying origin. At its most cursed (the Oedipus story), the son's trajectory outward must curve back toward the mother and end in tragedy (in examining "The Approach to Thebes" later we will see how Kunitz proposes to transform this grim story from within). At its most positive (in the very late poem, "The Knot"), we see how this fatality, this negation of being (the father's wound/knot "scored in the lintel of my door") is transformed utterly and marvelously into an affirmation of being: the phallic tree of life.

Returning to the narrative of "Open the Gates" we can assert that behind the "curious legend" of Kunitz' youth is in fact a primal scene capable of being transformed into an archetypical revelation. "Open the Gates" does not reveal or explain what the "curious legend" is; it merely refers to it. This curious legend is indeed the fundamental source of Kunitz' themes: both Alpha and Omega, beginning and end. Though he does not name it directly until "The Portrait," the legend seems clearly to refer to the fact that Kunitz' father killed himself before Kunitz was born. One consequence of this fact is a mother who "never forgives" the father and a father who is urgently needed by the son but does not exist except as spirit, ghost, or ideal. The son's sense of self and his struggle to achieve an adult identity (to learn "how to work" and remain "kind") are inextricable from this "curious legend." ("I am nobody's son," he says in the late poem "The Game," with both accuracy and anguish.)

Because of the curious legend of his youth, Kunitz is peculiarly inclined to imagine his end in his beginning: death (his father's) is there at the outset as well as at the end of his journey. What Kunitz witnesses when he stands on the "terrible threshold" is a vision so private, so intimately connected to the curious circumstances of his origins, that it paradoxically becomes un-private and impersonal. With the opening of the gates, the quest for identity has arrived at an absolute moment. Kunitz is simultaneously witnessing his own beginning (that moment of his engendering) and looking back from beyond his ending, his death. The phrasing for this vision is abstract (end and beginning) defeating our attempt to visualize it. Yet the erotic embrace that characterizes it draws force from the traditional pictorial motif of death and the maiden.

As the gates open, the hinges groan—a personification that overlaps sexual moan and death rattle. In the "rush of forms" (again archetypically ambiguous, potentially belonging to either eros or thanatos), the speaker's name is "wrenched" out of him. "Name" is another key-image word in the overall imaginative structure of Kunitz' work. It is central to Kunitz' quest for identity and is mysteriously connected to the father. In "Vita Nuova" he announces "the visor of my name is up." The poet's traditional task of naming is also linked to the father as the son struggles to understand his obscure self through language: "[Father] Teach me my reasons, I would know their names" ("The Guilty Man"). In the central drama of "The Testing-Tree," the boy Kunitz carves his name to a target tree and seeks the father's blessing on the three throws that will gain him love, poetry, and eternal life.

The precise imaginative link between "name," the father, and the quest for identity emerges in "The Portrait." According to the narrative of "The Portrait," Kunitz' mother's inability to forgive the father's suicide (while Kunitz was in the womb "waiting to be born"), extended to her never telling the boy Kunitz his father's name. The father's name was taboo—and the very act of making it taboo gave it (or its absence) a magical power. The dead father is alive for Kunitz: as ghost, as potential guide, and as healer. But he has no name. The oblivion and decay that threatens so many of the early poems is linked to a lack of name: "Anonymous sweet carrion / Blind mammal floating on the stream" ("Prophecy on Lethe"); or the "flying dreams" uncovered by the carvers of "My Surgeons":

> Father was prowling in a field
> With speckled tongue and a collar of flame.
> They labeled it "Polluted Streams,"
> The body floating with the name.

Both the father in "My Surgeons" and the speaker in "Open the Gates" "prowl"—a fierce, animal questing animates them. As

Kunitz struggles to work his way through the guilt and confusion of *Passport to the War,* his identity becomes uncertain: "My name is sand" begins the self-accusing speaker of "The Illusionist." If name is linked to immortality, fame, and intensification of being, then the lack of name and the lack of the ability to name represent the complete obliteration of being:

> Let sons learn from their lipless fathers how
> Man enters hell without a golden bough.

Finally, language throughout Kunitz' work is regarded as having a magical power—an attitude or article of faith shared by many poets who might be said to subscribe to the story of Orpheus, patron of magical poetry. Kunitz' poetry is the poetry of self—of the self seeking to know itself, to experience itself, and to grow. Our names can be said to be the locus in language of our personal self, and as such enormous power inheres in personal names. "Open the Gates" arrives at such a point that, in the fierce winds of revelation, "name" is torn away and the self stands in primal nakedness possessing nothing except the vision itself. The poem goes beyond its sources in the "curious legend" of Kunitz' youth and becomes a kind of personal Last Judgment or a transcendent vision of that phenomenon whereby one's life is said to pass before one's eyes at a moment of mortal peril. It has that intensity, but elevated to an existential grandeur. It is the final drama of the self—the self's last encounter with the mysteries of being; one that takes place after the physical life is over yet with all the intensity of which living beings are capable.

CHAPTER 3

This Garland, Danger
(Selected Poems)

Passport to the War appeared in 1944, while Kunitz was enduring the particularly bizarre purgatory to which the Army had as-
signed him after he was drafted as a 38-year-old conscientious
objector. By the time he was demobilized in 1945, the book was
already out of print. It would be another fourteen years between the appearance of *Passport to the War* and his *Selected
Poems*. Kunitz' output was slender; he lived his life apart from
the literary and academic mainstream. His peculiar combination
of rhetoric and intensity, of personal drama and elevated diction, was as out of tune with the taste of the fifties as it had been
with that of the thirties and forties. When he was thought of at
all, it was to be damned with faint praise for his technical vir-
tuosity. The manuscript of *Selected Poems*, which was eventually to receive the Pulitzer Prize, was rejected by eight publish-
ers, three of whom refused even to read it.

The thirty-two new poems that appeared in Kunitz' *Selected Poems* in 1958 appear in his collected volume under the
title *This Garland, Danger*, a phrase from the poem "Green
Ways." The new poems could be characterized as less private,
yet more personal.

The beloved is the presiding figure of *This Garland, Danger,* and her legend receives a new series of elaborations. She is no longer an entirely human figure defined by human dramatic terms as she is in *Passport to the War,* where she is often wife or lover. She is still a lover in *This Garland, Danger,* but she has been elevated above the human to become both lover and muse. The garland that is danger is lifted from the throat of Apollo's priestess and serves to link the beloved and the muse. It might well be the garland Keats' "wretched wight" makes for his faery mistress in "La Belle Dame Sans Merci," the first poem a young Kunitz committed to memory:

> I made garlands for her hair
> And bracelets too, and fragrant zone.
> She looked at me as she did love
> And made sweet moan.

The muse in Kunitz' poems isn't simply a female figure who inspires the poet to write; she is a powerful, magical figure akin to Robert Graves' "White Goddess," and the poet must encounter her physically, sexually, in order to create:

> Sister, my bride, who were both cloud and bird
> When Zeus came down in a shower of sexual gold,
> Listen! we make a world! . . .
> > ("Among the Gods," p. 101)

This sexual encounter is often stylized, often rendered in high or indirect speech, and sometimes even archaically as in the Elizabethan pun on "dying" that culminates "When the Light Falls":

> For the petals of her heart
> Are shaken in a night,

> Whose ceremonial art
> Is dying into light.
>
> (p. 100)

The encounter with the muse can also have overtones of incest: "Sister, my bride," "Mother and mistress, one" ("A Spark
of Laurel"). It's worth noting that the term "mistress" occurs
throughout Kunitz' work, both early:

> To mistress of the ruined hall,
> The keeper of the sacred heart
> ("The Signal from the House")

and late:

> Tell me,
> are you still mistress of the valley?
> ("After the Last Dynasty")

The term frequently centers on its second meaning, that of a
woman in authority, and is an indication of Kunitz' commitment
to that aspect of the courtly love tradition that involves the man's
respect for and fealty to the beloved.

The muse/beloved figure rises to great power and she takes
the poet/speaker with her. His confidence has returned—"We
played like metaphysic animals," he says in "The Approach to
Thebes." But the fate of the male, be he poet/speaker or father,
is still one of tragic mortality. The muse/beloved can exist both
inside and outside of time, but the male figures in the poems
exist inside time and are doomed, though they have a mitigating
self-awareness of their doom and thus a kind of dignity. If the
female is a "siren" or an "inhuman breast" ("A Spark of Laurel"), then in the same poem, the male is "Ulysses" or "Agamemnon"—an heroic yet human figure.

The powerful emergence of the muse/beloved figure is linked to a kind of delight in disorder (to borrow Herrick's phrase), which signals a fundamental shift in Kunitz' perspective: a shift toward acceptance of process and change, and away from the Platonic bias of his first book. In "The Thief," a poem set in contemporary Rome, Kunitz acknowledges his past attraction to pure fixities that are both sculptural and philosophical only to repudiate them in favor of motion and mutability:

> But the past that tempted me, the frozen pure,
> Was a pedagogic lie. All's motion here,
> And motion like emotion is impure,
> A flower flawed by mutability,
> Religion by its ruins, and yet thereby
> More lovely and more graced, perhaps
> More true. . . .
>
> (p. 117)

The muse/beloved's role in this shift is perfectly expressed in "The Class Will Come to Order," where the approving allusion to Donne is followed by a gleefully ironic reference to Plato:

> The poets love to haul disorder in,
> Braiding their wrists with her long mistress hair,
> And when the house is tossed about our ears,
> The governors must put it right again.
> How wise was he who banned them from his state!
>
> (p. 138)

More and more frequently Kunitz emphasizes process and change but always contained within the suspended moment that is the poem. He "hear[s] the sound / Of Matter pouring through eternal forms" ("Among the Gods"). He is becoming a poet of process at the same time that he remains a poet of essences. Magical language is capable of encompassing this paradox; the "transubstantial verb" of "A Spark of Laurel" can simultaneously embody process and immutability, can be (in the poem's terms) "both fire and stone."

In conjunction with the shift toward process, there is also a shift toward emphasizing chance. "I recognize the gods' capricious hand," the poet announces in "The Thief." In that most fated of stories, "The Approach to Thebes," Oedipus can state "On the royal road to Thebes, I had my luck." Fate, that was as powerful a force in his early work as the "frozen pure," is now set against "luck" and the unforeseeable encounter that alters all.

A new theme that might be said to appear in these poems could be called "out into the world." The speaker is more often a self among other selves, involved in social and economic relationships and moving through recognizable landscapes.

"The Way Down" is one of the few poems in *This Garland, Danger* directly concerned with the father/son legend, and it is a pivotal one in the quest-for-identity theme. Death, decay, and oblivion—those forces that conspired against the son's attempt to reach his dead father—are now assimilated into a cyclic view of nature and become part of a cycle of decay and renewal that offers great hope for the son.

The anguished pursuit of the lost father that characterized "Father and Son" now gives way to an encounter with a mythic father figure of the woods. The father has changed: he is a vegetative, phallic, cyclic father (death *then* rebirth). An alliance of son and father is achieved and death is in some imaginative sense overcome. A kind of phallic affirmation/celebration occurs in relation both to the father (final lines of "The Way Down") *and* in relation to erotic love with a woman ("The Waltzer in the House").

Nowhere is the increased authority and prominence of the female figure more clearly and convincingly dramatized than in

"She Wept, She Railed." This is an extraordinary poem, its central character a woman victimized by men and by her culture, though her own character and her mythic and historical analogues lend grandeur and dignity to her plight:

> She wept, she railed, she spurned the meat
> Men toss into a muslin cage
> To make their spineless doxy bleat
> For pleasure and for patronage,
> As if she had no choice but eat
> The lewd bait of a squalid age.
>
> (p. 107)

She is proud yet powerless, disdainful of men and the humiliations they inflict on women. Personal and transpersonal levels of being are paralleled in a characteristic Kunitz technique when, in stanza 3, the woman's words and behavior bring other figures to the listener's thoughts:

> I thought of Judith in her tent,
> Of Helen by the crackling wall,
> Of Cressida, her bone-lust spent,
> Of Catherine on the holy wheel:
> I heard their woman-dust lament
> The golden wound that does not heal.

The "golden wound that does not heal" is a mythic emblem of female sexuality that, at the degraded level, appeared earlier as "a marmoset with bloodied clout" (stanza 2). These enumerated figures existed in the world—that is important; they are not goddesses, but heroines whose physical sufferings were in proportion to their great power and presence in a world dominated by hostile men.

In stanza 4, the poem becomes the speaker's hymn of praise to this woman and all similar women. The exhilarated listener (we can't really call him the speaker of this poem) bursts forth: "What a wild air her small joints beat!" (1. 19). This praise and awe rise to a level of intensity and intimacy that becomes magically mutual in a kind of spiritual interpenetration of selves, a kind of transcendental sexual and spiritual encounter:

> I only poured the raging wine
> Until our bodies filled with light,
> Mine with hers and hers with mine,
> And we went out into the night
> Where all the constellations shine.

The poem has moved from its beginning in rage and despair to a postcoital quietness, courage, and mutuality: "we" has replaced "she" and "I." They go out into a night that is not dark but constellated with transcendental meanings.

There are clear indications throughout the poem of places where a reader of Kunitz' work can see that his characterization of the woman involves a great deal of identification: the despising of a "squalid age," the "golden wound" that parallels those images of wounds and the "stain of life" that are part of his story. What makes the poem work is Kunitz' restraint; for all his identification, Kunitz does not crowd his heroine.

It would be inappropriate to see the female figure in "She Wept, She Railed" as the beloved: she and her situation have an autonomous existence. But what this poem does have in common with the muse/beloved legend is the power of the feminine in relation to the male speaker. To put it simply, women, to the speaker in Kunitz' poetry, are usually "numinous" in the sense that Rudolf Otto uses the word in his *The Idea of the Holy:* women fill him with awe, wonder, and even terror. We could say that this awe and respect directed toward women is derived from the courtly love tradition, but that tells us nothing at all.

Kunitz expresses his attitude directly in the following lines from the late poem, "Journal for My Daughter":

> I'd rather sleep forever
> than wake up cold
> in a country without women.

It is clearly an essential aspect of Kunitz' vision throughout the work, and nowhere is it more apparent than in *This Garland, Danger*. Sometimes it can be seen in the relative size of the male to the female figure as in the mouse and mistress of "The Waltzer in the House," or the child Kunitz and his "first love," the governess Frieda in "The Magic Curtain" (from *The Testing Tree*). Kunitz' notion of the feminine is powerful, but not sentimental. In his poems the woman has her own center of being. Lovers are described as "contending" ("Lovers Relentlessly"), and a late love poem, "The Quarrel," ends with this address: "*Liebchen, /* with whom should I quarrel / except in the hiss of love, / that harsh, irregular flame?" The figure of the woman in Kunitz' poetry is powerfully sexual and encountered as a strong being; if she is sometimes dominated by the speaker, she also frequently dominates him.

Since Kunitz' poetry is so personal and it is "his" life that he strives to convert into legend, very seldom in the early poems does he create another figure whose story, separate from his own, dominates an entire poem. Such an event occurs magnificently in "She Wept, She Railed," where his role is literally that of cupbearer and sympathetic listener ("I only poured the raging wine"). Here Kunitz breaks out of the egocentricity of his solitude by projectively identifying with her, just as he does in "The Science of the Night" when he imagines the sleeping lover to be on a dream quest similar to those he has undertaken or leap-

ing toward those adventures in astronomical or astrological space
that he so values.

When critics discussing Kunitz' poetry get as far as recognizing the importance of the themes of "love and art," they usually conclude that "love" in Kunitz' work is more literary than
physical. In *This Garland, Danger*, the sensual and the mythic
are intertwined in such a way that the erotic is often present
only implicitly, and its presence could go unnoticed if the reader
were determined to ignore it. But in fact the imagery and the
dramatic situations of physical sexuality are consistently, impor-
tantly present in Kunitz' work and especially in *This Garland,
Danger*. The sexual encounter has cosmological power in "Among
the Gods" ("Sister, my bride, . . . we make a world!") and in
"As Flowers Are" ("Our skins . . . / Contending, as at first, that
the world might move"). In "The Science of the Night," both
lover and speaker are sexual beings ("Leaving my manhood on
a rumpled field").

But not even this awareness of the erotic prepares us for
the basic imaginative encounter of "The Waltzer in the House."
There are two characters: a "blue-eyed mistress lately wed" and
a white mouse. But the simple imaginative fact is that the mouse
is an extended metaphor for the man's penis conceived as an autonomous creature. The conceit is outrageous but delightful in
the intensity of its imagination and the mutual sexual delight it
expresses. We have only to compare it to a poem like Karl
Shapiro's "Buick," where a man drives a car as if he were making love to a woman, to see how successful Kunitz' poem is. The
Shapiro poem is vulgar because its language is derived from the
locker-room sexuality of the dirty joke; Kunitz' poem is original
and fresh in its mutual encounter—its discoveries and pleasures

are not derived from sexual stereotypes or preconceptions. The only appropriate approach to "The Waltzer in the House" is to quote it in full:

> A sweet, a delicate white mouse,
> A little blossom of a beast,
> Is waltzing in the house
> Among the crackers and the yeast.
>
> O the swaying of his legs!
> O the bobbing of his head!
> The lady, beautiful and kind,
> The blue-eyed mistress, lately wed,
> Has almost laughed away her wits
> To see the pretty mouse that sits
> On his tiny pink behind
> And swaying, bobbing, begs.
>
> She feeds him tarts and curds,
> Seed packaged for the birds,
> And figs, and nuts, and cheese;
> Polite as Pompadour to please
> The dainty waltzer of her house,
> The sweet, the delicate, the innocent white mouse.
>
> As in a dream, as in a trance,
> She loves his rhythmic elegance,
> She laughs to see his bobbing dance.
>
> (p. 103)

Kunitz is always a personal poet—he is not capable of writing a convincing poem about any subject unless it has, or his imagination can make it have, a powerful connection to his own life (the only exception to this rule occurs from time to time in his political poetry). We have noted at the outset Kunitz' ambition to convert life into legend, to transform the themes and events of his life into a form of spiritual allegory. "The Approach to Thebes" *begins* as legend, the legend of Oedipus, and its interest and intensity derive from how Kunitz will make this famous legend his own, how he will anchor it in his own personal themes and events. What we discover in a careful reading of this poem is that it is densely structured in relation to his personal life and the larger themes that the strange events of his early life gave rise to. As a poem of the spiralling self that centers its movement above key images and events, it is one of the darkest, most intense spirals—a tornado funnel rather than a gull's wheeling flight.

It might be good to begin by noting how Kunitz' version differs from Sophocles', since these differences are the main way that Kunitz makes the legend personal. In the first place, Kunitz' version makes no mention of Oedipus' killing of his father, one of the central episodes of Sophocles' tragedy. Since the mystery of Laius' death and the oracle's insistence that the murderer must be discovered are what precipitate the action in Sophocles' play, this is a major alteration of the story. Yet we, as readers, *know* that Oedipus killed his father, and so in a curious way, Kunitz' poem can eat its cake and have it too.

The violent, mysterious, haunting absence of the father in Kunitz' son/father poems is present in "The Approach to Thebes." We know that Kunitz has chosen the persona of Oedipus partly because of his own dead father, but this very knowledge allows Kunitz (and the reader) to focus on other aspects of the Oedipus story. We know the father's death is one of the central mysteries even without its being mentioned. There is one single detail of the poem which might be seen as referring to the father's death. "The color of my thrust" might also be a description of the slaying, but here it is part of Oedipus' complicated eroticized encounter with the sphinx. That this descriptive detail that sounds like a sword thrust is subsumed into the "parry and thrust" of magical language ("my riddling answer") and sexual combat is emblematic of the fact that Kunitz' son/father legend is subsumed in the beloved/mother legend in this poem. The father/son legend is allowed to stand silently behind Kunitz' poem so that the poem can focus its imagination on that other major theme: the beloved/mother legend.

This brings us to the second difference between Kunitz' telling and Sophocles'. In Sophocles' story the sphinx plays a minor role; in Kunitz' poem it is possible to say that the encounter with the sphinx is everything. The sphinx herself is a major character: a worthy companion and opponent of the hero. She is, in fact, the beloved/muse figure who dominates the new poems of this book, the muse/mistress with whom the poet grapples in a manner both sexual and spiritual and in a way that is capable of yielding what is most fervently desired: transformation.

When Kunitz chooses the Oedipus story, he is choosing one of the most fated, enclosed, hopeless stories known to the Western imagination; one that depicts the individual's fate as foredoomed in a way that bears no relation to justice. Kunitz chose this fateful, gloomy tale in order to transform it from within: to transform it toward joy by focusing almost entirely on one incident: the encounter with the sphinx.

The entire first stanza (half the lines of the poem) is given over to a description of the sphinx and this encounter. The encounter takes place at the nadir of being—"In the zero of the night"—but at a time susceptible to magic transformation: "when the heart is pearled [i.e., transformed as the oyster's bit of dirt is layered to pearl] / And the moon squanders its uranian gold" (Uranian refers both to heavenly and also to Venus as goddess of spiritual love). At this moment of desolation, transformation, and richness, Kunitz encounters the sphinx' riddle. The sphinx in Sophocles is a monster who oppresses the city of Thebes and her power resides in figurative language: the riddle which no one can answer. When various people fail to answer the riddle they are slain.

The riddle itself concerns human fate. One version of its statement is: "What goes on four feet in the morning, on two feet at noon, and on three feet in the evening?" The answer is always "man": the crawling four feet of infancy's morning, the two feet of noon's adulthood, the walking stick of old age. When Kunitz' Oedipus gives his answer, it is also referred to as a riddle: "my riddling answer"—magic is met with magic, power with power. The sphinx is a composite monster (lion's body, woman's head and breast, eagle's wings, sometimes a serpent's tail in the Greek conception); Kunitz' description narrows this to lion and woman. She has much in common with earlier beloved/muse figures in *This Garland, Danger*. She is a "shape-shifter" as was the "sister/bride" of "Among the Gods." But she is the most magical and powerful version of this figure, even the most dangerous (her Greek epithet was "the Strangler").

She occupies four levels of being, all of them eroticized: the vegetable, animal, human, and superhuman:

> Of shifting shape, half jungle-cat, half-dancer,
> Night's woman-petaled, lion-scented rose
> (p. 112)

She also brings into mind three categories of experience (nature, art, magic) while repudiating a fourth (logic):

> What if dog-faced logic howls
> Was it art or magic multiplied my joy?
> Nature has reasons beyond true or false

Throughout the first stanza these four levels of being are sexualized and the encounter is both sexual and spiritual ("[others]

could not guess the secret taste of her: / Impossible wine!"),
echoing lines from "She Wept, She Railed":

> I only poured the raging wine
> Until our bodies filled with light,
> Mine with hers and hers with mine . . .

Kunitz' ultimate vision of the encounter ("We played like
metaphysic animals") stresses the freedom and spontaneity *within*
the fated story: the transforming possibility of both sexual delight ("animals") and arcane knowledge ("metaphysic").

This brings us to the third major difference between Sophocles and Kunitz: the time frame within which the story takes
place. Sophocles' play takes place years after the encounter with
the sphinx, when Oedipus' children by his mother are grown,
when the discovery of the parricide and incest which took place
in the distant past precipitates the action of the play: the discovery of these events and the horror, punishment, and suffering
which result. Sophocles' Oedipus is a relentless detective seeking the answer to an ancient crime.

In Kunitz' "The Approach to Thebes," we are *in* that distant past. To be precise, Oedipus is poised on the outskirts of
Thebes. The ecstatic encounter with the sphinx has taken place
in the deep night, and now "the tragic curtain of the day" will
be raised, and the rest of the story will continue: Oedipus will
enter Thebes to be hailed as its savior, made its king, and be
given his mother as his wife.

If we are poised at a moment of transition, it is not a moment made tense by Kunitz' protagonist's ignorance of what awaits
him. Here we are at the essence of Kunitz' Oedipus: the future
in all its horror and squalor is foreknown to him. If "freedom"
was a key word in the first stanza ("We played like metaphysic

animals / Whose freedom made our knowledge bold"), then "fate" is a dominant word for the story's second half.

We can see this fate introduced first as the concluding line of the first stanza, where it is no more (or less) than the fate of mortality shared by all humans and the subject of the sphinx's riddle: "I can bear the dishonor now of growing old." Kunitz' Oedipus is so proud that he considers his mortal condition a dishonor. Such a pride in these matters is a consistent theme in Kunitz' poetry: it is a form of heroic, tragic protest. Nevertheless, as the second stanza begins, we see that Oedipus' foreknowledge of his unique fate is absolute and precise: "Blinded, and old, exiled, diseased, and scorned." He knows exactly what awaits him. As the stanza progresses, the incest theme emerges, but at this point we can see that the change from the final line of stanza 1 to the first of stanza 2 though at first appearing to be a change from "man" to "Oedipus" (i.e., from general to specific) could equally be an elaboration of the common human fate. In other words, there are still elements of everyman in Oedipus' fate.

The next two lines express the absolute dominance of preordained fate, a concept that presides over Sophocles' play, and has a major role in Kunitz' work as well:

> The verdict's bitten on the brazen gates,
> For the gods grant each of us his lot, his term.

In the most similar other recurrence of gates ("the monumental door / Carved with the curious legend of my youth," "Open the Gates"), the poem's revelation also intertwined sexuality and fate, and with a strong hint of their link to the parents. This intertwining is present, even more explicitly, and at a less abstract level, in Kunitz' Oedipus story, where the main characters are son, father, mother, and, conspicuously, sphinx.

We have seen before that the key image of gates is associated with fate and also with the feminine and revelation. The fatalism of this image is obvious (the word "verdict" even accepts guilt) but the other elements are also present, though in an understated way.[1]

Kunitz' Oedipus salutes himself in self-mockery.

> Hail to the King of Thebes—my self, ordained
> To satisfy the impulse of the worm

The image of "the worm" (as grave worm) points backward toward the common human fate of mortality, but it also points forward toward the morbid sexuality of the next passage where he contemplates his fated, incestuous marriage:

---

1. With this particular instance of the "gates" image, it is tempting to speculate about one of its possible literary sources: Book VI of *The Aeneid*. Aeneas stands before the temple of the Cumaen Sybil and examines its doors, supposedly made by Daedalus after his escape from Minos' kingdom.

Behind these gates carved with grim human stories is the temple where Apollo reveals, through his priestess (the "moon-breasted sybilline" of "Green Ways"), men's fates. Also behind these same gates is the entrance to the underworld, the land of the dead, about which Aeneas pleads with the Sibyl:

> "Teach me the way from here, open the portals
> That I may go to my beloved father,
> Stand in his presence, talk with him . . ."

Kunitz has referred ironically to this book of *The Aeneid* before ("let sons learn from their lipless fathers / How man enters hell without a golden bough"). I propose it as one source of the gates image in Kunitz' work, because of the powerful confluence of themes and images central to Kunitz' work: fate, story, the magical woman, sons and fathers separated by death, yearning and despair. To put it in more optimistic terms that apply equally to *The Aeneid* and the Kunitz of *This Garland, Danger:* a powerful woman associated with poetry and prophecy can help the son reach and commune with his dead father.

To satisfy the impulse of the worm,
Bemummied in those famous incestuous sheets,
The bloodiest flags of nations of the curse,
To be hung from the balcony outside the room
Where I encounter my most flagrant source.

The vision of sexuality here is in sharp contrast to the lyrical vision of sexuality associated with the sphinx in stanza 1. These bloodied marriage sheets vulgarly displayed from the balcony might well be the "tragic curtain of the day" that contrasts with the ecstatic night of the sphinx. As in the apocalyptic primal scene in "Open the Gates," the speaker "encounters" his source of being—only this story is being told at a much more rooted level: the "source" is literal: the mother. It is the primal taboo of incest, and its consequences are deeply destructive to the speaker. If the sphinx is the most complex and powerful version of the muse/beloved, then the mother/wife of stanza 2 is the most powerful version we have yet seen of the destructive power of the mother. Kunitz chooses the Oedipus story precisely because it is so heavily fated, because everything is against Oedipus.

In the Oedipus story we have a distorted version of the young Kunitz' life situation, a version whose distortion allows him to recast and fuse together his legends. The father is violently absent; the son is alone with a powerful mother. It is a grim situation from which there is no hope of escape ("the verdict's bitten on the brazen gates"). Nor does there seem any hope for the speaker's quest for the beloved: the sexual quest ends in the mother and the unredeemable agonies of incest. But Kunitz transforms that story from within so as to make the beloved quest at least a success. In Kunitz' version the sphinx becomes the lover, and the encounter is not one of solemn riddles and answers, but of ecstatic transcendent sexuality ("we played like metaphysic animals"). Kunitz shifts the center of the story away from its grim end and insists on the one moment of ecstatic freedom and joy in a fierce and unrelenting story. But establishing the ecstatic, positive encounter with the sphinx as prior to the destructive encounter with the mother would not by itself lead the poem to its complete triumph, only to the partial triumph of the mother/beloved legend.

There is still *fate* to encounter, and this is the key to the legend of being. Fate is to the legend of being what the mother is to the legend of mother/beloved. How does Kunitz/Oedipus triumph over that which he cannot alter? Free himself from that which he cannot escape? Being heroic, he will not seek to escape—his commitment is to survival and to powerful being:

> I come prepared, unwanting what I see,
> But tied to life.

He is the questing savior, determined to live, but undeceived:

> On the royal road to Thebes
> I had my luck, I met a lovely monster,
> And the story's this: I made the monster me

He embraces his fate so intensely as to transform it ("I made [it] me").

But such an embracing of his fate would not be possible unless the muse/beloved figure was present. "Open the Gates" has similar elements to those of "The Approach to Thebes" (gates, the issue of origins, apocalypse, sexuality), but it ends as fatalistic revelation rather than transformation; the difference between the poems is made possible because the beloved is present in "The Approach to Thebes": the lovely monster. She offers Kunitz a way out of the fatalistic story: the twin, simultaneous, magical transformations of love and art.

By poem's end the shape-shifter has been tamed and subsumed into Oedipus' own identity, has become part of him, has
become him: "I made the monster me." It is a mutual transformation: he is monster (especially in the sense of the deeds he
will do in Thebes), and her magical powers embodied in those
of the sphinx have been conquered by his own arcane knowledge in such a way that she yields to him; her last "shift" (it is
implied) is a shift not of shape, but being: she becomes him.

The speaker is in this poem not satisfied with *revelation*, as
he was in "Open the Gates," but struggles through his embrace
with the sphinx to achieve *transformation*.

In "Open the Gates," the crucial phrase was "I see," and
the speaker's stance was passive; in "The Approach to Thebes"
the verb is "I made" and the stance is active. The "making"/transformation comes out of the erotic embrace of the
muse/beloved. Yeats presented a similar erotic, magical encounter in "Leda and the Swan," a poem that stops in the full glory
of the dramatic situation with the rhetorical question: "Did she
put on his knowledge with his power?" Kunitz says: Yes—in the
poet's encounter with the muse/beloved, he not only puts on the
knowledge of the future (usually catastrophic) but also the *power:*
the active power of transformation. Kunitz' Oedipus "makes" the
monster into himself.

The terms "fate" and "will" function in relation to the legend of being in this poem precisely in the way "nostalgia" and
"desire" function in the late poem "King of the River": as "the
two-way ladder between heaven and hell"—as the twofold aspect of a survivor's being: despair and courage.

In "The Approach to Thebes," fate and will are reconciled.
Kunitz' Oedipus sees what's going on and accepts it, though he
does not desire it. Yet he accepts with such intensity that he is
transformed. The encounter with the sphinx doesn't simply precede the incest and attendant horrors and thus provide a "happy

memory" to contemplate. We see here one of Kunitz' basic imaginative strategies: through an individual act of will or desire, to internalize and (literally) incorporate fate. The encounter with the sphinx changes the nature of Oedipus' being, his identity. If the sphinx was a composite monster (half jungle cat, half dancer) he himself is now also a composite: he has become part human, part sphinx. He has enhanced his being, gained access to new levels of understanding and power that allow him "to bear the dishonor" of his human condition and the horrible deeds the gods have fated him to perform.

Although there are resemblances and differences between Sophocles' version of the Oedipus tale and Kunitz' version, no modern audience can read the poem without also thinking of Freud's interpretation. Kunitz' awareness of this is probably the occasion for the lines:

> Believe me, whatever sordid tales you hear,
> Told by physicians or mendacious scribes

Nevertheless Freud's version, with its focus on the family triangle, has great relevance to "The Approach to Thebes." Kunitz' poetry of identity begins in the tensions of the family triangle (the more psychological legends of son/father and son–mother/beloved) and moves forward through time and imagination toward its most metaphysical version: the legend of heroic being itself. If Kunitz/Oedipus was born into a fated psychological situation (absent father, powerful mother), time has moved him somewhat past it: "I came into the world / To fill a fate; am punished by my youth / No more."

We could say that Freud is present in the poem by his omission, in the way that the theme of parricide is significantly omitted. It is perhaps appropriate here to recall Jung's critique of Freud's model: that Freud offered no way out of the "sterile drama" of the family triad. Kunitz, by choosing such a doomful story, seems to be sharing Freud's determinism and yet, like Jung, discovering, within the grim circumstances of a life, possibilities of renewal and transformation.

The form of "The Approach to Thebes" is interesting. The first sentence is a full ten lines long. Stripped of its atmospheric clauses the sentence would read: "she taunted me, to whom I gave my riddling answer." This sentence is incantatory and sinuous with clauses that characterize the time of the drama, the sphinx, and the hero's motives. The sensuality and sinuosity of the first stanza's diction and syntax are in clear contrast to the final lines of the poem. Here the clarity of the syntax mirrors the authority and clarity of vision the hero has achieved. In the final four lines of the poem, rhyme and off-rhyme (see, Thebes, me), repetition ("monster" twice at, or near, line's end), and especially alliterative use of "m" sounds combine with the straightforward sentence structure to bring the poem to a powerful closure:

> I come prepared, unwanting what I see,
> But tied to life. On the royal road to Thebes
> I had my luck, I met a lovely monster,
> And the story's this: I made the monster me.

"The Way Down" is perhaps the key poem in *This Garland, Danger* and a pivotal poem in the full body of Kunitz' work. It is a poem of the father legend in which the father is no longer seen as a victim of death and decay ("the white ignorant hollow" of "Father and Son"), but as a part of the process itself and identified with nature. "The Way Down" establishes a phallic father-in-nature, a Father Nature, who will consistently symbolize the potency of being and its ability to renew itself.

When the title is traced to Heraclitus' fragment, "the way

up and the way down are one and the same," we have a micro-cosm of the poem at the very outset. Rather than attempting to transcend nature (the way up) and thus the terminal reality of death, the poem will descend into nature (the way down) and death will be seen to be part of a cycle of vegetative death and rebirth so that the way down into death becomes the way up out of it.

The poem is in three sections. This is the first time Kunitz has ever broken a poem up with more pronounced pauses than stanza breaks. Each section will echo the opening lines of sec-tion 1; indeed the first lines of section 1 and 2 are identical. This repetition reinforces the theme of recurrence and heightens an incantatory effect crucial to the rituals described and enacted in the poem.

The opening line, "Time swings her burning hands," echoes the closing image of "The Science of the Night":

My whirling hands stay at the noon,

> My whirling hands stay at the noon,
> Each cell within my body holds a heart
> And all my hearts in unison strike twelve.
>
> (p. 98)

There it was an image of ecstatic stasis, here it is of relentless, passionate motion. *But* the motion is that of the hands of a clock— the motion takes place within a circle and is cyclic and repeti-tious. The image is a key to the process of "The Way Down": time and mortality are real:

> Time swings her burning hands
> I saw him going down

Nevertheless, implicit in the image of the clock is the circle of the cycle of repetitions; the clock hand that descends will as-cend again.

In the first two lines we have three characters: time personified as a woman, an observer ("I"), and a third character ("him") whose descent is that of the hero's descent into the underworld of the dead:

> I saw him going down
> Into those mythic lands
> Bearing his selfhood's gold,
> A last heroic speck
> Of matter in his mind
> That ecstasy could not crack
> Nor metaphysics grind.

This figure's selfhood is of the natural world (matter) and is bound to the fate of mortality. It is an inmost integrity ("a principle of being" he calls it in "The Layers") that neither the passions of the senses (ecstasy) nor of the intellect (metaphysics) can obliterate. The self is "veridical with bane." (Its being speaks the truthfulness of death.) Having knowledge of its mortal fate, the self is able to embrace a tragic heroism.

Impelled by pride, will, and desire ("a speck of megalomania" is another image of selfhood in "Flight of Apollo"), this self is able to enter "mythic" lands, realms where the magical transformation and renewals of art and imagination are possible. But in "The Way Down," we find line 9 repeating line 2:

> I saw him going down . . .
> To a cabin underground
> Where his hermit father lives

So the poem's "he" becomes a son in quest of his father. The son/"him" is not the speaker—we have a displacement and distance here like that of the "white-lipped boy" and his quest in "Goose Pond." Descriptive clauses about the father come to a halt, and we shift back to the son:

> In his hermit father's coat,
> The coat without a seam,
> That the race, in its usury, bought
> For the agonist to redeem,
> By dying in it, one
> Degree a day till the whole
> Circle's run.

In the image of "the coat without a seam" we encounter a complex of relationships and qualities. It is the father's coat that the son now wears and thus a legacy from father to son—an important theme in Kunitz' work. Its primary allusion is to Jesus' garment that the Roman soldiers cast lots for at the crucifixion. As such it echoes back through the father-son legend toward the "fierce wild cry of Jesus" in "For the Word Is Flesh." But in "The Way Down" the son keeps the coat on and dies in it, and the coat may thus also function as an image for the human skin.

This reading seems reinforced by the earlier image in "The Way Down" of the father "escaping pound by pound / From his breast-buckled gyves [fetters]," which appears to be an elaborate image for the father's physical decomposition in death. One of Kunitz' favorite poets, Henry Vaughn, the seventeenth-century religious poet, uses a similar image when he refers in one poem to "fleshy dress" ("The Retreate"), and in another says "I'll disapparal, and to buy/But one half-glance [of God], most gladly die" ("Vanity of Spirit"). The relationship between the father and son is next expressed in cultural terms; the coat is one "that the race, in its usury, bought / For the agonist to redeem." To the extent that the image of the coat without a seam refers to Jesus we are involved in the story of the son as Redeemer sent by God the Father. But in earlier poems this story of Christ the Son and God the Father has been used by Kunitz to express his own vision: the son's suffering and his abandonment by the father. Here Kunitz' version of the Christian legend will be subsumed into a larger context of cyclic ritual derived in part from Fraser's *The Golden Bough.*

The relationship between father and son has expanded to include "the race." One generation "buys" the coat; another generation "redeems" it. Thus we are involved in a cultural, historical progression, a linear progression through time, rather than a cyclic one. Or, more precisely, we are involved in a *social* process that will be caught up in the governing process of cyclic, *circular* time. This passage in section 1 concerns a social, cultural pattern, just as section 2 will concern the cyclic pattern of natural seasons (winter through late summer), and section 3 will fuse both cultural ritual and cyclic time in the succession of seasons.

The two lines "That the race, in its usury, bought / For the agonist to redeem" still contain enigmas. There seem to be puns and paradoxes here: the coat is "bought," yet must be "redeemed." We have a play on redemption, as if some sin or error (usury?) was at issue, though the only sin may have been poverty and the redemption from a pawn shop—creating a paradox about exactly how "owned" the coat is. (It is as if the point of view is simultaneously that of the usurer who owns the pawn shop and that of the impoverished victim who must attempt to redeem the coat—his father's—that he has pawned.)

The phrase "the race, in its usury," may well refer to all of humankind, but it seems also to participate in a medieval characterization of Jewish culture. When we encounter the word "agonist" in the next line, we have an archaic word out of classical Greek culture—"a contender or combatant in games." By the third section we will understand that this "game" is none other than the ritual combat between the reigning King of the Woods and his pretender that Frazer describes in the opening passages of *The Golden Bough.* The son's quest is to contend, ever to suffer (the echo of "agonist" and "agony") until the cycle is completed, until the coat is completely possessed. The agonist completes its acquisition by "dying in it, one/Degree a day" (again the image of skin seems accurate here), thus bringing the central image back under the governance of circles ("one degree a day"—a compass) and the analogous image of the clock that opened the poem.

Section 2 begins the poem's action again by returning to the opening gesture of descent into death, but the point of view and distance from the events change rapidly. The "magician" of section 2, line 1, must be the "him" of section 1, whose other identities are: son of hermit father, wearer of the coat without a seam, and agonist. But the major change in section 2 concerns the role of the "I," the speaker who in section 1 simply observed from a distance and was characterized by the relatively passive verb "saw." Now the "I" collapses that distance by magically participating in that death:

> When the magician died, I wept,
> I also died, I under leaf forgot

The incantatory paratactic repetition of "died" and "I" interweaves the identities of magician and "I." Levy-Bruhl's concept of "participation mystique" seems relevant here—the dissolution of a separate self and its partaking of the identity of another thing or person. This death involves a removal from the upper world, a loss of the symbols and functions of supernatural knowledge and prophecy ("I under leaf forgot / The stars, the distaff, and the crystal bowl") and an embracing of physical nature: "I hugged the ignorance of stone."

Under the earth, the speaker has now entered the cycle of the seasons that characterizes vegetative nature. From being in winter ("the white chariot of the winter sun"), we move toward spring ("Why am I suddenly warm all over?") and finally pass from spring to summer:

> Great hairy seeds that soar aloft
> Like comets trailing tender spume
> Break in the night with soft
> Explosions into bloom.

When in the middle of the section ("Help me, my worldlings, leave / To the hoot owl") he leaves behind the winter's "empty branching halls," he is also making note of a spiritual shift in his being, a shift away from melancholy and toward the material world and the ecstasy that culminates the section.

It is as if he heeded Keats' advice in "Ode to Melancholy": "nor make the downy owl / a partner in your sorrow's mysteries." The "kingdom of blight" is the negative vision of vegetative nature, the one that dominates the early poems of *Intellectual Things*. What we are to understand through this image is that this is a diseased vision of physical nature (blight), and in its place is proposed a nature that dies and renews itself with a powerful, sexualized energy: "the fleshed root stirs." The speaker now experiences another change of being, a transition from vegetative renewal to a primitive animal life-force of "thunder bison" whose energy reinfuses the self with vitality:

> Where the fleshed root stirs,
> Marvelous horned strong game,
> Brine-scaled, dun-caked with mould,
> Dynastic thunder-bison, Asian-crude,
> Bedded in moss and slime,
> Wake, and the rhythm of their blood
> Shoots through the long veins of my name.
> Hail, thickets! Hail, dark stream!

He has participated in the cycle of seasons and now in different levels of being, as did Oedipus when he encountered the Sphinx in "The Approach to Thebes." The final three lines of the section enact the speaker's rebirth and his ecstatic affirmation of the bloodstream of being that moves through all the natural world. The magical link between name and being has occurred before but in a negative form. In "Open the Gates" the speaker was shriven for his being by the apocalyptic revelation that "shiver[ed] my name, wrenched out of me." In this poem his being has been enlarged—his name has "long veins" reaching back into prehistory and down through levels of being until it is a "fleshed root."

Section 3 begins by again repeating the opening line of the poem—"Time swings her burning hands"—signaling that we will again return to the story's beginning in order to arrive at yet a third level of understanding. But there is also a seasonal continuity with section 2. Section 2 went through the seasons of winter, spring, and summer; section 3 begins in late summer and fall:

> The blossom is the fruit,
> And where I walk, the leaves
> Lie level with the root.

The first line can simply mean that the blossom is now the fruit (i.e., spring has become fall harvest). But its verbal formula as paradox—"the blossom is the fruit"—has another function as well. It stresses the continuity of identity over time and through changes of state. For in terms of the seasonal story we have actually come full circle, and when we have the lines:

> My brave god went from me.
> I saw him going down

we are firmly a part of the rituals of sacred repetition by which human fates are tied to the cyclic processes of nature. Who is the "brave god"? The repeated phrase "I saw him going down" alerts us to his earlier incarnations as magician, son of the hermit father, and agonist.

The poem shifts to an invocation of another mythic figure, the hermit father of section 1 who has also assimilated aspects of the masculine animal identity of the thunder bison:

> O father in the wood,
> Mad father of us all,
> King of our antlered wills,
> Our candelabrum-pride

The father is a mythic father. We will see him again as "the inexhaustible oak, tyrant and target" of "The Testing-Tree." He is Kunitz' absent, awesome father taken up entirely into a mythical principle of phallic potency, of powerful being. "Candelabrum-pride" is an interesting phrase because it fuses three separate aspects of being in its image of the father stag's antlers. One aspect is the cultural identity of Jewishness that inevitably clings to the line "that the race in its usury bought." Here the candelabrum as menorah/antlers represents the triumph of cultural survival and potency in the father generation. "Pride" of course has been one of the watchwords of the self throughout Kunitz' work: it is the necessary pride of the lonely hero, but also a pride that has sometimes been destructive in the beloved legend. In this image of "candelabrum-pride" it is sexualized and linked to the phallic imagery of the legend of being.

This linking of pride and phallus occurred once before, when, in an atmosphere saturated with visionary sexuality, the speaker was "scourged by the black / Temptation of the blood grown proud" ("Open the Gates"). This is quite simply an imaginative linking of the potency of being, the process of erection, and the theme of pride and will—all important threads in the legend of being, bound together by the complex associative intelligence characteristic of Kunitz' work. We see another instance of the importance of phallic imagery as part of the legend of being in the final image of the child who is compared to a rooster's eye, in such a way as to introduce a phallic pun.

Here the mythic father is part stag, the male that dominates until defeated in combat. This animal story transposed to the human world yields the ritual of the Year-Kings or the King of the Woods Frazer describes: a priest king who rules until he is slain in combat by someone who then takes his place. The parallels and contrasts between the situation here and in "Father and Son" are striking. Both featured a descent: into the pond in "Father and Son," into the hermit father's cabin underground in "The Way Down." In "Father and Son" the son sought the father in a quest that took place on the personal level ("I" was Kunitz in the dream); an encounter was sought, but the father's flight dominated the poem, and the final encounter ("he turned to me") had the effect of paralyzing the son with revelation (as in "Open the Gates").

In "The Way Down" the quest takes place at the mythic level (the son is a "magician" with whose descent/quest the speaker identifies), the active encounter is far more likely to take place ("embrace him," "hold him through the night") and the son's/speaker's being is enhanced by it. The principle of "fibrous love" ("fleshed root") that the mythic father represents so penetrates the natural world that it endures beyond human or animal existence ("although the last heart die"), precisely because it is "rooted" in vegetative renewal: the sacred cycle of the seasons:

> Receive your dazzling child
> Drunk with the morning-dew
> Into your fibrous love
> Wherewith creation's strung
> Although the last heart die

Returning to section 3, we see that the invocation to the
father, potent though he is, ends with his death:

> King of our antlered wills
> . . . .
> That the pretender kills.

The human story of cultural and generational *succession* is being
assimilated to the seasonal successions. Who is the "pretender"
who will slay the King of the Woods? For all practical purposes
the pretender's identity remains extrinsic to the poem's main
movements. The relationship of son to father now dominates the
poem's drama, a relationship derived from solar myths of renewal. In such a myth the sun god (note Kunitz' pun on "son"
and "sun") descends into the underworld of the dead each night
and is reborn or resurrected with each dawn. Here the renewal
that takes place underground is linked to an antlered earth-god
father and the "dazzling child" has the "bright" attributes of a
solar sky god.

When the father and son enter their embrace, they renew
the culture and begin the cycle again. A much earlier poem,
"Poem" of *Intellectual Things*, also concerned cycles of death and
rebirth, but that was a poem of the mother/beloved legend and
involved repetition without renewal. The son was ritually slain
by the mother, then after being reborn twice, he was thwarted
in his reaching toward the beloved and enacted a suicide that
replicated the first death at the mother's hands. When Kunitz'
"Poem" identified the figure of the mother with vegetative nature, the cycles of death and rebirth were successions without a
purpose. Likewise, when the father alone was present, in "Father
and Son," the dominant story was culture ("teach me . . . in-
struct me"), and the pattern was one of linear pursuit that ended
with a devouring by Nature. Because "Father and Son" was
"outside" Nature, it was cut off from the cyclic renewal of the

seasons: the sacred, circular time. What Kunitz needed to do was to locate the Spirit Father in Nature in order that the cycles have a purpose (to redeem "the coat without a seam"—the human condition of mortality) and that the purpose be linked to forces of rewnewal powerful enough to overcome our mortal fate ("the night / our best hope's share"). The linear fate of fathers (they must yield their power to sons) is taken up entirely into the circular renewals of vegetative Nature.

From this point forward Nature and the natural world are far more likely to be identified with the figure of the father than with that of the mother. The "indomitable love" of the father is no longer an abstract spiritual principle, but is given flesh, located in a natural world that overwhelms that flesh, and is then renewed precisely because it is in and of that natural world. Kunitz' imagination was heading toward this principle of Nature as a "father" capable of dissolution and renewal in the poem "Invocation" from *Passport to the War*. "Invocation" stands midway between "Poem" and "The Way Down." The speaker "strays" into a forest where decaying Nature threatens his being ("Webbed in a dream, stagnating like a worm"), he succumbs to his "winter form" and burial ("beslimed, glued to a rock"). This underground descent leads to the discovery of a buried male principle (described in terms that mingle culture, Nature, and sexuality): "And sleazy men in cabins underground / Rose up and sang. Gleam of their eyes! by day / Harsh solar gold, and night's bleached lunar stone." Astonishingly, the male principle and its implicit phallic sexuality has appropriated *all* natural forces—both sun and moon. "Invocation" ends with a direct invocation to a supernatural figure whose power to free the speaker in a violent way makes him near kin to the "sudden Lord" of "Mens Creatrix":

Yet, Circler, one incendiary vein

I have defended, purified, to slake
You in the burning, whose daemonic beak
The clasp of bone about my heart O break!

The arrangement of the last three poems in *This Garland, Danger* allows Kunitz to dramatize his situation as a poet. The first word goes to the neglecting or disdainful audience as represented by the critic "reviewing me without undue elation" ("A Choice of Weapons"). "A Choice of Weapons" takes place primarily at the level of art and is Kunitz' opportunity to conduct an elegant public defense of his poetry against an imagined attack.

In "Revolving Meditation," Kunitz himself questions the basis of his art: he dramatizes his ambivalence about its nature and sources. The tone is less guarded, more intense and personal; not armored with wit. He is able, by poem's end, to overwhelm his misgivings and get on with his journey, concluding the poem with a powerful defense of his role ("the voice of the solitary / Who makes others less alone") and an assertion of the fundamental nature of his poetry's themes.

The third and final poem, "A Spark of Laurel," begins with intense affirmation of the value of Kunitz' work from a fellow poet. The strategy of beginning with someone else's opinion of his work makes it in ways a companion piece to "A Choice of Weapons." The tone also places it beside "A Choice of Weapons"—the speaker experiences none of the guilt or ambivalence of "Revolving Meditation." The "sprig or two of accidental laurel" Kunitz claims to have picked in "Revolving Meditation" has become the "spark of laurel" of the title: a magical intensity of language and being that does not question itself at all.

When the fellow poet recites an old poem of Kunitz', "A

Spark of Laurel," it discloses a series of connections consequent
on the belief that language in poetry is magical:

> And gravely then intoned
> Lured from the underground
> The greekness of my song
> Still melancholy-young;
> While she, long since forgotten,
> For whom the song was written,
> Burned wanton once again
> Through centuries of rain.
>
> (p. 146)

The metaphor is of the raising of the dead that Greek heroes
and demigods accomplished and represents a defeat of time and
mortality that can only be called magical. (Kunitz is not above
the play on "gravely"—serious puns being a part of his poetic
strategy.) The personified song that has been lured from the underground has the power to summon from oblivion the woman
for whom it was written: this power of conjuring is basic to many
of Kunitz' poems, and finally rests on the identity of word and
object that is at the source of magical language in poetry.

This figure of the beloved is from the past, perhaps from
the time of a poem such as "The Last Question" where "our
hooded shadows rise to play the stab scene." She stands for violent, disharmonious, melancholy love and is identified with Eu-
ripedes' powerful and fierce heroines. She might well be that
"dark one" of "The Dark and the Fair" who taught him "The
serpent's word, but yet the word." In Kunitz' legend of the dark
one, the beloved is also a muse and the link between poetry and
suffering is precise:

> Smiling, as she must do,
> To keep her legend true,
> [She] . . . struck the mortal blow,
> But not that blood could flow.

> Ha! Once again I heard
> The transubstantial word
> That is not mine to speak
> Unless I break, I break; . . .
>   ("A Spark of Laurel")

The *Oxford English Dictionary* provides two definitions for transubstantial which apply precisely to two forms of magical language in Kunitz' work. The first is "changed or changeable from one substance into another," and the second is "made of something beyond substance; non-material, incorporeal." This transubstantial word that is the essence of Kunitz' poetry can only be spoken from the intensity of authentic being. It has the power to transcend matter and thus to rise above death and time (second definition).

It also has the power to *become* what it describes; the language of the intoned poem becomes magically incarnated as the woman it describes: the word becomes flesh. This flesh is made partly of the historical woman herself and partly of legend, or, more precisely, this living flesh is waiting to be taken up and transformed into legend by imagination and by the transubstantial word, as it is in "A Spark of Laurel":

> The spiral verb that weaves
> Through the crystal of our lives,
> Of myth and water made
> And incoherent blood

The life is made transparent so that the inner pattern can be seen: a spiral motion made of myth, water, and blood. This is a more passionate, magically religious statement of his earlier assertion that "imagination makes / Out of what stuff it can, / An acton fit / For a more heroic stage / Than body ever walked on" ("Revolving Meditation"). It should be emphasized that the transubstantial word that describes and creates the pattern of weaving is a *verb*, a word of process, and that its motion is a spiral weaving. In fact, "A Spark of Laurel" is itself a continuous process of the spiral weaving of threads of myth ("lured from the underground"), water ("centuries of rain"), and blood ("struck the mortal blow" that later becomes the cry of Agamemnon's wounds)—a spiraling that constantly transubstantiates from language (lines 2–10) to person (lines 11–18), back to language (lines 19–26), and back to a final ambiguous state we might call consubstantial. This word, this spiral verb expresses the most ancient and intense experiences of desire and suffering (lines 27–36):

> What sirens on the coast
> Trilled to Ulysses lost,
> And Agamemnon's thigh
> Opened at last to cry:
> This laurel-sparking rhyme
> That we repeat in time
> Until the fathers rest
> On the inhuman breast
> That is both fire and stone,
> Mother and mistress, one.

We "repeat" [these rhymes] in time" just as the poet did at the poem's outset: we repeat them in time because our mortal condition confines us in that space, yet these rhymes have qualities capable of transcending time.[2] Thus far, we are in territory

2. The pun "in time" offers further complexities. We are mortal, as opposed to the immortality of the characters of an ancient story who cannot die until the story itself does—so we repeat their undying story (about death, though they die over and over in the story) from our mortal place in time. "In time" we talk about those who have escaped time by being turned into fictions. We also repeat their story before it is too late to do so. We repeat it "in time" to learn from it. Finally, because it is cast in metrical verse rather than in prose, we repeat it rhythmically, in, say, the trimeter couplets of "A Spark of Laurel," and so acknowledge its artistic medium: the formal measured "time" of accentual verse.

that has been well prepared for in earlier sections of the poem, but now we learn of another purpose for repeating the rhymes: "until the fathers rest." By one interpretation this image of the father could be an elaborate figure for the reciters' own deaths, their own mortal condition: we repeat these words in time until we die. But what's clearly happening is that a new figure has been introduced: a father. Glancing back to Ulysses and Agamemnon, we can see that these figures are both fathers also: Ulysses intently sought by his son; Agamemnon's violent death at his wife's hands mourned and avenged by his children.

In the terms of earlier discussions of Kunitz' poetry I could say we have switched from the muse/beloved legend to the father legend. But that is not adequate or sufficiently accurate, since both "mother" and "mistress" will recur in the poem later. The real subject of the poem is Kunitz' poetry itself, what its essential beliefs and purposes are. We know from "Revolving Meditation" that his themes are solitude, love, and mortality. But his themes and purposes are also intimately linked to the three figures of his legends: father, mother, and beloved. He is the central point that connects them all, whether his role is as son or lover. Somehow, in the midst of the mythic archetypal world of this poem, we are also about to encounter Kunitz' agonized family triangle. In the last lines of "A Spark of Laurel" all the three essential figures who haunt, thwart, and entice Kunitz in his quest for identity are taken up into his imagination, and all their unresolved stories are fused into one mythic vision. The restless, wounded father who haunts him is soothed to rest by the magical rhyme. The "inhuman breast" he rests on is "mother" (the father's mother)—which is mythically the earth of his grave. But the image also implies at the personal level the "inhuman [because not nourishing] breast" of the mother.

If the fathers sleep on the breast of someone who is both mother and mistress, then they enact a kind of incest. Incest is the most destructive image Kunitz can provide for his quest for identity: the one in which the mother's power succeeds in turning back toward regression the son's quest for identity, and turning back the son's most powerful drive outward toward quest, the drive of sexual desire. Kunitz encountered and imaginatively overcame this vision of incest in "The Approach to Thebes." He overcomes it again here, through two techniques. He displaces the incest onto the father. And he fuses the identities of mother and mistress. Ordinarily these three figures are at war with each other, but here the threads of their stories spiral together, and the powerful energy associated with each of the figures fuses into the ultimate unifying vision of the final four lines.

In some ways, "A Spark of Laurel" represents Kunitz' erotic quest in reverse—going back toward its origins in the family dynamic. The poem moves from the beloved ("she") back toward quest (Ulysses) and the dead father (Agamemnon) to a sexual fusion of the father-mother-mistress. Such a reversal of the quest takes us back to the sources of Kunitz' poetry. Near the poem's end, the consubstantiality of "fire and stone" alert us to poetry's source and to poetry as the product of its source. Its source is two stones (in Kunitz' case, father and mother) struck together; the poetry produced sparks and fire. "A Spark of Laurel" is an ars poetica. Poetry itself is also "both fire and stone." It is process (fire) and permanence (stone). It is the shifting nature of matter and the permanence of eternal forms. The prosodic structure of "A Spark of Laurel" heightens our awareness of the poem as poem. The lines are three stress lines, usually of six syllables, and are also rhymed couplets. The short lines and rhymes give "A Spark of Laurel" an archaic, incantatory quality as appropriate to its subject as the pentameter couplets were to the witty self-defense of "A Choice of Weapons."

CHAPTER 4

The Testing-Tree

Some men a forward motion love
But I by backwards steps would move . . .
Henry Vaughn, "The Retreate"

For years now I have tried to make my work more open and ac-
cesible, without sacrificing its complex inner tissue.
Kunitz' interview by Robert Boyers in *Salmagundi*

The change in Kunitz' work from *Selected Poems* (1958) to *The Testing-Tree* (1971) marks a decisive stylistic shift that has frequently obscured the unerring continuity of his basic legends and ambitions. Admirers of Kunitz' work frequently separate into those who profess admiration for the early work *(Selected Poems)* and those whose sensibilities are engaged by the poems of *The Testing-Tree* and later work.

The stylistic shift, from predominantly rhymed, formal verse to a free verse of varying line lengths with little or no rhyme, is certainly remarkable, especially when we realize that the praise Kunitz' work had received thus far tended to emphasize its formal accomplishments while failing to comprehend its themes and its irrational, lyric intelligence. Kunitz himself provides a perspective on this shift:

My early work was dense and involuted—so, I guess, was I. Now what I am seeking is a transparency of language and vision. Maybe age itself compels me to embrace the great simplicities as I struggle to free myself from the knots and complications, the hangups, of my youth. In my sixties I am astonished by my depth of affection for this life. It's equally true that I am no more reconciled than I ever was to the world's wrongs and the injustice of time. (*Order/Folly*, p. 301)

As Kunitz' remark about his astonished affection for the world indicates, we are not dealing simply with a remarkable stylistic shift between these two books. There is also a fundamental shift in Kunitz' relation to the world and to his life.

Kunitz' poetry has always sought the essence of a situation whether it was his own inner struggles he dramatized or those between son and father, lover and beloved. In *The Testing-Tree* Kunitz begins to seek essences in *origins*. Such a strategy has played a minor role before, as in the final lines of "Goose Pond" where "he meets his childhood beating back / To find what furies made him man." But heretofore the quest has been dream-like. What distinguishes many of the triumphant poems of essence-as-origin in *The Testing-Tree* is that they are concrete, realistic. They are able to locate an historical moment in which not "furies" but actual characters doing actual deeds embody and dramatize the forces that create Kunitz' being.

When, in "The Magic Curtain," Kunitz returns in memory to a childhood breakfast table where he sits across from his preoccupied mother while the young German maid, Frieda, bustles about, he has rendered concrete the legend of the beloved and the mother in a remarkable way. In this case, the return to the origin allows him to alter fate with love and forgiveness: to redeem the past. In "The Portrait," he takes the father legend to its historical, factual origin, and although this legend is not redeemed, an incalcuable amount has been revealed about "What furies made [Kunitz] man."

Even the third legend of Kunitz' poetry, the quest for being itself, finds its poem of origin in the title poem of this collection. We find the legend of being located in specific profound experiences from his boyhood and we see how this legend grows out of the son's quest for the father.

So much is new in these poems. For the first time we encounter characterized and named *others:* people who have independent identities from the speaker and do not seem to be either an aspect of himself used as a dramatized contrary or else abstracted away from their personal uniqueness until they are only "mistress" or "she." Related to this, but extending to objects and landscapes as well as people, is the enhanced role of detail in the poems. Perhaps the departure from high speech permits him to let more of the world in, perhaps his affection for the world has altered his stance toward diction. As would seem obvious from a poetry of origin, the role of memory is greatly enhanced in this collection.

In the three great poems of the three legends ("The Testing-Tree," "The Magic Curtain," and "The Portrait") and in "River Road," we see a central strategy—vivid memory dominates the body of the poem: we are *present* in the past; when the final liines of the poem bring us into the speaker's actual present state. This sudden shift at poem's end creates an effect of fusing meaning and intensity in one dramatic detail or gesture whether of tragic exultation:

> Give me back my stones!
> ("The Testing-Tree")

or the persistence of trauma:

> in my sixty-fourth year
> I can feel my cheek
> still burning.
> ("The Portrait")

The emphasis on poems of origin does not mean that the poems of cyclic, seasonal time are no longer an important part of Kunitz' imagination. On the contrary, one of Kunitz' finest poems, "King of the River," partakes of the cyclic structure that comes from identifying human being with the being of animals in nature. We see discoveries of cyclic awareness in relation to vegetative nature ("The Mulch") and in relation to the enterprise of poetry ("The Bottom of the Glass"), while the poignant, mysterious poem that Kunitz chooses to conclude the volume, "The Game," struggles to contain the tragic awareness of human fate within the double cycles of a wheel of fortune ("Let's spin the bottle," line 1) and the diurnal round ("but only for a day," final line).

As if to signal the major shifts at work in the new book, we find that the first poem, "Journal for My Daughter," focuses on a figure who has not been central to Kunitz' work before: a daughter by a failed marriage. Indeed the lack of her centrality, and the resentment it generated in her will be seen to be a main theme of the poem. But before discussing it, I want to consider the role children played in earlier poems.

In "The Tutored Child," Kunitz addressed a daughter, telling her the hopelessness of her parents' relationship, then characterizing her ("You are of nature's bright unlucky brood") and the hopelessness of her situation. His final stance toward her is pity and a kind of detachment: "My poor poor child whose terrors never cease, / Here is my pity penny. Buy you peace." We see him concerned with *legacy* in these final lines, even if the legacy is of a bitterly ironic sort. The same stance toward children and legacy emerged when Oedipus spoke in "The Approach to Thebes": "Children, grandchildren, my long posterity / To whom I bequeath the spiders of my dust."

At this point, Kunitz cannot get past the attitude that the

child is primarily a figure in the drama of his life-in-art. When an adult occupies such a position, usually a woman, that person is an opposite, equal other, and the Kunitz of the poem is free to unleash the passion, wrath, tenderness, pride, intelligence, and egotism that characterize him.

In terms of the child figure, Kunitz' poetry is more uneasy. There is a deeper reason for this, one that emerges most clearly in the story of "Journal for My Daughter." Periodically throughout his imaginative lifetime Kunitz sees himself as a child, especially in relation to the father quest. In "Father and Son," his stance is that of a child beseeching his father for a legacy that will help him grow into adulthood. A major theme of Kunitz' own imaginative life concerns seeking a legacy from a parent and his sense of a helpless, intense feeling of need. There is also a related sense of being haunted that can cause him to write as a man in his seventies, "When the messenger comes again / I shall pretend / in a childish voice / my father is not home" ("What of the Night?").

One clear meaning of Kunitz' work is that childhood traumas persist throughout a lifetime, that the fierce figures of father and mother, by their presence or absence, can dominate a lifetime's being. When, in "Journal for My Daughter," Kunitz for the first time confronts his own role as parent, his own part in a child's suffering, it is a major development in his work.

The opening two words of the poem tell us that Kunitz himself is entirely aware of the fact that his language and point of view dominated those early poems in which he confronted the child: "Your turn," he says to the daughter. The poem's strategy in the first section is to give us the child–parent relationship and history from the daughter's point of view:

> You say you had a father once:
> his name was absence.
> He left, but did not let you go
> (p. 39, ll. 2–4)

Kunitz has quite clearly bequeathed to his daughter the same legacy he received from his own father—a father whose absence becomes a haunting presence. How close this is to the situation of the absent father in "Father and Son" whose "indomitable love kept me [the son] in chains."

> Part of him, more than a shadow,
> beckoned down corridors,
> secret, elusive, saturnine
>
> (ll. 5–7)

The stance of this daughter, "abandoned" by divorce, is one of "resentment." Kunitz himself is characteristically ambivalent about his own suffering (alternately proud and apart or agonized and humiliated), and he recognizes himself in his daughter's behavior:

> Family   of   anthologists!
> Collectors of injuries!
>
> (ll. 13–14)

Throughout the poem we will see as a source of dramatic tension an identification with the daughter and a distance (generational) from her. In this section, the distance and identity are in these final two lines, whose content declares identification, but whose rhetorical exclamation creates a mild mockery.

How can this legacy of resentment and haunting be broken? When Kunitz as son faced his own father in this situation there was no resolution possible because "he turned to me/the white ignorant hollow of his face." The father was dead—therefore would always live on in the son's inner life. Then, in "The Way Down," Kunitz' imagination discovered a form of blessing and legacy that the father could give the son. By simply repeating the encounter at the mythic level of the spiraling self, he adapted a ritual of death and renewal originating in nature's cycles and extending to include the human.

But Kunitz is the father now and he is alive, so the encounter need not be so grim. The struggle and tension between the generations can be broken by a rebirth that leads to love:

> I wake to a glittering world,
> to the annunciation of the frost.
> (ll. 15–16)

The new, almost colloquial tone must not blind us to the deeper meanings of this event. Its parallel is found in "The Thief": "In the middle of my life I heard the waters playing"—it is a change of heart being described, heightened awareness of the physical world of "popeyed chipmunks" and field mice. This physical world has a spiritual dimension, and by poem's end we will eventually see that for all its vivid anecdotal quality it has a literary ancestor in Coleridge's "Frost at Midnight."

Much that has happened in the lives of father and daughter has unnaturally fused the human and natural world—has created the "resentment-weeds" of section 1. Section 2 proposes a careful observation of the natural world that will lead to a moral lesson for the human world:

> as the needle-nosed shrew
> threading under the woodpile
> deposits little heaps of land-snails
> for milestones on its runways,
> I propose
> that we gather our affections.
> Lambkin, I care.
> (ll. 20–26)

A gathering of affections is set against the anthology of grievances that concluded section 1, and Kunitz makes the first gesture toward that gathering—"Lambkin, I care."

The time has come to acknowledge all the human emotions, to trace the history of a life and a relationship (father–daughter) by reference to feelings. The poem's shifts are shifts of feeling and throughout the poem there is an assertion of the primacy of feelings: of passion, desire, and need. Section 3 continues the momentum of this new family history: "I was happy you were born." It begins in the past, with the daughter's birth and midway through shifts to the poem's present and to the "nation" of women rather than simply the daughter:

> Your nation gives me joy,
> as it has always given.
> If I could have my choice
> on the way to exile
> I think I'd rather sleep forever
> than wake up cold
> in a country without women.
> (ll. 32–38)

These last three lines seem earned, true, and central in the context of Kunitz' entire work.

Section 4 returns to the daughter's infancy, the shared experience of her illness and discomforts:

> You cried. You cried.
> You wasted and you cried.
> Night after night
> I walked the floor with you
> (ll. 39–42)

and the gift of a song ("the only tune / I ever learned to carry") that he sang at that time. Again, as in section 3, we shift to the present, but this time it is the daughter who speaks to the father:

> You do not need to sing to me.
> I like the sound of your voice
> even when you phone from school
> asking for money.
>
> (ll. 56–59)

Throughout this poem there is less a sense of guilty self-justification than of Kunitz' wanting to give belated testimony. The poem takes place in the social, political, and economic world and tells its story at the human, not the magical or mythical levels. Centered in the give and take of human relations, the poem seeks its meanings there. It is the triumph of this book as of this poem to find many of its answers in the human world and the natural world.

Section 5 continues its anecdotes from the distant but shared past. This one begins as if it was a scary children's story and most surely concerns Kunitz' dear friend and fellow poet, Theodore Roethke:

> There was a big blond uncle-bear,
> wounded, smoke-eyed, wild,
> who shambled from the west
> with his bags full of havoc.
>
> (ll. 60–63)

Kunitz endorses the intensity of his relationship to Roethke at the same time that he registers his awareness of how frightening the world of adults can be to children:

> Both of us were drunk,
> slapping each other on the back,
> sweaty with genius.
> He spouted his nonsense-rhymes,
> roaring like a behemoth.
> You crawled under the sofa.
>
> (ll. 67–72)

This section is not only a casual tribute to Roethke's "My Papa's Waltz," a poem fusing intensity and terror and told from the child's point of view, but also a splendid example of Kunitz' capacity in this late work to incorporate literary reference without being dominated by it. The voice is entirely Kunitz' own voice yet we can sense Roethke rumbling like distant thunder somewhere in the background. In his early work, Kunitz sometimes slapped his allusions on the page with a very heavy hand. Here, it seems to me, he is masterful in hinting the quality of another man's work without self-conscious histrionics or imitative subservience.

Section 6 continues the tone of the preceding section with its childlike diction: "Goodies are shaken / from the papa-tree." But the legacy now is not entirely material (the "money" of section 4) but is in the form of aphoristic wisdom, advice, and slogans: *Be what you are, Give / what is yours to give. / Have style. Dare.* We know Kunitz well enough to realize that these bits of wisdom are seriously intended, but we are unprepared for what follows ("such a storm of fortune cookies!") a line whose humor is genuinely self-deflating without being masochistic. This important section is structured by urgent messages at beginning and end that frame a drama. The drama is one that has occurred elsewhere, a subtheme of the father-quest that could be called "the mysterious summons":

> Outside your room
> stands the white-headed prowler
> in his multiple disguises
> who reminds you of your likeness.
> Wherever you turn,
> down whatever street,
> in the fugues of appetitite,
> in the groin of nightmare,
> he waits for you
>
> (ll. 80–88)

But here the nightmare figure is a version of Kunitz himself haunting his daughter, not Kunitz' dead father haunting him. Here the legacy of haunting Kunitz received from his father seems most powerfully to replicate itself in his relationship to his daughter. It is the situation that the "gathered affections" must combat and overcome. But Kunitz has one advantage over the dead father: he is alive and can interpret the mysterious summons—he can deliver the message that his own father's ghost never could. He intervenes to deliver his message:

> His agents are everywhere,
> his heart is at home
> in your own generation;
> the folded message in his hands
> is stiff with dirt and wine stains,
> older than the Dead Sea Scrolls.
> Daughter, read:
> *What do I want of my life?*
> *More! More!*
>
> (ll. 90–98)

The "fortune cookie" messages were directed at the daughter—wisdom or advice she could make use of. This second message concerns Kunitz himself—his most overt effort to explain himself in the poem and perhaps to justify himself as well. Essentially, the message is a manifesto from his quest for being and says: "I am driven by being. I *crave* being." I say he is driven because the message is more ancient than himself ("older than the Dead Sea Scrolls") and more powerful than his personal identity.

The private slogans of section 6 give way to public, social, and political slogans as section 7 continues the shift of focus from the daughter to himself:

> Demonstrations in the streets.
> I am there not there,

> ever uneasy in a crowd.
> But you belong
>
> (ll. 99–102)

He separates himself from his daughter's identity at the same time that he strengthens the link of generations:

> We come of a flinty maverick line.
> In my father's time, I'm told,
> our table was set in turn
> for Maxim Gorky, Emma Goldman,
> and the atheist Ingersoll.
>
> (ll. 107–11)

Pride in family heritage asserts itself, and in an understated but important way, Kunitz has brought into the harmony that third, most intransigent of generations—his own father's. If pride momentarily links daughter, father, and father's father, then the flintiness quickly separates them again:

> If your slogan is mis-spelt
> *Don't tred on me!*
> still it strikes
> parents and politicians down.
> *Noli me tangere!* is what
> I used to cry in Latin once.
> Oh to be radical, young, desirable, cool!
>
> (ll. 112–18)

From Kunitz' pride comes the impulse to chide the ignorance of the younger generation, to admire their rebellious energy even when he recognizes it as directed at himself. Not to be outdone by his daughter, he presents his own youthful slogan—"Noli me tangere"—"Do not touch me"—one that could not be outdone for a proud solitude that verges on arrogance, since it is derived from the risen Christ's warning to Mary Magdalene. The final line of the section—"Oh to be radical, young, desirable, cool!"—is the triumph of nostalgia, backward-facing desire and saves the section from the danger of smugness. The exclamation at the end of section 6—"More! More!"—was the self's forward thrust of desire; the exclamation at the end of this section is the self's backward longing. As "King of the River" will make explicit, nostalgia and desire are the two main energies of the quest for being but the quest for being is a theme that now subsides in this poem, as we turn quietly and resolutely to the shared distant past again.

Section 8 begins as anecdote: ("Your first dog was a Pekinese") that becomes first death, with its confusion of feelings, and with its hint that the pain of loss can be healed, that being can triumph over loss:

> You sobbed for half an hour,
> then romped to the burial service
> in the lower garden
> by the ferny creek.
>
> (ll. 125–28)

Then, with the powerful understatement of simple speech so characteristic of this book, Kunitz juxtaposes the dog's death and that deeper trauma that we first heard about in section 1. Kunitz quickly follows this with a shared experience of the natural world, as if to say: death is real but brief—renewal and rebirth happen also. The father asserts his leaving was an unusual but natural phenomenon, a transient one like an eclipse, or a leaf sliding over the light:

> I helped you pick the stones
> to mark his shallow grave.
> It was the summer I went away.

> One night I carried you outdoors,
> in a blitz of fireflies,
> to watch your first eclipse.
> Your far-off voice,
> drugged with milk and sleep,
> said it was a leaf
> sliding over the light.
>
>   (ll. 129–38)

The final section is a gesture of analogy, an anecdote about Coleridge carrying his crying child outside, just as Kunitz did his daughter. The suffering Kunitz knows his daughter felt is displaced onto Coleridge ("heavy-hearted") and his child. The final section in the poem about Kunitz and his daughter is suffused with sorrow, but a distant sorrow.

The poem ends with an exquisitely precise perception (so typical of Coleridge at his best) of a suspended moment of feeling and communion, of sympathy (both the child and Coleridge are miserable), and of intimacy. Coleridge and his daughter enact the mutuality of suffering and sorrow, but at a distance from Kunitz and his daughter, as if to say: this is both unique to us and also shared by other human beings. In a poem occupied with anecdote and personal detail, this final section focuses on a transcendent moment the deepest purpose of which is not to take us out of the world, but momentarily to lift the heaviness of the personal burden by recognizing the transpersonal within the personal.

Section 8 asserts that suffering is real but transient, that healing is possible. Section 9 tells us how that healing can happen: looking with intensity and care at a natural phenomenon (the child's brimming eyes) the poet sees *transformation:* the suspended tears become sparkling moons. Kunitz' final gesture in the poem is wonderfully modest, especially when so much of the earlier language concerned his pride and egoism: he allows

Coleridge to speak for him. He allows the final magnificent lines of blessing that conclude Coleridge's "Frost at Midnight" to shine up through his own final lines:

> Therefore all seasons shall be sweet to thee,
> Whether the summer clothe the general earth
> In greenness, or the redbreast sit and sing
> Betwixt the tufts of snow on the bare branch
> Of mossy apple tree, while the nigh thatch
> Smokes in the sun-thaw; whether the eave-drops fall
> Heard only in the trances of the blast,
> Or if the secret ministry of frost
> Shall hang them up in silent icicles,
> Quietly shining to the quiet Moon.
>   ("Frost at Midnight," ll. 65–74)

What were icicles in Coleridge are human tears of suffering. Nor do they simply reflect back the moon's light in a secret sympathy that bespeaks the harmony of all things. Kunitz echoes Coleridge but emphasizes more directly the link between the human and the natural world.

Also, and most important, Kunitz emphasizes the active transformative power of imagination. Kunitz' daughter transformed the eclipse by her imagination into a leaf sliding across the light: terror and mystery rendered comprehensible and simple. When Kunitz says the tears "made" a sparkling moon he has chosen an *active* verb of transformation when he could as easily have chosen a passive verb—like "became." "Made" emphasizes the will, and the role of the maker, whereas "became" would emphasize the process of metamorphosis. The meaning here is in the power of transformations. In poetry this transformation is called imagination, but Kunitz here emphasizes its healing power in all of human life. We end with a sparkling moon, not an eclipsed one. The tears that are the outward sign of human suffering and the light from the world make a third, a new thing, which is beautiful and mysterious.

"The Illumination" begins in a state of spiritual desolation that is evoked through several images. The first is architecture: we have in the hotel the most transient of shelters, the most tenuous of securities. If in some sense the house is the image of the intact self (a self Kunitz feels as "lost" by the father's death), then a hotel with its numerous rooms and guests is a self in jeopardy. The hotel setting combines with another image: that of puppet strings. The image, by reducing the protagonist to a puppet, mocks the self's autonomy and integrity. In addition, Kunitz' imagination associates puppet strings with still another image, that of coils, thereby extending backward into a guilty past. The twisted strings above and the coils behind are image variations on the same theme: the self twisted awry, inauthentic, thwarted (by the condition of puppethood) and self-thwarting (through the gestures of flailing about).

So the poem begins in a state of deep desolation:

> In that hotel my life
> rolled in its socket
> twisting my strings.
> All my mistakes,
> from my earliest
> bedtimes,
> rose against me
>
> (p. 45)

This self is haunted by guilt and self-accusing. In seeking the essence of its crippling guilt, the self goes to origins—to "earliest bedtimes." But though we have a column of "mistakes," which lists them sometimes specifically ("the parent I failed"), some-

times generally ("the hearts I spoiled"), the total is a general-
ity—"a history of shame." The poem is a poem of spiritual desolation, not psychological inquiry. By line 13 the poem has
reached that nadir of despair that so frequently precedes spiritual illumination, the vision the title refers to:

> "Dante!" I cried
> to the apparition
> entering from the hall,
> laureled and gaunt,
> in a cone of light.
> "Out of mercy you came
> to be my Master
> and my guide!"

We have seen earlier how Dante is a presiding spirit over
Kunitz' ambition to have his life "perish into work" and emerge
transformed as "legend" or spiritual allegory. When a proud and
confident young Kunitz "unfurled the banner" of Dante in "Vita
Nuova," the young poet himself did the choosing as an act of
will. Now Dante's appearance is an act of "mercy." He appears
to Kunitz as Virgil appeared to Dante in the opening cantos of
The Inferno.

"The Illumination" is a poem that occupies a border area
between the legend of the father-quest and the legend of being.
Dante is both a father figure and far more than that. Dante has
been associated with Kunitz' father in "Vita Nuova"; he is a kind
of Spirit Father who embodies solutions to the central dilemmas
of Kunitz' life, dilemmas that are derived from the father. He
has overcome death by descending into the underworld and returning, unlike the "lipless" mortal fathers. He has fused life and
art by writing a poetry in which he himself is the main protagonist. Dante has converted life into legend—he is that self that
has spiraled up out of the squalor of experience: the "cone of

light" is an emblem of spiraling ascent that contrasts with the "twisted strings" of Kunitz' life.

But the Kunitz of "The Illumination" is no longer the confident poet of "Vita Nuova," and Dante himself enacts a transformation that has elements of mockery in it: yes, it *is* Dante, but can he guide?:

> "I know neither the time
> nor the way
> nor the number on the door . . ."

Throughout the poem Kunitz indulges in a kind of undercutting or self-deflation of the poem's seriousness, as if to guard against pomposity, guard against the fact that the poem *is* about a vison and an illumination:

> And he held up in his hand
> the key,
> which blinded me.

Even at the very end, we are held suspended between the ludicrous and the sublime. The "key" is a grand symbol of that which unlocks the great mysteries and enlightens the seeker. For a befuddled someone to enter your hotel room by accident is the stuff of slapstick. "To spoil hearts" (l. 10) is to be a demon lover; to spoil your "own left ventrical" (l. 12) is not so impressive. For the spiritual guide to "not know the way" is terribly portentous, but when he also does not know "the number on the door" we have returned to a kind of comedy.

The point is that these two levels of discourse are held in perfect suspense: this is a serious poem in which the speaker undergoes a deep experience of wretchedness and then a spiritual transformation. But it is a cagey poem—its claims are resonant yet curiously guarded and terse: I saw the key—it shone—

it shone so brightly I was blinded—end of poem. We can see that the *key* has great power, and yet the holder of the key is bewildered, both lost and not lost. As always, Kunitz will not interpret his dramas. He will work them for every possible resonance, be it literary, metaphysical, psychological, or comic, but again and again when the story ends, the poem ends. As he will tell us in "The Testing-Tree": "Never explain!"

I have said before that Kunitz is a poet who makes extensive use of intelligent, nonrational connections to communicate. One form of this that Kunitz uses to the fullest is the arrangement of the order of poems within a book, the juxtapositions of poems. In "The Illumination" we are informed that the speaker's mistakes go back "to my earliest bedtimes," and where does "Three Floors" begin but at those earliest bedtimes of awareness?

"Three Floors" is a quiet, unassuming poem that contains the essence of Kunitz' work: the son's quest for identity understood in relation to the parents and the beloved (played here by the sister). The "Three Floors" of the title might well be the three figures of mother, lover, and father. What makes "Three Floors" rare is that all three figures are present in the same poem. We have many instances of son–father, son–mother–father, but only three others where all four figures could be said to be present: "The Fitting of the Mask," "The Magic Curtain" (where the father is present indirectly—as Frieda's lover), and "A Spark of Laurel."

This unusual situation, plus its stylized historical "reality" (its claim to essence as earliest experience of something), allows Kunitz to define himself in relation to the central figures of his work. Mother of course is first: the primary, censorious presence—the watchful, critical eye:

> Mother was a crack of light
> and a gray eye peeping
>
> (p. 47)

Rather than longing, she inspires a quiet fear and evasion:

> I made believe by breathing hard
> that I was sleeping.

Stanza 2 introduces the sister—rarely mentioned in his work—but we see that the language of companionship and erotic attachment overlap, and she is the child's imagined lover as well as sister:

> Sister's doughboy on last leave
> had robbed me of her hand
>
> (ll. 5–6)

The metaphor of incest is relevant to the poem's meaning, although the deliberately innocent child's voice of the poem makes this assertion seem bizarre. It's ambiguous in this poem, but when Kunitz is tempted to turn desire back toward a family figure (usually the mother, here the sister), it presents a self-thwarting of his identity quest. The energy that sends Kunitz out into the world in search of identity and intensity of being has a strong erotic component.

The poem takes place in the fictive unity of a single night and three floors of the same house. Stanza 1 gives us the mother on the second floor; stanza 2, the sister-beloved on the first floor. The third stanza concerns the attic and a mysterious identity whose emblems Kunitz discovers:

> Under the roof a wardrobe trunk
> whose lock a boy could pick

> contained a red Masonic hat
> and a walking stick.

The powerful key that shone in the last lines of "The Illumination" might well have unlocked this mysterious trunk, since it contains arcane emblems of an unknown person. At this point we can ask why, in such a carefully structured formal poem with three floors and three figures, we do not also have three stanzas? What we have is a delayed revelation (as in "The Illumination" where not Dante but the key had the power). What stanza 3 presents is a legacy: emblems of a mysterious masculine identity.

In stanza 4, the third figure appears: the father's ghost—released from the trunk with the emblems of his identity. The power in those emblems, and the power in the father's ghost are communicated to the son in the imagery of phallic erection—"bolt upright in my bed that night." "The Illumination" alluded to origins, but sought revelation and grace. "Three Floors" confronts origin and discovers essence (in the figure of the father).

The legend of being and the legend of the father-quest fuse in phallic intensity. The father appears to the terrified son as a vision and a haunting, like Dante in "The Illumination" or Lincoln in the late poem, "The Lincoln Relics." This represents a variation on the father theme that could be called "the miraculous appearance." The "father" is not summoning the son, merely appearing before him in a startling manner. The meaning of each particular appearance is revealed by its dramatic context, the details, and the tone. The details here are of phallic intensity and terror and wonder:

> The wind was walking on my neck,
> the windowpanes were crying.

The rhythmically weak feminine ending of the crucial final rhyme—"flying/crying"—has a curious effect. It undercuts the seriousness with which we take the events and reinforces the child-as-speaker identity that the lilting rhythm and the alternating tetrameter and trimeter lines have created.

In both "Three Floors" and "The Illumination," it is as though Kunitz has developed a new strategy to accompany his new style. High speech and high seriousness went well together. Now that he is writing what might be called "possible speech," he has begun to guard against portentousness. He is, after all, writing respectively about a vision and the seeing of a ghost—and he is writing to an unbelieving age. This strategy of slightly undercutting the content, slightly mocking himself, allows him to expound his theme without seeming pompous.

We could begin a discussion of "The Flight of Apollo" by saying that it was occasioned by the July 20, 1969, landing of Apollo XI on the lunar surface, but Kunitz is not an occasional poet unless those occasions suit his deeper purposes. Nor does he assume personaes casually. The speaker of this poem is a moon-walking astronaut, but he is also the poet whose imaginative journey into space is sponsored by Apollo, the god of poetry. Kunitz' fascination with space travel stems from his days as a cub reporter in Worcester when he interviewed Charles Goddard, the father of the modern, liquid-fuel rocket. Goddard predicted to the then young Kunitz that man would walk on the moon in his lifetime. The vision of space travel stuck deeply in Kunitz' imagination as an ultimate human adventure—an image for the individual's constant outward questing and searching.

In earlier poems, like "Science of the Night," these voyages were taken in dreams. They were also linked to the Neoplatonic spiritual journey that involves the soul's flight out of the body and up through the crystal planetary spheres toward ecstatic communion with God. Such a transcendent flight to young Kunitz was an escape from the world of time, mutability, and death. The older Kunitz who speaks in "The Flight of Apollo" is a poet of the quest for being: he discovers as much or more meaning in the process, the journey itself, than in any goal.

Section 1 is written in prose, something new to Kunitz' work. By a paradox of tone, the flatness of prose somehow permits Kunitz to make his baldest statements of exalted tragic awareness:

> Earth was my home, but even there I was a stranger .   .   . I know what I know: I shall never escape from strangeness or complete my journey. Think of me as nostalgic, afraid, exalted. I am your man on the moon, a speck of megalomania, restless for the leap toward island universes (p. 48)

We see here another paradox that frequently attends on persona: Kunitz is most himself when he is other. This condition of alienation, restless questing, exaltation, fear, nostalgia—these are essences of Kunitz' being that have animated all his work. The view is tragical, as the first half of the following sentence indicates, but heroically tragical: "Infinite space overwhelms the human heart, but in the middle of nowhere life inexorably calls to life."

Section 2 is in free verse. It begins by repeating an assertion from section 1: "I was a stranger on earth" and begins the theme of the journey into space as a spiritual journey to "new Jerusalems." The final phrase—"the intelligence of the stars"— is strongly reminiscent of Plotinus' description of the soul's homeward flight from earth to Intelligence and from Intelligence to God. We have here a poem of the isolated pilgrim on the journey of being, a representative human ("your man on the moon") who nevertheless makes "the flight of the alone to the alone."

The next poem, "Around Pastor Bonhoeffer," is well placed to act as a contrast and counterbalance to the egotism celebrated in "The Flight of Apollo." If the astronaut embodies the heroism of the isolated self, then Bonhoeffer represents the heroic surrendering or transcending of self in order to combat evil. There is little that can be said about the poem, except that it magnificently dramatizes three moments in the life of Deitrich Bonhoeffer, the Lutheran minister who, although a pacifist, joined in a conspiracy against Hitler's life.

The first section concerns the tense moments of waiting to hear whether the plot was successful. The second section is a dramatization of the ethical crisis that forced Bonhoeffer to forsake his beloved solitude and privacy:

> In the chapel of his ear
> he had heard the midnight bells
> jangling: *if you permit*
> *this evil, what is the good*
> *of the good of your life?*
> And he forsook the last things,
> the dear inviolable mysteries—
> Plato's lamp, passed from the hand
> of saint to saint—
> that he might risk his soul in the streets
>
> (p.50)

Just when Bonhoeffer is leaving this world, a magnificent "reversal" occurs. He is "turned" around. We must remember that the verb "turning" has powerful significance in Kunitz' work—it is the physical gesture that signals a transformation. In a sense, when Bonhoeffer meets the "Master," who is presumably Christ—he is "turned around," so that he faces life again, faces the world, and in a sense reenacts Christ's resurrection. Only it is not so much a resurrection as it is a judgment: Bonhoeffer is turned around to face us and we see that he died for us, that he was an example to us of great courage and integrity: his image fuses with that of the Master. It is as though Kunitz is saying: no, Bonhoeffer is not led *away* from this world into heaven; he is led back into his world—a world whose "brotherhood" he and his deeds have made believable.

We realize that like Christ, as understood by Christians, Bonhoeffer "died for us," and that the "brotherhood of man" is a believable phenomenon if based on as authentic and selfless a deed as Bonhoeffer's.

It is possible to call politics a theme in Kunitz' work, but it cannot be given the status or importance of the three legends. Why? It is too distant from the central concerns of the work— the self-involved nature of the lyric and the spiritual quest Kunitz is on, a quest that is undertaken in solitude or in relation to only a few significant figures (parents, beloved).

Politics does succeed periodically in attracting the energy of Kunitz' imagination, but across a great distance, often as a kind of ire. Kunitz himself tells us how far the state is from poetry in "Grammar Lesson":

> Each substantive drank light,
> Required no definition,
> Embraced its opposite,
> As even poet, nation
>
> (p. 105)

This embracing of the nation by its opposite, the poet, seldom takes place. When it does they grapple, of course, not embrace with love. We can say that it is a question of the attraction of opposites, but the theme does not come easily to Kunitz. His motto was "Noli me tangere!"—he was "ever uneasy in crowds," and though, like many intelligent and principled individuals, he is engaged by political issues, they seldom bring forth his strongest poems. His political poems are best when he has an individual figure he can focus on: Bonhoeffer, Lincoln—representatives of individual integrity and strength of spirit.

"King of the River" is quite possibly the ultimate expression of the legend of being in Kunitz' work. It is a masterpiece. A reader wishing to understand its full power should begin by reading it aloud, becoming aware of the incantatory power of its rhythms, its syntax of spiritual longing and contradiction: "If . . . if . . . but. . . ."

With this poem it is not possible to quote lines that illustrate the commentary; commentary is appropriate and possible, but it is a violation to break up the unfolding wholeness of sentences that are actually stanzas (1 and 2).

I say without hesitation that "King of the River" is a great poem of spiritual questing. A part of its greatness, a primary source of its strength and beauty, is that it is entirely anchored in a phenomenon of the natural world: the "King" of the river is a king salmon "heavy with milt" whose struggle against the current of a northwestern river structures the poem at the literal level.

Even the image of the "two-way ladder / between heaven and hell" which seems entirely metaphysical has its source in the object world: the "fish ladders" constructed so that the salmon can climb high, man-made dams. As never before Kunitz finds a phenomenon that permits him to "see himself" as in a mirror that reveals the deepest secrets and paradoxes of being as he experiences it.

The poem begins with contradictions reminiscent of the opening strategy of "Revolving Meditation," but far more incantatory:

> If the water were clear enough,
> if the water were still,
> but the water is not clear,
> the water is not still,
> you would see yourself,
> slipped out of your skin,
> nosing upstream,
> slapping, thrashing,
> tumbling
> over the rocks
> till you paint them
> with your belly's blood:
> Finned Ego,
> yard of muscle that coils,
> uncoils.
>
> (p. 52)

The stanza conceives the possibility that "you would see yourself" (line 5), that a revelation of identity is possible, but lines 1–4 surround the possibility with impossibility. To propose the desired possibility (clarity, knowledge, power, purity of heart) only to state that reality contradicts it, will be the pattern for the opening of each stanza—to extend hope and withdraw it.

How many metamorphoses we've seen in Kunitz' poetry, but this is the profoundest—the one that contains the revelation of identity and essence. It is not simply "yourself" that you would see, but "yourself slipped out of your skin"—another being that is intimately connected to your being. It is not your soul understood as some spiritual essence distinct from your physical body. In fact it is a paradoxical entity: a creature self whose being and drives incarnate the speaker's spiritual essence *in* or *as* a physical, mortal creature—a "Finned Ego."

"Finned Ego" is capitalized to exalt it just as the title, "King of the River," entitles the fish while it plays against the species name. Like the king of a river in a fairy tale, or a river god in mythology, this creature seems to possess secrets and powers that would attract a questing mortal to the banks of his domain.

In the early lines, the flux of the water seems the dominant reality, the controlling phenomenon that has the power to obscure the image of the other self. But when the Finned Ego appears, we see that it is an incarnation of process: a concentration of being so powerful that its movement dominates three-fourths of the stanza with its verbs and verbals: nosing, slapping, thrashing, tumbling, coils, uncoils.

The second stanza begins with an abstract word, "knowledge," having replaced the first stanza's physical word, "water":

> If the knowledge were given you,
> but it is not given,
> for the membrane is clouded
> with self-deceptions
> and the iridescent image swims
> through a mirror that flows,
> you would surprise yourself
> in that other flesh
> heavy with milt,
> bruised, battering toward the dam
> that lips the orgiastic pool.
>
> *Come. Bathe in these waters.*
> *Increase and die.*

Knowledge is the key word at the outset—self-knowledge is the revelation proposed and then withdrawn because of inner reality ("for the membrane is clouded / with self-deceptions") and outer reality ("and the iridescent image swims / through a mirror that flows"). The outer reality is one of movement within movement, a Heraclitean flux that frustrates our need for a fixed truth. We no longer even have that consolation of formal fixity that poetry offered—"the sound of Matter pouring through eternal forms" ("Among the Gods"). Now *all* is movement; the subject of the poem is not poetry but our creature self—"yourself / in that other flesh."

When Kunitz spoke of the "difficult truth that we are living and dying at the same time," he expressed abstractly one of the central dramas of the legend of being. Unlike the pure journey of the astronaut in "The Flight of Apollo," the salmon's journey is heavy with mortality and sexuality.

In the isolated couplet a "power" speaks to him—"*Come. Bathe in these waters. / Increase and die.*" It is similar to the "power" that speaks the final lines in "The Illusionist"—"Kneel, spirit. At this beheading / Thy spongy faces fall." What is interesting about "King of the River" is that the poem continues *past* these lines, that the poem has the ritual power to begin again and renew itself *even* after a seemingly climactic exhortation by the Spirit of generative Nature. How can this be? Because paradoxically the most powerful force in this poem is the Spirit of being—the Finned Ego—even though that power is trapped within mortality.

When the Spirit speaks we again see the triumph of verbs: of movement and process. The language eliminates all nouns that might bespeak goals or arrival; even procreation is seen as a process within the self (the verb "increase") not as a purpose (that would make use of a noun like "offspring"). The tone here is of erotic solipsism that has somehow become transcendent, so that we do not feel confined within any particular self, certainly not Kunitz' self, but participate in a kind of essential self.

The key word in the incantation that begins stanza 3 is "power." Power is quickly related to "imagination" and the magical enterprise of poetic transformation. This power is also a power of transcendence—the power to "break out of your cells." We see another serious pun of Kunitz': "cells" continues the biological metaphor and also refers to the mortal physical body as a jail from which imaginative release is sought:

> If the power were granted you
> to break out of your cells,
> but the imagination fails
> and the doors of the senses close
> on the child within,
> you would dare to be changed,
> as you are changing now,
> into the shape you dread
> beyond the merely human.

This third occurrence of an opening sentence that is "interrupted" by a clause that completely undercuts it ("but the imagination fails / and the doors of the senses close / on the child within") is the most poignant and agonizing yet, perhaps because the image of the imprisonment of the "child within" is such a powerful image of the defeat of possibility. We are used to "doors" opening in Kunitz, perhaps to some terrible revelation, but at least to possibility, to a new reality.

When we read the sentence without its interrupting clause, we see other things:

> If the power were granted you
> to break out of your cells,
> . . . .
> you would dare to be changed

Here we have the triumph of courage and the desire to be transformed. Continuing, we have:

> as you are changing now
> into the shape you dread
> beyond the merely human.

These final three lines have complex, multiple meanings. The speaker is the human protagonist. If he had the power to change, and break out of himself, he would dare to do it, *but* these final lines say: you are changing anyway, regardless of your assent or desire. Into what? There are two possibilities, neither excludes the other. First you are changing toward death—your mortality is transforming you toward death—"beyond the merely human." Second, the "you" of the poem is becoming the salmon—his creature self—who incarnates a condition of intense mortality:

> A dry fire eats you.
> Fat drips from your bones.
> The flutes of your gills discolor.
> You have become a ship for parasites.

The linguistic continuity of "you" across the threshold of transformation ("as you are changing now, / into the shape you dread / beyond the merely human. / A dry fire eats you.") accomplishes with swift magic the metamorphosis that earlier lines hinted at as possibility. This moment in the poem is analogous to Keats' oneness with the bird that imagination accomplishes in the lines—"Already with thee! Tender is the night . . ."—except that Keats' gesture is a temporary loss of self. Imagination will fail Keats, and he will fall back from the bird to his "sole self" and the human condition. Kunitz will not return from this identification, because it is not "imagination," not "the viewless wings of Poesy," but a natural process. For Kunitz this is a fated process: metamorphosis is inextricably woven with inevitable mortal decay. The shape he dreads is the salmon but also his own mortality as it approaches death:

> The great clock of your life
> is slowing down,
> and the small clocks run wild.
> For this you were born.

The movement here from specifically fish-derived images to the wonderful image of the clocks broadens the possibilities of assertion. The "small clocks" echo the body's "cells" in this frenzy of approaching death, as they did to different effect in the final triple image of cells, clocks, and hearts in "The Science of the Night."

The wind, which is all movement, the essence of process and change, speaks the first of several aphorisms about being that the stanza rises toward:

> You have cried to the wind
> and heard the wind's reply:
> "I did not choose the way,
> the way chose me."

The wind is a little like Dante in "The Illumination," who knew "neither the time / nor the way" and yet the key he held had great power. Here it is "the way" that has power over human fates, its power of direction *is* their fate. We are moving now toward a central assertion of Kunitz: that there is a human fate more powerful than individual will (in this poem the most inclusive fate of all: mortality) and that what the individual must do is *embrace* that fate with such intensity as to transform it and himself:

> You have tasted the fire on your tongue
> till it is swollen black
> with a prophetic joy:
> "Burn with me!
> The only music is time,
> The only dance is love."

The "dry fire [that] eats you" is transformed into the fire that you "eat"—you embrace the agony of mortality and become one with it—you join with the process: "Burn with me!" becomes part of the motion of mortality that is agony and sexual ecstasy both.

The tongue that tastes the fire is not unlike the "strenuous tongue" of Keats' melancholic who "bursts joy's grape against his palate fine," and whose "soul shall taste the sadness of [Melancholy's] might." Keats' tongue goes past joy to melancholy; Kunitz' tongue goes past agony to a sexual intensity of motion. This tongue is another of those transcendent erections that stand for intensity of being, its closest counterpart being the visionary, apocalyptic sexuality of "Open the Gates," where the protagonist was "scourged by the black temptation of the blood grown proud." Here the erect pride is present in the "Finned Ego" and its heroic journey of desire ("the only dance is love").

As with the preceding stanza, we think when we read the magnificent final lines of this third stanza that we have arrived at the poem's resolution, that it cannot continue past this marvelous, all-encompassing rhetorical flourish. Yet it does, beginning as always, with its quiet conditional:

> If the heart were pure enough,
> but it is not pure,
> you would admit
> that nothing compels you
> any more, nothing
> at all abides,
> but nostalgia and desire,
> the two-way ladder
> between heaven and hell.

Everything is now process—a movement of longing up or down the ladder of being. It is the movement forward—of desire, (whose emblem is the "orgiastic pool"). Or it is the looking backward of "nostalgia," a nostalgia that for Kunitz involves the illusion of having once belonged, of having once been secure, and whose emblem is often a "house" that is jeopardized or long lost. We will soon see another emblem for it: the "salt kingdom" (ocean) where the salmon was born and that he has left to make his journey.

By making the ladder "two-way" he again emphasizes movement and also interposes an odd perspective between the terms nostalgia/desire and heaven/hell as if to foil a simplistic and isolating polarization of terms. The final sentence begins with "threshold"—one of the most powerful of Kunitz' key images:

> On the threshold
> of the last mystery,
> at the brute absolute hour,
> you have looked into the eyes
> of your creature self,
> which are glazed with madness,
> and you say
> he is not broken but endures,
> limber and firm
> in the state of his shining,
> forever inheriting his salt kingdom,
> from which he is banished
> forever.

Perhaps it adds to the intensity of the poem to realize that we are reading the poem of an old man, and that fact cannot help but add authority to the opening image. It is the "brute," absolute hour—the ultimate confrontation with the "creature self" that is the incarnation of mortal being. The "madness" with which its eyes are glazed is the madness of driven being—of wanting "More! More!" ("Journal for My Daughter").

When the "creature self" forever inherits and is forever banished, it is a paradox, it is a doomed fate that utterly surrounds the individual consciousness, and it transforms the ladder image of nostalgia and desire into a perpetual circle: desire's fulfillment is to inherit the kingdom, to be banished from it creates nostalgia; hence the cycle is perpetual—the meditation on being continues to revolve, the fathers do not "rest / On the inhuman breast" ("A Spark of Laurel"). Instead, the creature self endures "in the state of his shining." The "state" of shining is another of Kunitz' puns: he has and loses a kingdom perpetually, but what he keeps is a *state*. This state is the state of being, of intensity of being that he predicted in "Vita Nuova": "My dark will make, reflecting from your stones, / The single beam of all my life intense." Again with "limber and firm" we have the phallic imagery Kunitz uses for intensity of being, for a creaturely cycle of falling and resurrection.

Somewhere within or surrounding the inevitable decline of mortality is the final cyclic paradox. The poem does not end saying: we grow old, decline, and die. Nostalgia and desire (the backward and forward motion of the self) remain, *and* the *causes* of nostalgia and desire remain (perpetual inheritance and banishment): the circle (or spiraling circle) replaces the image of the ladder.

The presence of death, decline, and cycles brings up "The Way Down." There Kunitz confronted decline and death but linked them to a magic ritual that connected the human being to the cyclic deaths and renewals of vegetative nature. He used the animal kingdom (the "thunder-bison") as *bridge* between human and vegetative nature. "The Way Down" is also a poem of the father-son legend and accepted a human death in one generation so long as the blessing was passed on. "King of the River" is a poem of the legend of being: the individual self is being confronted, its essence dramatized: nothing is present but the self's own impulses, longings, and the external conditions of its being (mortality, flux, the failures of power, knowledge, purity). The "King" is no longer the father ("father in the wood, / Mad father of us all, / King of our antlered wills"), but is the self: the individual human consciousness shorn of all magic. The *legacy* issue is still present, but it is not bequeathed by the father as blessing or lesson: it is the legacy of being itself.

The human self is a creature with consciousness but no magical links to vegetative nature to sustain its courage as it faces the last mystery: death. On the threshold of this last mystery the paradox of being is made manifest: a driving intensity of survival ("endures," "shining") that is contained within an endless cycle of satisfaction and defeat, inheritance and banishment.

The meanings of "Robin Redbreast" start with the title. The subject is not simply robin, but robin redbreast. The "redbreast" of the folk name applies most precisely to the English robin, whose scarlet is that of a wound and might account for its role in the ballad "Who Killed Cock Robin?" "Robin Redbreast" is a poem of the legend of being, but one entirely eclipsed and thrown into shadow by the wound image. It is one of Kunitz' major poems of the tragic sense when tragic is defined as a simultaneous awareness of man's dignity and vulnerability in relation to the universe.

The poem begins in diminishment and desolation:

> It was the dingiest bird
> you ever saw, all the color
> washed from him, as if
> he had been standing in the rain,
> friendless and stiff and cold,
> since Eden went wrong.

(p. 56)

The bird has been linked to the human world and the source of human desolation at the mythic level. The next lines shift to the speaker and his context:

> In the house marked For Sale,
> where nobody made a sound,
> in the room where I lived
> with an empty page, I had heard
> the squawking of the jays
> under the wild persimmons
> tormenting him.

The key image of the house plays an important role here. The house is desolate, lost, just as our home in Eden is; we have here the backward look of the self that reveals desolation at the source—a mythic orphanhood, a homelessness. This desolation is also in the present, in Kunitz' life as a creator—"an empty page."

He's brought out of this trance, awakened to a phenomenon in the natural world: jays tormenting the robin. His gesture of rescue fuses the identification—the parallel levels of being between the human self and the creature self:

> So I scooped him up
> after they knocked him down,
> in league with that ounce of heart
> pounding in my palm,
> that dumb beak gaping.
> Poor thing! Poor foolish life!
> without sense enough to stop
> running in desperate circles,
> needing my lucky help
> to toss him back into his element.

But a misperception has occurred. Although the speaker is "in league" with the bird's wish to live unmolested, he clearly feels superior to it in power and understanding. This is a similar misperception to that of "The Dragonfly" in *This Garland, Danger:* a human self is too taken with its role in the natural universe, too proud of its relative power and knowledge.

The poem's strategy, as in "The Dragonfly," is to set up the speaker for a revelation that devastates his sense of himself in the universe and even of the nature of the universe itself. Nothing of this sort is explained; all meaning is subsumed into gesture and fact. The speaker looks down on the bird, condescends to his helplessness, lifts him up as if he, the human, had the power to "restore him." From the new perspective of his upraised arm, the speaker sees something he failed to notice before, something that changes the meaning of all that went before:

> But when I held him high,
> fear clutched my hand,
> for through the hole in his head,
> cut whistle-clean . . .
> through the old dried wound
> between his eyes
> where the hunter's brand
> had tunneled out his wits . . .
> I caught the cold flash of the blue
> unappeasable sky.

Suddenly with this new fact (that a hunter's bullet had passed through the robin's head, lobotomizing it without killing it), forces larger and more powerful than the speaker are present. The first is fear, personified as having the power to arrest the speaker's actions, to overwhelm him. The second force more powerful than the human is not even personified: it is a cosmic force of malevolence: "the cold . . . unappeasable sky."

With the "unappeasable sky" we are brought back to the poem's beginning: to Eden and the angry, punishing God who banished us forever (and who condemned us to mortality and suffering). But what we have at the poem's end is not an angry God, but an angry Absence—a malevolent, hungry Absence.

The robin cannot be restored; the wound cannot be healed; the desolate wretchedness of the human condition cannot be overcome. Something that is real and unalterable wishes us ill. Its coldness is "unappeasable"—a powerful, perfect word, precisely and dramatically juxtaposed to the brevity of "sky." How we hear the serpent's hiss as our voice lingers over its third syllable!

The salmon in "King of the River" is a creature self that triumphs—its intensity of being, its mad commitment to its journey result in a triumph within the context of its mortality. The creature self as robin is doomed and helpless from the start: a malevolent fate whose source is in the past (either the mythic past, Eden, or the material past of the hunter's bullet) leaves it without resources to transform this fate. It is a poem of awful revelation like "Open the Gates," not awful transformation like "The Approach to Thebes." According to Kunitz, what is revealed in this poem is a part of man's spiritual being as surely as the red breast is part of the bird's physical being.

The poem is completely autonomous—all of its meanings are present in its diction, its facts, and its gestures. But we can also see in the figure of the wounded robin a transformed figure of Kunitz' own suicide father. A careful reader of Kunitz' work knows by now that the father's death is the major source of Kunitz' desolation as far as the poems are concerned. The robin's wound is the father's wound, and it is the son's wound as well—a legacy from the father.

But the father is also the terrible unappeasable Absence glimpsed through the bird's wound: he is God the angry Father who is God the Absent. He is the father "whose indomitable love kept [the son] in chains"; he is the hungry ghost who stops him on the stairs in the early poem "Master and Mistress." And he is the human father whose death shattered Kunitz' childhood and made the key image "house," which stood for belonging and family, always a "lost house" or a house desolate and "For Sale." All these links between "Robin Redbreast" and Kunitz' father are extrinsic to the poem. But they are there beneath the poem as the powerful ingathering force that constellates the poem's language, and they also shine up through the poem, giving each word its peculiar intensity. We can't call "Robin Redbreast" a poem of the father legend, but we can call it a poem of the legend of being dominated by an image from the father legend: the wound shining like an unchangeable malevolent star. Kunitz' poems have often dramatized the fact that childhood trauma persists; here that fact is projected from the past onto the heavens and dominates totally.

Throughout *The Testing-Tree* there is an opening outward, an enlarging of the self's spirit to include other selves and other possibilities. In the "love" poem "After the Last Dynasty," we encounter another new possibility for Kunitz: humor.

Stylistically, he now explores the ways in which short free verse lines can be used to further tone and subject. In the following passage he uses the suspense between enjambed lines as a way of creating and controlling the reader's response:

> Reading in Li Po
> how "the peach blossom follows the water"
> I keep thinking of you
>
> (p. 62)

(so far a sensitive, predictable opening for a love poem, bordering on the sentimental) because you were so much like

(suspense of uncompleted thought)

Chairman Mao,

(deflation of the opening's pretensions; humor of the absurd)

naturally with the sex

(beginning again, stringing the reader farther along)

transposed
and the figure slighter.

(a second punch line).

How marvelously the one word "naturally" entirely transforms our notion of what sort of person the speaker is: he is neither the delicate sentimentalist of lines 1 to 3 nor the buffoon of line 5, but someone whose dominant character is "nimbleness;" he has an ability to move quickly and precisely from love to humor to affection.

This is a poem of lost love—the self, stopped in its journey, gazing back over its shoulder into the past. The poem makes dazzling use of its governing conceit—"Loving you was a kind / of Chinese guerrilla war"—especially when it permits Kunitz to adapt Mao's aphoristic style to express the troubled relationship:

In the cold spring rains
when last you failed me
I had nothing left to spend
but a red crayon language
on the character of the enemy
to break appointments,

to fight us not
with his strength
but with his weakness,
to kill us
not with his health
but with his sickness.

The poem shifts in its second stanza—the speaker wants to pin a new note on the door to replace the angry slogans of the "red crayon language." The note is a plea ("Tell me") that acknowledges her power through the second sense of "mistress"—as a female authority figure ("are you still mistress of the valley," line 36), that returns us to line 2 and the Li Po poem ("what trophies drift downstream," line 37) and finally concludes with an anguish that indicates how much feeling still persists—("why did you keep me waiting?" line 38).

Again, "nimble" seems the only appropriate word for a poem that can be flippant and genuinely moving at the same time. Much has been said about the influence of the English Metaphysical poets in Kunitz' early work, but it seems obvious that in a poem like "After the Last Dynasty," which bears no stylistic trace of this influence, we are closer to seeing the truth: imagination in Kunitz' later work is genuinely akin to the Metaphysical spirit: the associative imagination, the ability to fuse the imagistic disparities into a convincing emotional unity. Or, in "Robin Redbreast," the passionate intellect fusing a literal situation (injured bird on a lawn) with the most profound metaphysical implications. Perhaps it is the elusive quality of affection and feeling that marks the difference between "After the Last Dynasty" and a "love" poem governed by elaborate and ingenious conceits such as "Foreign Affairs" from *This Garland, Danger*.

The "new note" Kunitz leaves, although it is ten years late and "you are nowhere," represents a triumph of imagination over reality, but it is crucial that this triumph is incomplete. It triumphs over time, but not over feeling: the speaker's feelings of loss, hurt, caring, and abandonment remain unalterable.

"River Road" seems about to continue a theme that the preceding poem also touches on—the failure of relationship: "That year of the cloud, when my marriage failed." But if the opening line appears to announce a theme, the lines that follow appear to evade it, or at the very least shift the focus first to the self, and then to anecdote:

> I slept in a chair, by the flagstone hearth,
> fighting my sleep,
> and one night saw a Hessian soldier
> stand at attention there in full
> regalia, till his head broke into flames.
> My only other callers were the FBI
> sent to investigate me as a Russian spy
> by patriotic neighbors on the river road
> (p. 64)

We have an isolated self who has three visitors. The first is a ghost from the distant past (not the first genuine ghost we have encountered in Kunitz' work). The second set of visitors bespeaks the paranoia of the social and political world, and the third set of visitors is from the creature world:

> and flying squirrels parachuting from the elms
> who squeaked in rodent heat

whose sexuality is somehow contagious:

> Even my nervous Leghorns joined the act,
> indulging their taste for chicken from behind.

in a way that is alarming—"they caught a kind of dancing-sickness"—and finally ends in death:

> they flapped and dropped and flapped again.
> The county agent shook his head;
> not one of them was spared the cyanide.

We have heard anecdotes from the summer of failed marriage—and by stanza's end we are uncertain whether the subject has been evaded, or whether the supernatural, paranoia, and a rampant sexuality that eases into disease and death are not somehow related to the subject. Ultimately, the stanza remains both clear and cryptic.

As if aware of this paradox of incompleteness, stanza 2 begins by reiterating the poem's opening line: "That year of the cloud, when my marriage failed." But stanza 2 places us firmly in the natural world, away from the house and away from others. This movement to the natural world is presented as another anecdote—the planting of seedling trees—but it quickly takes on aspects of ritual and seems, in its precise description of repetition, to function as a stabilizing act for the self:

> I paced up and down the bottom-fields,
> tamping the mud-puddled nurslings in
> with a sharp blow of the heel
> timed to the chop-chop of the hoe:
> red pine and white, larch, balsam fir,
> one stride apart, two hundred to the row,
> until I heard from Rossiter's woods
> the downward spiral of a veery's song
> unwinding on the eve of war.

Any attempt to understand the poem's first stanza falters on the opacity of the anecdotes and the protagonist's reticence. By recognizing the poem's underlying polarity of social world (stanza

1: marriage, house, poultry yard, games) and natural world (stanza 2), we can arrive at a clearer understanding of the poem's true subject: not the marriage and its failure but the self's struggle to survive desolation and abandonment.

Stanza 3 opens with a sudden rhetorical exclamation:

> Lord! Lord! who has lived so long?
> Count it ten thousand trees ago,
> five houses and ten thousand trees

We are suddenly aware of the self looking back over its history in terms of the human, social world ("five houses") and the natural world that is associated with the solitary self ("ten thousand trees"). Both the social world and the natural world as transformed by the human (the rows of the trees, the ritual—like that of words on a page for Kunitz) are part of the self's long history. We are in the present looking back in *memory* to the events of stanza 2:

> since the swallows exploded from Bowman Tower
> over the place where the hermit sang,
> while I held a fantail of squirming roots
> that kissed the palm of my dirty hand,
> as if in reply to a bird.

Suddenly, in *memory*, this scene is intensely animated and interconnected: every object responds to every other. The "downward spiral" of the veery's song—that introduced a further descent of the self into the chaos of the human world ("the eve of war") has been replaced by "swallows" exploding "from Bowman Tower" (an image of phallic intensity out of the legend of being) and by the singing of the "hermit"—who is both a hermit thrush and Kunitz himself in his solitude. Even the roots of the nurslings are alive with intimate affection.

In mid-stanza we shift again—this time into the physical landscape of the dramatized present:

> The stranger who hammers No Trespass signs
> to the staghorn sumac along the road
> must think he owns this property.

We have shifted from the ecstatic intensity of nostalgia to the matter-of-fact present. But this present is the same place if not the same time as the past—and what the self made out of its desolation it now moves through:

> I park my car below the curve
> and climbing over the tumbled stones
> where the wild foxgrape perseveres

The self, like the foxgrape, has persevered. As it moves backward into his own history ("the woods I made"), it moves through a landscape that is poignant with the tragedy of mortality and yet also represents a triumph of the transforming, creating self. The woods as landscape have become an emblem of the transformed self—like the poem. The nature of that landscape—"dark and resinous, blistered"—is as descriptively appropriate to Kunitz' self (stanza 1) as it is to a coniferous woods. "River Road" in its final stanza is a poem of the legend of being, but one where the journeying self stops its journey forward ("desire") and yields to a kind of celebration of nostalgia's backward pull:

> I walk into the woods I made,
> my dark and resinous, blistered land,
> through the deep litter of the years.

Wonderfully sudden shifts of consonants and vowels go a long way toward creating the dignified cadence of these final three lines.

The opening line of "River Road" announced a subject—
the failure of a marriage: "That year of the cloud, when my marriage failed"—whose language echoed that of the preceding poem:

> In the cold spring rains
> when last you failed me.
> ("After the Last Dynasty")

despite the differences of tone and strategy. There is also a link
to a third poem, "Robin Redbreast," through what I would call
the "architecture of desolation": in both poems the speaker is
alone in a house, in a state of utter desolation. We have seen
how the key image of the house is linked to the father legend as
an image of utterly undermined security at the beginning of a
life. "House" in Kunitz' poetry is an image that mocks its con-
ventional meanings. When "house" appears in relation to the
failed marriage, we are perhaps encountering a second source of
desolation in adult life, a second "origin" that reveals essence.
The failure of a marriage does, after all, represent the failure of
one of the two ambitions—"love and art"—that raved in the
speaker's breast in "The Tutored Child," a present-tense poem
from *Passport to the War*. "The Tutored Child" and its companion poem "The Reckoning" both fit into the historical-biograph-
ical framework of the poem "River Road."

However, the point is not that all these poems might refer
to the same failed marriage, but that, as legend, the failed relationship becomes the origin of the self's second traumatic desolation and anguished solitude. In *The Testing-Tree*, the failed
marriage becomes the negative origin of the beloved legend, just
as the father's absence is the negative origin of the father legend, and just as nostalgia is the negative pole of the legend of
being.

The role of desolation in Kunitz' work is best expressed by
the opening lines of the late poem, "What Of The Night?":

> One summer, like a stone
> dropped down a well,
> I sank into myself
> and raked
> the bottom slime.
>
> (p. 2)

For Kunitz a descent into the self, its desolation and despair, often necessarily precedes the act of creative affirmation and renewal that his poems strive toward. In the three poems of this "second source" of desolation ("After the Last Dynasty," "River Road," and "Robin Redbreast"), it is the self's backward motion, the desolation, that dominate the poems. But it is necessary for this desolation to be acknowledged and its "origin" in the beloved legend to be located in order that poems of affirmation and renewal be written. In these poems of the desolate pole of the beloved legend there is a breakthrough into the language of feeling that is more direct and convincing than anything yet encountered in the father legend.

Perhaps this is because the second experience of desolation is more direct and more personal than the father's suicide—which existed as legend from the start. Without wishing to overstress the connection, I'd speculate that this second desolation and its feeling tone of sorrow, hurt, and despair make possible the poems of affirmation and renewal of love in *The Testing-Tree*. Certainly a poem that seems to bridge the negation and desolation of the "failed marriage" and the renewal of affirmation and love is "Journal for My Daughter." In that poem, the daughter experiences as her first, formative trauma what I have called Kunitz' "second source"—the breakup of the marriage. In relation to her primary trauma (father–daughter), she has the opportunity to forgive and be reconciled, something Kunitz could not do in relation to his primary trauma (father–son). But, and this is a cen-

tral message of *The Testing-Tree*, Kunitz can forgive and choose
love and reconciliation in relation to the beloved legend even if
he cannot in terms of the father legend. If "Journal for My
Daughter" is the bridge between the theme of failed mar-
riage/abandonment and intimacy/affection, then "The Magic
Curtain" is the poem that explores the other shore: the triumph
of the beloved legend and its affirmations of intimacy, affection,
and delight. The quest for the beloved is accomplished, and the
legend located within the life, as if it were there all the time, at
the source—in childhood—only waiting to be acknowledged, to
be called by its name. And for the first time, the beloved has a
name: Frieda.

"The Magic Curtain" seems to me to be one of Kunitz'
masterpieces. It is another triumphant location of essence in origin—in this case the healing essence of love and forgiveness. In
"The Approach to Thebes," Kunitz confronted and eluded the
destructiveness implicit in the son–powerful mother dilemma by
interposing the lover (as Sphinx) between the son and the mother.
This triumph at the mythical level is brought down to earth and
enacted in terms of personal history in "The Magic Curtain."

The poem opens as a vividly realized scene from Kunitz'
childhood. The figure of the mother dominates the first four lines,
and Frieda is "behind her." But Frieda will not be obscured for
long:

> At breakfast mother sipped her buttermilk,
>   her mind already on her shop,
>   unrolling gingham by the yard,
> stitching her dresses for the Boston trade.
> Behind her, Frieda with the yellow hair,
>   capricious keeper of the toast,
>   buckled her knees, as if she'd lost

> balance and platter, then winked at me, blue-eyed.
> Frieda, my first love! who sledded me to sleep
>   through snows of the Bavarian woods
>   into the bell-song of the girls,
> with kinds of kisses mother would not dream
>
> (p. 66)

As, at section's end, the mother sends the child off to school in the keeping of Frieda, the intimate erotic conspiracy between them becomes explicit: "How could she guess what we two had in mind?" (1. 24).

Section 2 continues the story:

> Downtown at the Front St. Bi-jo (spelt Bijou)
>   we were, as always, the first in line,
>   with a hot nickel clutched in hand

This section is a paean to the world of imagination that is the shared world of early motion pictures:

> School faded out at every morning reel,
>   *The Iron Claw* held me in thrall,
>   *Cabiria* taught me the Punic Wars,
> at bloody Antietam I fought on Griffith's side.

The movies in section 2 occupy the analogous but larger role of the tales, lieder, and counting songs of section 1. Kunitz strings together one movie or movie scene after another. It is a quick tour of the silent movies, one that gives a sense of their imagistic richness, but also a sense of the wonder and pleasure they brought to a small boy in a bourgeois town.

Near the end of section 2, romance returns—this time transposed from Frieda onto a mock-serious debate about movie actresses:

> Blanche Sweet, said Frieda, had a pretty name,
>   but I came back with Arline Pretty,
>   and, even sweeter, Louise Lovely.
> Send me your picture, Violet Mersereau!

The boy's naive pleasure in the actresses' names makes this passage the charming and convincing equivalent of that scene in Truffaut's *The 400 Blows* where the child protagonist steals a movie poster. Frieda's waywardness is inspirational. Her childish delight makes her the perfect companion and accomplice for a truant boy.

Section 2 ends with our leaving the theatre we entered in the first line and moving "to the Majestic for the two o'clock show." In fact, time is moving far more rapidly than the confident child-narrator of section 2 realizes. Section 3 opens with time, just as section 2 closed with it, but it is a different kind of time:

> Five . . . four . . . three . . . two . . . one . . .

What appears at first to be the numbered frames of an old-fashioned movie leader for a movie about to commence becomes, more sinisterly, a countdown. Numbers and time move backward not to begin another movie like those we saw in section 2, but to signal a kind of crisis seen from adulthood:

> Five . . . four . . . three . . . two . . . one . . .
> The frames are whirling backward, see!
> The operator's lost control.

It is an adult now who is the section's central character, and the movie is the story of his life:

> Your story flickers on your bedroom wall.
> Deaths, marriages, betrayals, lies,
>   close-ups of tears, forbidden games,
>   spill in a montage on a screen,
> with chases, pratfalls, custard pies, and sores.
> You have become your past, which time replays,
>   to your surprise, as comedy.

In another poem from *The Testing-Tree* that is specifically about the artist's plight, we have a similar statement: "Life aims at the tragic: / what makes it ridiculous?" (lines 9–10, "The Bottom of the Glass"). The tone of "The Bottom of the Glass" is kept jaunty by its short lines and occasional feminine rhymes, and we detect in it an opening to the possibility of the self's defeat. It is, after all, the *self,* Kunitz' self, and not *life* that aims at the tragic. "The Bottom of the Glass" resolves this defeat by humorous paradox:

> In age as in youth
> the joke is preposterous.
> And nothing shall save me
> from meanness and sinning
> but more of the same,
> more losing like winning.
>   (p. 85)

Such a paradox appeared first in "Postscript" from *Intellectual Things*, where the entire poem's tone clearly and unambiguously "aims at the tragic":

> I lost by winning, and I shall not win
> Again except by loss.

In the later poems, the human range of possibility is vastly extended: the tragic and the ridiculous are reconciled by paradox and humor ("The Bottom of the Glass"). And in "The Magic Curtain," the defeat of the self's ambitions and expectations for the life (that it should achieve the dimensions of tragedy) are overcome by the poem's final gestures.

The comedy which "time replays" in "The Magic Curtain" is the serious comedy of mortality:

> That coathanger neatly whisked your coat
> right off your back. Soon it will want your skin.

We then encounter a perfect echo of Frieda's German counting song/riddle from section one:

> *Five . . . four . . . three . . . two . . . one . . .*
> *Where has my dearest gone?*
> *She is nowhere to be found,*
> *She dwells in the underground.*

The song is no longer, as in section 1, about a love who has fled to America but has become a lament for Kunitz' lost love who has fled back from America to Germany!

The tone shifts to an assertion of will on the part of the speaker: "Let the script revel in tricks and transformations" (line 73). Now he insists on the magic of imagination as a serious thing, not just the entertainment of section 2. The imagination can heal and restore, can bring back the beloved from the underground as Orpheus could not:

> When the film is broken, let it be spliced
> where Frieda vanished one summer night
> with somebody's husband, daddy to a brood.

We learn that Kunitz' dour mother was right all along, that Frieda was more hussy than Eurydice and that such frivolity and lightness must inevitably lead to terrible trouble. Frieda has absconded:

> And with her vanished, from the bureau drawer,
>   the precious rose-enameled box
>   that held those chestnut-colored curls
> clipped from my sorrowing head when I was four.

To begin with the smallest detail, the rose-enameled box is subliminally linked to Dresden, a city that in the *next* war will be destroyed utterly although it is a civilian city. This subliminal link echoes one of the poem's main themes, love against destruction, and reinforces the poem's greatness in subtle ways.

Frieda is not only Kunitz' love, but the poem emphasizes that she runs off with a *father*. Frieda's scandalous behavior rescues Kunitz and "fatherness" from the oppressive, loveless seriousness that Kunitz' mother represents. Kunitz and "fathers" in general are rescued from death-in-life by Frieda: by love, by delight. Kunitz knows this, he recognizes Frieda's significance: the "one word: *Liebe*."

And here, the boy Kunitz and his mother part ways forever:

> "I'll never forgive her," mother said,
> but as for me, I do and do and do.

In this final line Kunitz makes a triple, magical affirmation: "I do" represents the simple act of forgiveness. "Do" is also a pun on the German intimate form, "you" or "thou." Finally, it is a marriage vow.

Kunitz the boy, though abandoned by his beloved Frieda, forgives her. Why? Because she has rescued him from his mother and her most destructive human trait: an inability to forgive. To be unforgiving is to be closed to human possibility. As the poem

"The Portrait" will establish, it is the mother's unforgiveness that deprived Kunitz of the knowledge of his father and thus of an essential aspect of himself. Frieda rights this wrong by running off with a father who might well have been Kunitz' father: that is, he's not simply "some man," but is identified as both a husband (bourgeois respectability) and a daddy. Frieda is the scandalous "other woman," but she is the one who opens Kunitz' life up to love—not only to "first love" but to a constantly reaffirmed, active principle of love in the world: I do and do and do. She is like the dark woman in "The Dark and the Fair," "who taught [him] the serpent's word, but yet the word."

"The Magic Curtain" is not simply a poem in which the major legends of Kunitz' poetry become triumphantly affirmative—it is a great poem. In its understated way, it is as absolute and profound an affirmation as "King of the River." It is completely successful in locating the fundamental archetypal structures of human life *within* the events, details, and circumstances of everyday experience. The story is pure feeling intelligence completely subsumed into its characters, gestures, details, and events.

"The Portrait" is perhaps the pivotal poem in Kunitz' oeuvre. Beneath its limpid surface, its clarity of diction and event, fundamental mysteries of his being are enacted. If we are correct in asserting that a dominant strategy of this book is the seeking of essence in origin, then "The Portrait" concerns multiple origins: biological, historical, psychological. These origins fuse in three characters (father, mother, child), who enact a single drama that reveals Kunitz identity (through a backward look toward his dead father) and determines his future being (the persistence of pain resulting from the mother's harshness).

"The Portrait" begins where "The Magic Curtain" ends. The identity of Kunitz' mother remains true to itself: unforgiving and intransigent. Now she has a new object of unforgiveness: the husband who committed suicide and left her with a child in the womb. (We could, parenthetically, assert that this is also a poem that discloses the mother's identity—the origin of her anger in the humiliating, traumatic circumstances of her husband's violent "desertion" of her.) We can, because of the events detailed in the first six lines of the poem, compassionately comprehend for the first time the mother's negativity and destructiveness as a figure throughout the work. On the other hand, we also see the terms of the drama between mother and child: she will not forgive, she has been scarred for life by the suicide, and at poem's end, we see that she has managed, by her violent act (the slap) to scar her son for his lifetime.

We have here the theme of legacy. In "Journal for My Daughter" Kunitz as father struggles not to perpetuate the legacy of the absent father that haunted his life and now (with himself as the father) threatens to similarly afflict his daughter's life. In "The Magic Curtain" we have the most effective response to the threat of this legacy: forgiveness and love. Eros overcomes Thanatos. Or, as "My Surgeons" puts it: "Tell them I say the heart forgives / The world. Yes, I believe. In love."

"The Portrait" is a poem in which Thanatos triumphs. The mother's intransigence, which was overwhelmed by the force of Kunitz' love in the final line of "The Magic Curtain," here encounters no resistance and entirely dominates the poem's action. Nor is there, in "The Portrait," any figure who might stand for love: no Frieda, no beloved or muse. This is Kunitz' quintessential poem of the only child and the powerful mother. The child's only ally, his father's portrait, is torn to shreds; he has no power to resist the mother's onslaught.

The opening lines give us the mother's stance and the circumstance that gave rise to it:

My mother never forgave my father
for killing himself,
especially at such an awkward time
and in a public park,
that spring
when I was waiting to be born.

(p. 86)

What a weird pleasure the poem takes in its own unfolding. The first line is categorical, but curiously neutral in tone. Then the punch line of the second line: dramatic information we could not possibly have anticipated and thus carrying a great shock value that mocks the matter-of-factness of its presentation. While the reader is trying to link the sensational circumstance of line 2 back to the mundane content of line one, he encounters in the next three lines what is almost a flippant tone in the story's further developments: as if Kunitz knows he has a good story and is relishing its sinuous unfolding. How line three tantalizes the reader far more than it informs him: we, as readers, want to know what the phrase "such as awkward time" could possibly mean in relation to suicide. It, and the following line, emphasize the social disgrace attendant on the survivors of a suicide; the suicide, line 3 subtly hints, is a scandal. Given the pact the reader has entered into, we want to know (and the poem promises to tell us, but not yet, not yet . . .) *why* it is an awkward time, what the scandal is, what makes a shocking event also a public awkwardness.

How sparingly, artfully, Kunitz doles out the details of the event: one new piece of information per line: suicide (l. 2); hint of scandal (l. 3); location of suicide (l. 4); season (l. 5); link to Kunitz' life; and also fulfillment of the scandal hinted in line 3. How each new detail changes *all* that went before: how our imagining of the event (which wants constantly to be complete, contained, closed-off) is kept open by Kunitz, as he adds a new, significant, detail in each line. Kunitz toys with the reader's curiosity, and also with the reader's desire to "complete" a dramatic scene as quickly as feasible: he draws out the story. A poet/storyteller can only risk that if their last detail tops all the rest—as this one does; there is a kind of ironic bemused detachment in the way he unfolds the details of this first sentence, *exactly* as if he had taken his cue from the lines of section 3 of "The Magic Curtain" or lines 9 and 10 of "The Bottom of the Glass" and understood the paradoxical possibility that tragedy, from the right distance in time, can be seen as comedy or at least as the ridiculous. I am not suggesting that Kunitz regards these events as humorous; I am simply asserting that, as much to his surprise as to that of his listeners', "time replays" his past as comedy. We know Kunitz' sensibility sufficiently to realize that humor is not the antithesis of the tragic but is a component of it.

Line 7 begins the second of the poem's four sentences:

> She locked his name
> in her deepest cabinet
> and would not let him out,
> though I could hear him thumping.

We see here a magical linking of "name" and being: the name has the power of a living thing, and in fact, by a sleight-of-syntax, "name" becomes "him" and "him" takes on the power to act in the physical world ("thumping").

In three key earlier poems we have seen aspects of the theme of name and power. The clearest example of the magical identity of language and being is "Mens Creatix":

> He comes, the sudden Lord,
> a rhythmic Spike of Light,

> To cleave you with that spike:
> Himself, His flowing Word.
>
> Strike, O Poem, Strike!

The "flowing Word" has magical, powerful being. We've noted already the subliminal link between this "sudden Lord" and Kunitz' Spirit Father through such key images as "flowing"—a verb associated with the rhythmic flow of language in a poem and blood from a wound. The second poem to explore an aspect of the theme of language and being was "Open the Gates." It is worth noting that the opening scene/sentence of "The Portrait" and the final lines of "Open the Gates" have in common a fusion of death and birth. In "The Portrait" they are linked matter-of-factly—my father's death occurred while I was about to be born. In "Open the Gates"—the death and the engendering in the final line are archetypal ("and I see / The end and the beginning in each other's arms").

"Open the Gates" shares a similar concern in its linking of name to revelation:

> I brandish the great bone of my death,
> Beat once therewith and beat no more.
>
> The hinges groan: a rush of forms
> Shivers my name, wrenched out of me.

Here, at the moment of revelation, the speaker's name is torn from him by what is released from behind the door: he is shriven of personal identity as opposed to having an identity revealed to him; but what the two poems have in common is their insistence on the power and importance of "name." In "Open the Gates," the hinges of a monumental door groan open to reveal; "The Portrait," in keeping with its realistic narrative, insists on the lifting of a trunk lid as the gesture of revelation. But what is revealed is equally powerful—this trunk is the same attic trunk encountered in "Three Floors" that produced mysterious emblems of the father's being and, ultimately, the father's ghost itself. What is at stake in "The Portrait" is the revelation of the father's identity which is fundamentally and intimately tied to the son's identity.

The third key poem that asks us to consider the link between "name" and being, and to understand how fundamental this link is for the quest for identity in Kunitz' work is "Vita Nuova." "Vita Nuova" is that early poem which stands at the source of Kunitz' poetry of identity quest. It is about spiritual rebirth as the title indicates—but it is that form of rebirth peculiar to Kunitz: the son is born through the father, and the quest for identity will be fulfilled when the son *is* the father. We see "name" present as Kunitz, the mysterious knight persona of "Vita Nuova," announces: "now the visor of my name is up." The quest begins with the lifting of the visor to reveal his face, but it will not end until Kunitz' face is transformed, until "shadowless / With inner light, I wear my father's face." The mutual identity of son and father exists as a prediction, a vow, in "Vita Nuova"— we will see how "The Portrait" is a poem, perhaps *the* poem, that fulfills that vow.

The discussion of precursor poems emphasizing the powerful and magical link of name and being might lead us to misapprehend the drama of sentence two of "The Portrait." If the magic that gives the father's name physical, vital being is powerful, then the mother's negating and confining power is even stronger. *She* locks his name away, confines him, *buries* his name, even though his name is not dead and "thumps" away like an actor trapped in a trunk in one of "The Magic Curtain's," movies.

At the simplest narrative level we must also understand that the embittered, unforgiving mother has forbidden all mention of the father, has kept from the son his father's name. She thus withholds the father's legacy from her son: a mysterious legacy the son yearns for. In "Three Floors" the legacy took the form of a Masonic hat and a walking stick: objects sufficiently eccentric as to be the magic wand and cap of a magician. In "The Portrait," the legacy is a "pastel portrait"—the "father's face" so fervently sought in "Vita Nuova."

As the third sentence of "The Portrait" unfolds its story, the boy Kunitz, the "I" of the poem, has begun to assert himself in the narrative, taking over the initiative from the mother: "When I came down from the attic. . . ." This gesture of self-assertion will, by sentence's end, prove to be premature and unable to withstand the mother's destructive power:

> When I came down from the attic
> with the pastel portrait in my hand
> of a long-lipped stranger
> with a brave moustache
> and deep brown level eyes,
> she ripped it into shreds
> without a single word
> and slapped me hard.
>
> (p. 86)

In the first five lines of this sentence, the boy has found (and describes) his prize: his father's face. A physical emblem of the source of his being, a source of his actual physical identity (the "deep brown level eyes" will return as the "albino walrus" with the "gentlest eyes" in the recurring dream of "The Testing-Tree"). If the thumping trunk could be a scene from one of the movies described in "The Magic Curtain," then this pastel portrait could be seen to transform make-believe to reality: it is human, yet subtly heroic: a "brave" moustache and "deep" eyes.

Now the mother performs the third of her four powerfully destructive acts in the poem (the first: never forgiving; the second: locking his name). She rips the picture to shreds: she destroys the identity the son has been seeking; she "kills" the father a second time. This symbolic second death of the father is something the son was aware of early on: "O ruined father, long sweetly rotten . . . / Beware a second perishing" ("For the Word Is Flesh"). In Kunitz' imagination, this second killing is the real crime: the first death preceded his existence—he bears no grudge against the father for killing himself (although he consistently yearns for his blessing and his teaching as a means of achieving his own identity). On the other hand, the boy Kunitz is a witness at the second symbolic killing of his father by the mother. In addition, the mother's wrath transfers instantly into the fourth destructive gesture: she slaps the boy. By this slap she shows that her destructive power is capable of and intended to harm both the father and the son. She reveals herself as the source of destructiveness, just as the father has always been the parental source of love ("whose indomitable love kept me in chains") even though he existed only in Kunitz' imagination.

All Kunitz' imaginative life he has sought his identity through his father, whether in vows of mutual identity ("Vita Nuova") or in questing, pursuit and beseeching ("Father and Son"). The mother's slap accomplishes what all the questing has failed to do: it links father and son—it makes them one. The slap across the face is so linked to the tearing to shreds of the father's face that it fuses son and father. The boy/adult Kunitz at last (final sentence) "wears his father's face."

It is a face that is scarred: the father's face scarred by Kunitz' imagination of the suicide wound (he will call it "a scald" in "Quinnapoxit"), the son's face permanently (though invisibly) scarred by the mother's slap:

In my sixty-fourth year
I can feel my cheek
still burning.

In "Vita Nuova" Kunitz wanted an inner light to come from his
face: what he has is the "burning" of shame and pain. But in
"Vita Nuova's" final line he also sought intensity as a highest
goal—and "burning" is surely an intensity of feeling and a source
of light.

When Kunitz pursued his father's ghost in "Father and Son"
he sought a blessing from him, a blessing that would "teach him
the way" and help him grow into an honorable adult. Such a
blessing was denied him. In "The Way Down" the poem's cli-
max is again a son's request for a blessing from a dead, magical
father. The dream quest of "Father and Son" is thwarted; the
ritualistic encounter of "The Way Down" ends on a note of high
yearning as far as the theme of blessing goes. In "The Portrait"
we again see that the thematic triumph is linked to the poem's
seeking the legend *within* the life and its events. The son Kunitz at last receives the blessing that links him to his father: the
mother's slap is that blessing.

It is a negative blessing, but it does the job, and as the adult
Kunitz of the final sentence acknowledges, it is a blessing that
has sustained him for an entire lifetime. If this preceding sentence sounds flippant it isn't meant to, for surely the poem itself
is a form of gratitude toward the mother: her very harshness
helped the boy to identify *with* his father and escape from the
enormous psychological gravitational power of her identity—a
power which throughout the work threatens to overwhelm him.
By the deepest of paradoxes, her destructive gesture frees him
and guides him.

Does the poem, in deciding to straightforwardly tell "the

curious legend of [Kunitz'] youth" ("Open the Gates"), become a confessional poem? Does it become private by virtue of the oddness of its events? Hardly. Among other things, the final four lines concern a universal experience, not a unique one: the fact that when we are young, our parents (intentionally or not) hurt us or punish us arbitrarily—and that the particular incidents of these early hurts persist with such vividness throughout our lives that we can re-experience the original sensations no matter how old or mature we are.

It is a simple matter to distinguish Kunitz' "The Portrait" from so-called "confessional" poetry by pointing to its final lines and their clear aspiration toward the universal through the personal. But by placing "An Old Cracked Tune" on the next page, Kunitz asserts emphatically that he is defined but not confined by the unique events of the past. Both are poems of identity: self-portraits as well as portraits. The dramatis personae in both poems are identical: mother, father, son/speaker.

If "The Portrait" concludes that pain and trauma define the speaker, then "An Old Cracked Tune" insists that "joy" is the final, dominant experience. A reader familiar with Kunitz' work will recognize the poet in "Solomon Levi." The circumstances of Solomon's life are those of Kunitz': "my mother's breast was thorny / and father I had none" (p. 87, lines 3–4). But this brief poem and the adoption of this persona tells more than any analysis why Kunitz is not a confessional poet. Kunitz is a poet of the self and the self's struggle for identity. In these two poems Kunitz is *defined* by events, but not *confined* by them: he does not aspire to, or arrive at, an *enclosed*, private self, but a self that goes through the personal to a transformed, transcendent self beyond.

Stanza 1 of "An Old Cracked Tune" would define and confine Solomon-Kunitz by his circumstances and origins, but stanza 2 goes beyond toward a level of general wisdom: "The sands whispered, *Be separate*, / the stones taught me, *Be hard*" (lines 5–6). The speaker of the poem fulfills the implications of his name: as Solomon he seeks and achieves wisdom, that which is achieved when circumstance is transformed into meaning. It is just such a transformation that Kunitz seeks in "The Portrait" and indeed in all his poetry. The transformation of tragic circumstance toward tragic joy dominates "King of the River" and all his great poems of the legend of being. Solomon Levi is a desert hermit-saint, a holy fool perhaps: half-cracked, but not bitter or cynical; deeply cut off from the social world, but capable of approaching it, of choosing "the edge of the road" as the place for his ecstatic dance.

It is interesting to compare Solomon Levi's dance to William Carlos Williams' ecstatic dance in "Dance Russe": Williams' dance, despite its uninhibitedness, is buried deep *within* "the household" and the social experience: it is a privacy (behind locked doors) within a social context. Kunitz' Solomon Levi tells us in the second line that his condition is not one of privacy but of deep solitude, even an alienation from the social community: "the desert is my home." From such a solitude (born perhaps from the family circumstances we encounter in "The Portrait" and lines 3 and 4 of "An Old Cracked Tune") and the ordeals it imposes comes a wisdom (survivor's wisdom: be hard, be separate) and finally a joy. It is with this joy that Solomon Levi reapproaches the human community (the road where people journey) to dance his dance, share his song. Solomon Levi's coming to the edge of the road to share with the passing world his dance and his song makes him a type of the solitary artist, an artist whose adverse circumstances of origin and whose ordeal in the desert have led him finally to a celebratory stance.

The four sections of "The Testing-Tree" comprise one of Kunitz' finest poems of origin as essence written in a tragic mode. It is also one of his ultimate poems in which the world of legend and the world of experience fuse completely. It begins (as do so many of the poems in this book, e.g., "The Magic Curtain," "River Road," "Three Floors," "The Illumination") by reinhabiting a precise moment in the distant past in such a way as to make it vividly present.

If we were to make a slight but crucial distinction between the strategy of section 1 of "The Magic Curtain" and section 1 of "The Testing-Tree" it would be this: the scene of the past reinhabited in "The Magic Curtain" is unique and happened only once; the scene in section 1 of "The Testing-Tree" at first seems to be a unique occurrence, but has actually occurred many times and in its recurrent, repetitious behavior contains the seeds of ritual. In section 3, this ritual will rise to the surface; for now we see it in the repeated behavior and in the crucial adjectives: "tribal," "magic."

"Tribal" introduces the theme of the Indian past that the boy Kunitz identifies with explicitly in the final lines of section 2:

> as I followed in the steps
> of straight-backed Massassoit
> soundlessly heel-and-toe
> practicing my Indian walk.
> (ll. 45–46)

In section 3, the Indian theme is linked to the ancient target oak itself when Kunitz describes it as having "locked King Philip's War / in its annulated core." We thus see the tribal theme as the boy's imaginary journey into a further past: a past of belongingness that is irrecoverably lost, entirely obliterated by the history of Model A's and tanks that dominates section 4. This longing for a tribal past is linked to the longing for the lost father through the figure of the target oak.

In section 1, the important thing is the quiet introduction of tribal consciousness whose time is the sacred, cyclical time of seasons marked by ritual repetitions accentuating key moments in the circle of seasons. The primary contrast is with linear, historical time, that notion of time that dominates the final section with its distressing image of progress:

> That single Model A
> sputtering up the grade
> unfurled a highway behind
> where the tanks maneuver,
> revolving their turrets.
> (ll. 98–102)

One movement of the poem involves a lament for the lost, cyclic tribal time (sections 1 to 3) and its replacement by linear, historical time (section 4). In terms of the dramatized self in the poem, we would say that cyclical, tribal time calls up the spiraling self. When linear historical time triumphs in section 4, we see the spiraling self replaced by the journeying self:

> It is necessary to go
> through dark and deeper dark
> and not to turn.
> (ll. 106–8)

The second adjective in section 1 that foreshadows the whole poem in the characteristically subtle way of late Kunitz is the "magic" of "magic Keds." What appears to be childish hyperbole is actually the necessary access to tribal consciousness. What separates the repetitious "play" of the Academy ballpark from the ritual stone-throwing of the target oak is the presence of magic. (Baseball is to the target oak ritual as a carnival's Kewpie doll is to Cupid, son of Venus: a desacralized phenomenon.) Magic is fundamental to this poem and to Kunitz' work in general. Without the power of magic, imagination would be nothing more than idle fantasy, whereas in Kunitz it is always potentially transformative of reality in accordance with human longing (for love, poetry, immortality) or capable of revealing truth beneath appearance (the recurring dream of section 4).

A lesser phrase confirms the implications of "tribal" and "magic": "perfect stones / rolled out of glacial time." The necessary perfection of the stones indicates the longing for an absolute and unconditional state that underlies ritual (ritual being man's attempt to make contact with the supernatural). That these perfect stones come from "glacial time" calls up a faint echo of the "Dynastic thunder-bison, Asian crude" who played a crucial role in the powerful rituals of "The Way Down."

When the final lines of section 1 recount the boy's race down the road, we recognize an aspiration typical of Kunitz' poetry:

> as I poured it on
> for the prize of the mastery
> over that stretch of road,
> with no one no where to deny
> when I flung myself down
> that on the given course
> I was the world's fastest human.
> (ll. 15–21)

This is a theme that runs throughout Kunitz' work: the solitary self in quest of heroic accomplishment. In an early central poem like "Vita Nuova" the heroic was confused or fused with the archaic and noble and expressed itself in terms of "visors" and "gentleness" (with its secondary meaning: of noble birth). In early Kunitz, the heroic quest and the desire to "convert life into legend" often meant an elevation of diction and imagery, a transcendence of the recognizable world that verged on rejection of it in favor of an ideal or idealized legend. In a poem like "Vita Nuova" both the social and natural worlds are transcended in favor of the solitary, supernatural world of the heroic quest. What is so amazing about a poem like "The Testing-Tree" is that Kunitz remains true to a fundamental principle of his being—the value of the solitary heroic quest—but no longer needs to reject the natural physical world. The heroic can be subsumed into the recognizable, mundane world of Keds and baseball without losing its essential nature.

But a distinction must be made between Kunitz' ability to locate his quest in the world of nature and his ability to locate it in the social world. As with the distinction between Williams' "Dance Russe" and Kunitz' "An Old Cracked Tune," we must again recognize that the boy Kunitz "could never hope to play" in the Academy ballpark, though his solitary ritual calls for a pitcher's skills. The quest is extrinsic to (living) human society, and the race that ends section 1 can be seen as a race away from the social world of schools, home, and ballpark and toward the world of nature that so dominates section 2.

The tension between the magnetic power of the social world and the pull of the world of nature (which is the "natural" setting for the heroic quest) is dramatized quietly in the opening lines of section 2:

> Around the bend
> that tried to loop me home
> dawdling came *natural*
> (ll. 22–24; my italics)

Again with subtlety and understatement, Kunitz puts forth the underlying terms of his drama: the road is personified as an agent of constraint and confinement: its purpose is to bring people home to their social identity and responsibility. In section 4, the image of the road has risen to an overtly sinister status as the "single Model A / unfurled a highway behind / where the tanks maneuver." In contrast to the power of confinement manifested by the image of the road is the power of nature that causes the boy Kunitz to break away from the road, wander across a field rich with plant and animal life, and finally to approach the mysterious "umbrageous trail" that will lead him to the place of the ritual encounter. This mysterious, ancient trail contrasts with the road, and it can only be reached by crossing the trackless natural area of the field. The "flickering presences" that give the boy "right of passage" are Indian ghosts: he has left the modern, historical world and entered the tribal, nonhistorical world. These ghosts are his spirit guides—they are analogous to the Spirit Fathers whom Kunitz often seeks for guidance, but they are now tribal and collective, not personal guides. Certain words are crucial here: "I owned the key / to an umbrageous trail"—key implies door and lock: the unlocking of a door to reveal what is beyond. It was a key which Dante held up in "The Illumination." The phrase "right of passage" is a perfect example of what I can only call a deep pun: a form of layering of meanings that is an essential form of intelligence in Kunitz' work. In this case, "right of passage" means "permission to pass," but its deeper meaning is rite of passage: the anthropological term for the ritual a young person undergoes as he is initiated into membership in the tribe. It is a ritual characterized by ordeals undergone, symbolic death and rebirth to a new identity, and initiation into the sacred knowledge of the tribe. Here we can see that the boy has been initiated into a long-vanished New England Indian tribe whose ghosts lead him further into the forest as he practices his new tribal knowledge: the soundless heel-and-toe Indian walk. Massasoit is not a tribal name, but the name of a specific Indian chief who was the father of King Philip. In 1675 King Philip led an Indian alliance against the encroaching settlers; to follow Massasoit's steps is to become an heroic son.

The trail and the road are contrary in nature and purpose: the former primitive, winding through nature and leading toward a solitary sacred space; the latter geometrical, and rigid, imposing itself on nature, leading to a social space. Between lies the "nettled field"—a place of transition. In the field the animal and plant world triumphs over the human social world. The human world is overwhelmed, almost obliterated by the natural world, and we have a sense of passing back through time toward the era of wilderness and forest represented by the Indians and their trail.

But in the precise detail of the remnant lilac we see the key image of the house and the complex meanings it enfolds:

> and a stringy old lilac
> more than two stories tall
> blazing with mildew
> remembered a door in the
> long teeth of the woods.
> (ll. 29–33)

Again, as with the road, we have quiet personification: the lilac remembers. The accuracy of this image is a hallmark of later Kunitz: nineteenth-century home owners planted lilac "in the dooryard" as Whitman puts it—and the plants tended to long outlast even the house's ruins. The lilac remembers the house: it is a ghost-house, a house long lost in the past. In the context of Kunitz' work it is the image of intimate belonging that was associated with the father and is as irrecoverably lost as is the dead father himself. This house is tied to memory and to nos-

talgia. But in the precise context of this poem the image is mod-
ified—we never hear the word "house," only the word "door."
A few lines later, we hear of a "key to the trail" that the boy
owns, and it becomes clear that the old lilacs form a kind of
ghostly threshold the boy passes through with his key in order
to enter the trail. The images of door and key link up so that
the boy must make the following series of movements to fulfill
his quest: first he must leave the social world and the road; then
he must cross the natural world of the field and pass through
the phantom house that is a central image at the source of his
own sense of personal loss (linked to his missing father); then,
having crossed this threshold "blazing" with the mildew of death,
he can at last enter the Indian trail where he is reborn *beyond*
his personal self into the prehistorical tribal identity of the ghost-
Indians.

In other words, the lost house that in "Father and Son" was
seen as being the symbol of the anguish and loss at the source
of his life ("the house, the stucco one you [father] built / We
lost") is now seen as a threshold: something to be passed through
toward a further truth. In "The Testing-Tree" the further truth
is *backward* toward a primordial ritual and a tribal identity that
partly relieves Kunitz of his personal anguish. In "King of the
River," the threshold looked forward toward the last mystery that
we call death. In each case "threshold" intensifies the drama of
transition, and in "The Testing-Tree" it finally succeeds in alter-
ing the negative connotations of the house image.

Though Kunitz successfully passes through the field in section 2 and is not impeded in his quest by the sinister and fateful
image of the lilacs and the phantom house, this very image and
space will return to haunt him in the apocalyptic "recurring
dream" of section 4 where the adult Kunitz is pulled back into
the personal psychological torment of his family dynamic. In
section 4, the mother is no longer evaded by not returning

home—she has taken up fearful residence in the field. And the father is there as the albino walrus (recognizable to us in this transformation by his "gentle" eyes—like those of "The Portrait"). All is tragic defeat in the early part of section 4; all is collapse out of the timeless tribal into the anguished personal. For now let me point out that the first two-and-a-half sections of the poem are all movement (indeed section 1 is a single continuous sentence). The boy Kunitz, certain that he has the key to the trail and the tribal identify, can "pass by" all the impediments both physical and personal on his way to the sacred ritual. He can even go

> Past the abandoned quarry
>   where the *pale sun* bobbed
>   in the sump of the granite
>   (ll. 49–51; my italics)

and not recognize that this pale sun/son is himself *and* his father: that it is a prefiguration of the albino walrus trapped in the well and an ominous sign that the boy is a paleface not an Indian: that his link to his biological father is one of mutual identity confirmed by the mother's presence and gestures in section 4 as powerfully as her slap linked them in "The Portrait."

In the first two sections, the poem has passed through three kinds of space: road to field to forest. In section 3, the boy continues his journey toward the fourth symbolic space: the clearing, a space in the midst of the wilderness where the ritual encounter can at last take place. At the very moment that the boy enters the clearing a transformation shows that it is a sacred space where magic is operative:

> with stones in my pocket
>   changing to oracles
>   (ll. 56–57)

The "testing-tree" itself has analogues in Frazer's *Golden Bough*. It is also Kunitz' Spirit Father conceived as a transpersonal manifestation of Nature itself: a life force of the kind we could call "tree of life," except that it is distinctly linked by gender to the father principle. An analogous encounter was dramatized in the final section of "The Way Down" where the "brave god" was addressed as "O father in the wood, / Mad father of us all." There the father-king was ritually slain so that the son could succeed him and rise to his own full power and identity. In "The Way Down" the Spirit Father was staglike ("King of our antlered wills, / Our candelabrum-pride"), a part of animal nature. In "The Testing Tree" the Spirit Father has donned branches rather than antlers and is part of vegetative nature. Unlike animal nature, vegetative nature lays deeper claims to the life-force— can be inexhaustible.

But the testing-tree is not simply a symbol of the inexhaustible life-force of vegetative nature. The tree is also the ultimate Spirit Father: Jehovah, the One God, the autonomous male creator principle raised to its highest level. The tree also contains a noble yet human-scaled male figure: the Indian chief King Philip who waged war against those early New England colonists who were clearing the wilderness for Henry Ford. With King Philip we have the tragic-heroic, finite male contained within the infinite male principle that is Jehovah. That King Philip's War is "locked" in the tree's history and that he is specified as being there "beneath the cut of my name" (i.e., the boy's name carved on the tree bark) completes and fulfills one of the poem's main themes: the son's search for identity that entails a search for the lost father who is the potential source of a potency of being. King Philip's War is "locked" in the tree just as the mother of "The Portrait" "locked" Kunitz's father's "name" in her deepest closet and would not let "him" out. Name and being are magically one; King Philip's spirit is imprisoned, but the son "owns the key."

When Kunitz in section 2 follows in the steps of Massasoit, King Philip's father, he is the dutiful son whose heroism will honor the father. King Philip is "immortal" in the sense that his glorious *name* remains. In "The Testing Tree" the key consists of going backward in history to a prepersonal identity and a prehistoric time where the game of the three stones and the tree has the power to transfer enormous power of being directly to the boy/son from the Spirit Fathers.

The Spirit Fathers who are present include: Jehovah, King Philip, and Kunitz' own personal father: *"Father wherever you are / I have only three throws / bless my good right arm"* (ll. 70–72). The ritual of the stone is a game, but a sacred game: beneath its simple surface are the deepest meanings. The three goals that the boy Kunitz aims for (presumably one goal is attained for each stone that hits the tree) are partly personal ideals (love, poetry) and partly representative human longing for the unconditional (eternal life). We recognize love and poetry as the "two ambitions" that raved within him in "The Tutored Child" Eternal life is the ultimate wish, the ultimate goal the boy seeks in his encounter with the supernatural. In a sense though, he has already transcended the limits of his personal condition by traveling backward in time, shedding his personal identity, and becoming reborn in imagination as an Indian.

"The Testing-Tree" describes a parabola of imaginative transcendence roughly analogous to Keats' "Ode to a Nightingale." When the boy Kunitz becomes, through imagination, an Indian he has transcended his individual identity and suffering and is in the same transcended state as Keats when he has traveled upward into the tree boughs on the "viewless wings" of imagination and can say to the nightingale: "Already [I am] with thee." The parabola of transcendence has reached its highest point at the end of section 3 of "The Testing-Tree."

If the poem ended here it would be untrue in that it would

not honor the tragic nature of the human condition. The lyric impulse (and human yearning) to transcend the finite human condition is fulfilled and then (emblem of the poem's greatness) the poem goes on to say transcendence is truth, but only half the truth. It is at that point that Keats says "Forlorn, the very word is like a bell / that tolls me back from thee to my sole self." We rise up out of time and out of entrapment in our individual selves only to fall back into them. The boy Kunitz rises up out of his schoolboy self into the tribal identity and an heroic identification with King Philip only to fall back into the psychological and circumstantial limitations of family and history that rule section 4.

In the opening lines of section 4, we have entered a new space which is actually an earlier space transformed:

> In the recurring dream
>   my mother stands
>   in her bridal gown
> under the burning lilac
>   (ll. 79–82)

The new space is the personal psychological space of the dream: an interior landscape that is the field of section 2 transformed and inhabited. The dream-field replaces the clearing as the center of the poem's drama, and the phantom house with its sham doorway and fierce mother has replaced the testing-tree and its Father Spirits.

To say that the dream "recurs" is to link it with the world of ritual (section 3) that is based on recurrence, repetition, and cycles. But with one important difference: in the ritual of the testing-tree the boy seeks out the encounter of his own free will, establishes the necessary strict rules for his encounter with the supernatural, and hopes to rise to power through skill and strict adherence to the rules. In the "recurrence" of dream, it is the dream that has power and authority over the passive dreamer: the recurrence is endured, the dream imposes its images on the dreamer.

The recurrent nature of the dream establishes it as a parody and reversal of the sacred ritual that dominated the first three sections. Sacred, cyclic time and primitive consciousness (Jehovah and the tribal) dominated the testing-tree ritual. Tribal ritual is sacred recurrence: the sacred spiral of transcendence. The recurrence of the dream is the individual neurotic recurrence that indicates a psychological impasse—a circle that cannot be broken or broken out of—a circle from Dante's *Inferno*.

Where can Kunitz go: in what direction can he proceed, if the poem's drama has collapsed out of the sacred spiral into the circle of neurotic repetition? The poem's answer is to replace the spiraling self with the journeying self—to accept journey as the governing metaphor in the fallen, historical world of section 4:

> It is necessary to go
> through dark and deeper dark
> and not to turn
> (ll. 106–8)

In the opening of section 4 the figure who dominates the dream is the mother. The paternal has been replaced by the maternal with all the negative power she implies. She is being courted by "Bernard Shaw and Bertie/Russell"—two fantasy fathers who represent Western civilization and culture as opposed to the primitive Spirit Fathers the boy would have chosen (Massasoit, King Philip) and *also* as opposed to the father's primitive (i.e., animal) form: the albino walrus. The walrus is at the bottom of a well that is filling with dirt: it is a grave (the key image-verb, "staining" of "staining the water yellow," alerts us to the image cluster of mortality-wound-father). Since the well is reached by passing through a doorway, it is also the foundation hole of the long-gone house with which the father's loss has always been linked.

The mother's menacing gesture is analogous to her slap in "The Portrait": it confirms that the boy's identity and fate are inextricably tied up with his doomed father. King Philip follows his father Massasoit, and leads the New England tribes in a heroic, doomed war; the "pale sun bobs in the abandoned quarry," just as the albino walrus huffs from the bottom of the well. (These water-sources, ponds and lakes, have been the settings for encounters between the living and dead before in "Goose Pond" and "Father and Son" and later in "Quinnapoxet").

Suddenly, the feeling content of the dream surfaces:

> If the dirt keeps sifting in,
> staining the water yellow,
> why should I be blamed?
> (ll. 94–96)

In the final lines, we see Kunitz' quest for an heroic identity collapse entirely into the personal, psychological identity that results from the family drama of mother–father–son. The tone is one of guilt: "Why should I be blamed?" We sense here the speaker's helplessness and powerlessness in relation to the recurring dream and the stalled psychological drama it enacts. In this line the son Kunitz tries to break the link of identity between himself and his father. At this point, the inner, emotional drama of the poem becomes clear: if the son identifies with a transpersonal, imagined father and son (Massasoit and King Philip) he might be saved and gain access to what he longs for; if he identifies with his personal father then he will in some mysterious and disastrous way share his fate.

With the line about blame, the poem has touched a secret source of the drama: the son, by denial, acknowledges his own feelings of implication in his father's death. The next line shifts tone and strategy entirely, as if to wrench the drama out of its descending spiral of guilt and morbidity: "Never try to explain" (l. 97). The linguistic form of the line is that of a *motto*—a pure product of the intelligent will oriented toward behavior and survival in the world. Mottos abound in Kunitz' poetry and they function to reorient the self in the midst of crisis. In terms of the poem itself (and by extension, the dramatic lyric form), this motto asserts the poet's ability to dramatize the truth, but not to interpret it. That is, the complexities of human experience can be presented in the many-leveled gestures, descriptions, puns, and contraries of a poem like "The Testing-Tree" but any attempt on the poet's part to explain, or interpret this drama would reduce it to a false simplicity. An explanation is a reductive gesture: an attempt to present *human* reality as having two dimensions; but the key dimension in a poem like Kunitz' "The Testing-Tree" is *depth*. In *Meditations on Quixote*, Ortega y Gasset speaks about our knowledge that depth is a constitutive dimension of reality. Using the example of an orange, Ortega points out that when we look at the fruit, we see only two dimensions: its extension of height and width. We *know* the third dimension is present, is constitutive of the orange's reality, but this third dimension of depth must manifest itself through the other two dimensions—depth must shine up through those other two dimensions that are all we actually perceive. This is exactly the strategy of the dramatic lyric as practiced by Kunitz in "The Testing-Tree." The depth of the poem: its stories and meanings about the mysteries of human identity, human beliefs, the natural and supernatural must shine up through the apparently simple events and details of the poem: "the magic Keds" and "the pale sun" that bobs in the abandoned quarry.

Motto is one more form that the irrational intelligence takes in its desire for meanings and orientations. But it is a form aware of the need to resist the explanations and interpretations that (to its way of thinking) falsify experience. Interpretation substitutes the dimension of abstraction for that of depth; it disembodies the human experience, whereas the ethos of the dramatic lyric is precisely that the meanings to be disclosed in human experience should be incarnated in dramas whose meanings are present in their dimension of depth.

Will, in the form of the motto, "Never try to explain," rescues the poem from the power of a dream it cannot control and a feeling (guilt) it cannot resolve. But if the poem breaks away from a dream centered in the insoluble conflicts of Kunitz' family, it next encounters a dream, a waking-dream, or vision whose dramatic center is in the world of Western history and progress:

> That single Model A
> sputtering up the grade
> unfurled a highway behind
> where the tanks maneuver,
> revolving their turrets.
> (ll. 98–102)

We shift from personal family to the nonhuman, technological "march of progress": from the field to the road. The self of the poem has gradually lost momentum—as Thoreau would say, "Things are in the saddle and ride man." The journey forward through section 2 toward the clearing is replaced by a backward movement in which the protagonist is a passive observer: first of the field, now of the road. The power of this highway is the power of Western civilization in general and technological "progress" in particular. It means the triumph of the civilized over the primitive, culture over nature. In terms of the poem's values, this triumph is a triumph of destruction. The triumph of

technology in the poem is roughly coeval with the boy Kunitz'
"fall" out of the timeless-time of adolescence: that is, the Model
A Ford was "born" just about the same time the boy Kunitz of
the early sections of the poem "died." The "murderous time" is
the twentieth century whose beginning Kunitz witnessed.

The nightmare vision of triumphant destructive, antihuman
technology closes itself off with a descriptive detail that links it
to the opening line of section 4: "revolving their turrets." Like
"recurring," revolving is another sinister circle. It is in complete contrast to the sacred circle of seasons that is the basis for
the ritual of section 3. The sacred recurrence of ritual and the
human encounter with the supernatural that occurs in ritual can
be best conceived as an ascending spiral: an upward spiral of
transcendence. The recurring dream and the revolving turrets
are circles that offer no escape to other levels of meaning. They
are like the suicidally depressed "Back and forth, back and forth"
pacing of the painter in "The Artist" (p. 84).

The dynamic, spiraling self of the tree ritual has been defeated—has collapsed out of sacred time back into the flat circle
of neurotic repetition. The tribal transpersonal self has collapsed
back into the psychological self ensnared by the family drama.
The heroic questing self has become a powerless, passive observer of events. Sacred, cyclical time has been replaced by linear, historical time.

What must the self do? What can the self do? The first thing
is to survive at a feeling level, to survive by feeling:

> In a murderous time
>   the heart breaks and breaks
>   and lives by breaking.
>   (ll. 102–5)

There is a need not just to recognize reality ("the heart breaks
and breaks"), but to *transform* the fate of reality by an act of

moral will: the heart, the feeling self, can *only* be nourished by opening itself to suffering—the third line in this tercet transforms the implied fatalism of the first two lines.

In the next tercet we have returned to the journey motif, though there is no dramatized self journeying:

> It is necessary to go
>   through dark and deeper dark
>   and not to turn.

"Dark and deeper dark" parallel and reinforce "breaks and breaks." The journey has returned as the dominant metaphor for the self in the world, but it is not the same journey as that in which the boy moved toward the sacred clearing where time was suspended and the self could encounter the supernatural. This journey goes through dark and deeper dark: it is the self after it has fallen into historical time, into the personal self whose journeys have beginnings and ends. The journey of self in section 4 begins with the ruined house, the harsh mother, and the lost father—it ends with personal death. Again, the third line of the tercet transforms fate/necessity by an act of moral will—in this case courage.

In the final tercet, the "I" of the poem (the adult, old man self of the deeper dark) reappears with great forcefulness: three end-stopped lines in a row: an assertion; an anguished, demanding question; and a powerful demand each of whose five syllables is heavily stressed:

> I am looking for the trail.
>   Where is my testing-tree?
>   Give me back my stones!
>   (ll. 109–11)

These lines express the essence of the tragic sense (as defined by Kitto in *The Greeks*): a simultaneous insistence on the dignity and vulnerability of the human individual in relation to the universe and the limits of his condition. Because journey through time (rather than journey to the sacred center) is now the governing metaphor, we know that the testing tree is at the beginning—as hopelessly lost in pastness as the father's house. "Where is my testing tree?" is a cry of anguish in which Kunitz' "nostalgia" and "desire" fuse absolutely; heaven and hell are reconciled in one emblem of the unconditional world against which the self hurls its exultant, hopeless demand:

Give me back my stones!

In the final poem of *The Testing-Tree*, simplicity and complexity fuse. "The Game" has the reality of *voice*, of song: not of landscape. It is a pure lyric: a voice in the void that refers to the things of this world, but these things (tree, stone, bottle) have been lifted up out of their worldly context. The movement from "The Testing-Tree" (and especially its final lines) to "The Game" is a movement from the tragic heroic mode to the lyric mode. And yet they are intimately related: as though "The Game" was an echo of the longer poem—a quietly poignant echo from a transcendent world.

Why does this book culminate in "The Game"? In part it is because "The Testing-Tree" protests ("Give me back my stones!") where "The Game" accepts. The game of the title is several things, but its first echo is with the line about the testing-tree ritual in the preceding poem: "I played my game for keeps." The colloquial nature of the expression "for keeps" served to partially mask the fact that the game had the deepest implications for the speaker's life in the world. The game of the final poem's title is thus no less than the game of the human condition, of being in the world—a portentous fact that is immediately undercut and anchored by the most specific and mundane possible reference in the first line:

> Let's spin the bottle
> No, I don't want to be kissed
>
> (p. 93)

"The Game" does not go from the cosmic to the mundane as though this were a great journey: the cosmic and the mundane are identical: the child's game of spin-the-bottle contains universal implications about our situation in the world (the role of chance, the separateness of selves that even affection cannot bridge).

Spinning the bottle combines fate (the closed circle of the bottle's spin) with chance. It is like Fortune's wheel: a closed circle—yet a circle where luck is possible: a prize is to be had. When the bottle stops spinning, it points outside itself to an object of desire in the world. But the second line speaks to the issue of the prize:

> No, I don't want to be kissed

and thus shifts the terms away from the exclusive definition of the game as a child's game. The speaker is *beyond* desire: makes his proposal ("Let's spin the bottle") not out of any hope of gain or goal.

I think of "The Game" as being spoken by Solomon Levi, the hermit, alone in his desert. If it's also a kind of prayer, it's not addressed to God but to the Spirit Father. The human, imaginative power to transform is at an ebb: the speaker is not *transformer* but *transformed:*

> Sometimes I feel my arm
> Is turning into a tree
>
> Or hardening to stone
> Past memory of green

The speaker lacks now the artist's power to transform the conditions of being and must acknowledge that he himself lives (and dies) *within* these conditions, unable to transcend them. He passively experiences changes, metamorphoses that are magical but ambiguous; to become a tree might be interesting, but the stony permanence is a kind of death that undercuts all possible positive connotations of the first metamorphosis. He does not dance for joy and surviving is not possible.

There are poems that no one else can write, poems locked so deeply in the mystery and circumstance of an individual life that no one else could write them, and even to read them frightens us. "The Game" is such a poem: without knowing Kunitz' life through his work, it would be impossible to understand the way that it phrases and rephrases its imagery of father and son. It is a poem of essences and yet precise as well.

Who else could say so accurately and yet with such a grasp of its resonance: "O the night is coming on / And I am nobody's son"? It is both a negation and an affirmation, which is the structure of the whole poem. It is a phrase that fuses a violent physical fact and a metaphysical conundrum.

Only Kunitz could have the courage and integrity to insist simultaneously on his old age, his awareness of oncoming death *and* his sense of still being a son. Again, he resists orthodoxies and the easy answers; he "never learned to pray" and the "Father" he addresses is not a patriarchal God. One of Kunitz' achievements has been consistently to refuse those consolations: to insist that the absent father, though numinous, must remain a *human* mystery, must be understood in terms of the human world and its limits (which we simultaneously protest against—"Give me back my stones"—and acknowledge).

"The Game" is the most poignant, vulnerable poem in Kunitz' oeuvre. Kunitz is again, as he is in essence, a *son:* there is always a higher figure above him, whether it be the benign Father Spirit or the Mother. Odysseus, the wily, the triumphant, was "Nobody" or "No man" in the cyclops' cave; Kunitz is "nobody's son"—not Odysseus the brave wanderer, but his son, who endures suffering, humiliation, and confusion because the mystery of his father's absence haunts him and prevents him from succeeding to an adult identity. If one's father simply dies when one is young, there is tragedy perhaps, but not mystery. It is the mystery of his father's death that enslaves Kunitz—that makes him forever a son and also "nobody's son": he simultaneously belongs to his father and is totally alone. This is the deepest level of meaning that Kunitz can extract from the "curious legend of his youth" and it is one that permits him to connect meaningfully to the deepest realities of the human condition: our longings, our despairs.

Solomon Levi survived his past and his *origins*, but the speaker of "The Game" faces the future ("O the night is coming on") and cannot survive because the rules of this game (which is life) concern mortality and transience. Time and mortality triumph. Within those limits though the human spirit can rise up to an unconditional assertion, an absolute:

Father it's true

but only to circumscribe truth with time:

But only for a day.

"The Game" is a great, small poem, a great "whole" fragment. Its poignancy results from its giving itself over to the truth

of impermanence, the truth of metamorphosis despite our longing for security and stability, for "father." Its intensity results
from the fact that it is both a poem that partakes of poetry's permanence and yet is written/spoken by an old man trapped in
time: "O the night is coming on." He is a child playing a game,
and he is an old man facing death. "The Game" expresses the
ultimate dilemma of the self trapped in time yet yearning for
the unconditional. The anguished demand/cry of the final lines
of "The Testing-Tree" gives way to the quiet human voice of the
final line of "The Game":

> Father it's true
> But only for a day

Though the human has the power to make a gesture toward truth,
toward a statement of its personal truth, this urge toward the
unconditional truth is rendered conditional and transitory.

In the line "No I don't want to be kissed" we can hear the
hermit Solomon Levi talking, but also the self *beyond* desire:
the self that has moved with time and in time so far (old age)
that its story has become part of the impersonal legend of being.
Similarly, when Kunitz says "I am nobody's son," he speaks accurately from the peculiar circumstance of his own birth, but he
also asserts that orphanhood and loss are an essence of being ultimately shared by all of us. This poem is absolutely personal,
and yet it centers itself in the legend of being, beyond the personal. The poem's simplicity is utmost and awesome. In the first
line a bottle spins in a child's game. In the final line, the earth
spins and a single day stands for our mortal span. The genuine
essence of the tragic is present: our human dignity and vulnerability side by side.

CHAPTER 5

The Layers

The surfaces of the poems that comprise *The Layers* are deceptively quiet and flat. We have to carry with us all of Kunitz' previous poems—their key images; their legend themes; their complex, nonrational, dramatic intelligence; their emotional intensities. On the simplicity of the late poems, their severity of story, syntax, and diction, we must bring to bear the preceding poems, the way Schliemann consulted Homer's *Iliad* so that he could point to one hill resembling all its neighbors and say: within that hill is Troy. The intelligence of Kunitz' poems is now below the surface, archaeological.

We might have said of Kunitz' earlier style that it was architectural: built up above the surface with allusion, rhetorical and metrical complexities, philosophical and scientific concepts as image sources. The architecture would be that of a castle— appropriate to young Kunitz' notions of the nobility of the poetic enterprise. In the late poems the humble has replaced the noble: the "unknown makers" of folk art have replaced Helen and St. Catherine. Late Kunitz is "drunk . . . sweaty with genius" ("Journal for My Daughter"), no longer seeking the mask of "youth, the undefeated, / Whose falcon-heart, winged with the golden shout / Of morning, sweeps windward from his native city" ("The Fitting of the Mask"). The surface of the late poems is flat—only slight rises or depressions in the ground tell us that there is something down there: a depth of meaning beneath simple words and phrases, simple gestures.

Imagination supplies new strategies to the self for its struggle to transcend the condition and the limits of the self in time. These strategies (metamorphosis, transformation, "changes"), though present in earlier poems, here take on the authority to resolve the endings of poems and to move the poems triumphantly toward the legend of being.

At the same time, other personal legends, especially the father legend (or what is really a parental legend), are isolated specifically in the context of Kunitz' personal life ("Quinnapoxet"). The parents are brought together in the same story—as though they offered two ways of life to the son: either the maternal notion of duty and sternness, or the father principle linked to nature and its violence, but also to a potency that comes from suffering, from a heart that breaks and breaks, and ultimately learns how to live by breaking. Later, in "The Unquiet Ones," the parents are reconciled and given a mythic dimension: Janus, mysterious god of origins and thresholds.

The beloved legend is no longer a source of the intense dramas it once was when mother or culture ("The Class Will Come to Order") stood between self and beloved. This legend is capable of flaring up as the drama of a poem like "The Quarrel" whose ultimate human relationship is recognized as "the hiss of love / that harsh, irregular flame." but it is as though the negative feminine that the mother represented has been overcome by such a positive figure as Frieda of "The Magic Curtain," and it is now possible to pass on to a stance that acknowledges and celebrates the "unknown makers"—women who have suffered and/or triumphed in the making of folk art in America. Put another way, "A Blessing of Women" is a clear instance of a poem that could only come after Kunitz had in some sense "forgiven" his mother and opened himself to the positive qualities of endurance, determination, shrewdness, courage, and creativity her life (as seen in section one of "The Magic Curtain" and "The Portrait") exemplified. The women celebrated in "A Blessing of Women" are clearly sisters of Kunitz' mother but free of the personal onus of having distorted Kunitz' own growth as a person. When Kunitz' mother stitched dresses of her own design "for the Boston trade" ("The Magic Curtain"), she harnessed her creative energy to necessary, practical purposes. To go from her life to the celebration of women's folk art is to acknowledge the mother's creativity, to elevate it to art (one of Kunitz' two ideals) and to "forgive" the mother for the life she led and its impact on young Kunitz, forgive her mode of life by acknowledging it as part of a larger social and economic context—what our culture has done to women. The price of Kunitz' survival was high ("sometimes I feel my arm / Is turning into a tree / Or hardening to stone / Past memory of green," "The Game"). In "A Blessing of Women" he obliquely acknowledges how terribly difficult and costly his own mother's survival was.

The title of the book's first poem, "The Knot," is itself a pun. The knot is also "The Not"—the phenomenon of the negation of being (a wound) that is transformed into the affirmation of being (tree) in the course of the poem itself.

The poem's ostensible story is so clear that it becomes almost impossible to discuss. We must instead discuss the complexities below the surface and acknowledge that the poem's power results in part from the tension between a quiet, lucid surface and those psychic and metaphysical complexities hidden beneath it. The layering of meanings in "The Knot" begins with the title itself. The knot is, at the literal level, the knot in a board that shows where a branch once was when the board was a tree.

The knot is also a projection onto the physical world and concretization of the psychic state of the speaker as the word "trauma"
indicates ("out of the trauma / of its lopping-off," p. 1). The knot
is a psychic scar as much as a physical scar on the lintel. The
story of "The Knot" is the history (lines 1–6) of the self's past
attempts to deal with the situation; and then, from line 7 to the
end of the poem, the way in which the situation manifests itself
in the present.

It is a poem of the legend of being which orchestrates key
images from all three major legends. The "knot" is the wound
from the father legend. The "lintel" above the door has to do
with the fatality and revelation of the mother–beloved legend.
The phallic tree-of-life image that dominates the latter part of
the poem is an image of creative energy from the legend of being.
These three images are orchestrated into a hymn to being whose
anguished and ambiguous ejaculation is "Let be! Let be!" There
has been talk in recent years of a "deep image" poem. According to that critical term, "The Knot" would be a deep image poem,
by which is meant a poem whose central image is symbolically,
nonrationally complex. In contemplating the meanings of this
image we uncover the meanings of the poem. Such a poem as
"The Knot" is the product of a projective imagination: the knot
is a concretization of the poet's subjective state. A deep image
reveals less about the object world than about the inner world
of the self: the world of being. The deep image is equally the
"deep I": the "moi profond" of Bergson—where being and world
meet, and what is revealed is the complex interpenetrability of
self and object. The deep image poem is the deep-I poem: the
poem of being and of being-in-the-world. Such a poem is the
natural product of the poet of symbolic intelligence, just as the
didactic poem is the natural product of the discursive intelligence. Kunitz is the poet of dramatized symbolic intelligence par
excellence.

"The Knot" is pure psychic process—the opening line (whose second meaning is repression) emphasizes *process:*

> I've tried to seal it in

rather than the static nature of the thing itself

> > that cross-grained knot
> > on the opposite wall,
> > scored in the lintel of my door . . .

The knot itself is active and urgent:

> > but it keeps bleeding through
> > into the world we share.

The layered meaning of the verb "bleed," the shape of the knot, inform these lines with their psychic story: the recurrence of trauma—its ability to reassert its negating, disruptive force in our psychic life. For Kunitz the image for violent, haunting trauma is the father's (imagined) wound. The concentric rings of a wood knot might give us an ideal structure for the effective key image: its most inner core circle is the biographical source in the poet's lived life; the outermost concentric rings are those reverberations of the image that are most universal.

Thus the knot's center is the father's imagined suicide wound and the outer concentric rings might be: the violent absoluteness of mortality ("Robin Redbreast"); the way the living carry personal loss with them through their lives; and the recurring, negating power of trauma (how it functions in "The Knot"). The concentrtic rings of a wood knot in some ways resemble a collapsed spiral. It is the spiraling self that discloses the power and meaning of key images, because key images always resonate backward toward the past and toward the personal. The outer rings of the knot, like those of the spiral, take their shape from the ring at the center; thus, even when we do not trace an image to its source (as we do the wound to Kunitz' father), the successful key image carries in its form an echo of the personal source.

When the knot/wound image fuses with the lintel/door image at the poem's very outset, it is as though the speaker labors under a double fatality. He senses the knot's behavior as threatening and sets himself against it ("I tried to seal it in"). At this point a crucial fact is revealed: the power of the self is not equal to the renewing, regenerating power of the knot:

> Mornings when I wake,
> curled in my web,
> I hear it come
> with a rush of resin
> out of the trauma
> of its lopping-off.

All is now verb and process. The knot has undergone several transformations, become more primitive and powerful. It no longer "bleeds"—the verb that linked it most grimly to the father/mortality source: now its fluid is "resin," the proper fluid of life for vegetative nature. The transformed knot's power of regeneration is now absolute: it becomes a bud, then shoots up, finally grows into an entire tree. That this tree is a magical tree, a tree of life, that incarnates the impersonal life-force of being itself seems clear. An equally clear image that parallels the tree of life image is that of magical phallus, whose power of regeneration establishes it as an equivalent bodily based image of the tree of life. We see what the phallic image has to add to the tree of life image most clearly by going back to the wound image. When the "lopping-off" of the tree limb that created the knot/wound is understood as the disappearance of the

father/masculine principle in Kunitz' life through both the suicide and the mother's intransigent wrath, it is apparent that a
kind of psychic castration is one way of describing the curious
circumstances into which Kunitz was born: the "curious legend"
that haunts and impels his work.

The search for the father is the search for identity; the search
for the father principle is the search for the potency of being
that is the human analogue to the tree of life. For Kunitz, this
potency of being is a masculine principle whose image is a phallus that is also the tree of life. The story of "The Knot" thus becomes a perfect retelling of Kunitz' life as legend. Everything
(father and mother/beloved stories) is left out, yet everything is
present. Everything is present in two intertwined stories: one
magical, about a wood knot "rising from the dead" to become a
tree; the other natural, about a man waking in the morning with
an erection. These two stories fuse into a hymn to being that
recapitulates the whole process of Kunitz' life from his beginnings in denial and repression to his later yielding to powers beyond his control, powers that he finally affirms.

The poem is structured on a double rebirth: that of the tree
and of the speaker. The final image of the self held within the
boughs of the phallic tree of life has an earlier analogue in the
image of the self "curled" fetus-like in its web. In each the self
is contained within a larger principle and we could almost say
that they represent both feminine and masculine creative principles, though as always in Kunitz, the masculine is most emphasized. The lines "Mornings when I wake / curled in my web"
echo lines from "The Mulch":

> Birthdays for him are when he wakes
> and falls into the news of weather.

and "Journal for My Daughter":

> I wake to a glittering world,
> to the annunciation of the frost

and represent once more the strategy of locating the cosmic (death-birth) within the mundane (waking up in the morning).

We have only to compare "The Knot" (the first poem in the collected poems) to "Vita Nuova" (the last) to note major changes and major continuities in Kunitz' imagination. As he says in "The Layers": "and I am not who I was, / though some principle of being / abides." In "Vita Nuova" the final emblem of the success of Kunitz' quest would be wearing his father's face. In "The Knot" there is no mention at all of father: Kunitz' quest for identity has gone past the personal. He now sees, *beyond* the father, the principle of creative being which takes a masculine, phallic form. Even in the early poem, this focused potency was present in the final image: "the single beam of all my life intense." But, just as the personal father no longer plays a part, the personal heroic I ("the visor of my name is up") is also no longer at center stage. The "I" of "The Knot" is acknowledged to be out of control of processes in line one. Relative to the mysterious forces of being that surround him, he is weak and undergoes a regression ("curled" toward the womb and toward a more primitive form of being "in my web"—perhaps spider). Later, the self metamorphoses to bird or, less likely, a quasi-angel.

Transformation of self is present in both poems. In "Vita Nuova" transformation is a predicted outcome ("I will . . . until") dependent on willed powers centered in the self. In "The Knot" transformation is something that happens to the self whether it wishes or no: a process to which the self can choose to yield and participate in.

When the young Kunitz asserts as his final, highest goal that "the single beam" of all his life be "intense," he is not far in spirit from the final lines of "The Knot." In the third line from the end, Kunitz cries "Let be! Let be!" The repetition itself is a kind of intensification of meaning that is a characteristic device throughout Kunitz' work. But the meaning of the phrase is also manifold; it is an ejaculation that affirms the power of being: "Let there be more being: Let Being exist more intensely!" (as in the message from "Journal for My Daughter": "*What do I want of my life? More! More!*").

But in "Let be! Let be!" Kunitz also cries out "Desist! Desist!" It is the anguished cry of the self aware of being a physical form trying to contain powerful forces. In the preceding lines the regenerating limb has a parallel agony: it "racks itself with shoots." This "racking" is both the torture caused by such potency of being and potency of being itself: the "rack" of shoots like the "antlered will" of the father/stag/magician in "The Way Down." The two most potent forces of the legend of being, nostalgia and desire, coexist in this exclamation. Desire wins. Or, more precisely, the onrushing power of being wins and Kunitz' final gesture is to yield to it and actively take part in the process: to shake his wings and fly into its boughs.

In the poem "Quinnapoxet," Kunitz takes his stand in relation to the figures of his two parents. He rejects the mother and makes a gesture of communion toward the father. For the first time, Kunitz overtly links the key image of the wound (here a "burn/scald") to the father and thus to the father's suicide:

> in his dark worsted suit,
> with his face averted
> as if to hide a scald
>
> (p. 5)

The image of the wound is also seen here as a link between the self and nature. The opening lines are descriptive of an intense, intelligent link between Kunitz (as a man dreaming about his boyhood landscape) and the natural world:

> I was fishing in the abandoned reservoir
> back in Quinnapoxet
> where the snapping turtles cruised
> and the bullheads swayed
> in their bower of tree-stumps,
> sleek as eels and pigeon-fat.

The "abandoned reservoir" is a variant of the key image of ponds and has been consistently linked with the father/son legend and with death. Here instead of death we have a wounding that is not fatal:

> One of them gashed my thumb
> with a flick of his razor fin
> when I yanked the barb
> out of his gullet.

This is all precise, fascinating nature description (especially the description of bullheads), but from "The Way Down" on, nature has been masculine in Kunitz' imagination, and it remains for "Quinnapoxet" to make the thematic link between the two most sustaining principles in his life (Nature and Father) through the imagery of wounding and phallic renewal.

When the two parents' ghostly figures approach and hail him, he ignores the mother's reprimand and instead gestures to his father. We might note that here, at the end of the father quest, the father approaches the son, no longer flees—though he still is ashamed of his scald/wound. It is to this scald that the son Kunitz ultimately signals with his own wounded thumb:

> I touched my forehead
> with my swollen thumb

and splayed my fingers out—
in deaf-mute country
the sign for father.

The son's gesture is one of communion: the wound received from his intense, active relationship with nature is now part of his connection to his father. Nature-son-father form a trinity of communion that contains the mystery of wounding and of renewal or rebirth (the phallic, swollen thumb). The "sign" Kunitz gives to his father is a sign of love whose purpose is to heal the rift between them and to transform the father's shame (the wound/averted face) with the power of the son's pride.

The mother remains what she is throughout the work: a human figure possessed of and by a negative complexity of moods centering in resentment, anger, and intransigence. The father on the other hand is part of a masculine principle—a life-force that animates the terrible ambiguities of nature (could the sun's "terrible coals" have caused the father's scald?) and forms the deepest bonds between people. "Quinnapoxet" takes the transcendental phallic energy of the tree of life in "The Knot" and turns it back toward the world: the natural world and the world of human relationships. The legend of being whose highest image in Kunitz is one of phallic renewal and phallic intensity is here shown to have its sources in *this* world and to animate the most important aspects of it.

"Words for the Unknown Makers" (p. 8) is a set of poems anchored to an occasion in the world: an exhibition called "The Flowering of American Folk Art" held at the Whitney Museum in 1974. It is the ideal opportunity for Kunitz to celebrate an art form he has always admired and also to dramatize and illuminate the processes by which an artist creates his or her art.

These are all plain-style poems, characterized by simplicity of diction and an approximation of a speaking voice. Again the complexity of intelligence has been layered below the surface of the story and diction rather than built up above the surface, like the raised embroidery of literary and philosophical allusion. For example, "makers" is the right word, the properly inclusive word, for the variety of folk artists the poem discusses, but it also contains within it the Greek meaning of "poesis": "to make." It also quietly echoes William Dunbar's fifteenth-century "Lament for the Makers" that extols and laments dead English poets of his time, most of them "unknown" to us except through his poem. Both Dunbar's poem and the Greek word take us to the historically primitive and humble origins of art and thus are perfect echoes of a poem about folk art on the occasion of the recognition of its importance and beauty by the culture descended from it. Dunbar's poem looks back to both celebrate and lament, as does the Whitney exhibit and the Kunitz poem.

These "unknown makers" were craftspeople whose work we now recognize as an enormously rich creative outpouring funneled narrowly into the few forms of expression permitted it by a society harsh in its physical conditions and in the limits it imposed on blacks' and women's expression. An interesting contrast is provided by "She Wept, She Railed" with its historically "noble" and doomed women (Catherine, Cressida) versus the patiently enduring, "humble" creators of this poem—"makers" who could be said to have learned the lesson of "The Testing-Tree," or that the heart "lives by breaking." They have learned the wisdom of the journeying self: "it is necessary to go / through dark and deeper dark / and not to turn" rather than the earlier poem's wisdom of the spiraling, ascending/transcending self whose final gesture had its human protagonists look upward to a heaven where "all the constellations shine" as emblems of the "frozen pure" element of the human story. These are unknown makers not saints of suffering; the night is something to be walked through, not the appropriate spot from which to gaze toward a transcendent, static, emblematic world.

Folk art, like poetry, is a constant reminder that when creative expression is censored and confined, it frequently intensifies. (The political equivalent of this cultural phenomenon is seen for Kunitz in Russian poetry under Stalin: how Akhmatova's personal lyrics and figurative language subvert the state that seeks to oppress them.)

Kunitz identifies with his poem's protagonists: an identification that acknowledges a paradoxical sameness and difference. This technique or psychological phenomenon has been with him from the start in his identification with his dead father, but now, it is disciplined by external reality: the historical otherness of the person he identifies with ("To a Slave Named Job") or whom he identifies with his father (Lincoln of "The Lincoln Relics").

The slave of "To a Slave Named Job" is not unlike Kunitz or his biblical namesake; he is the "bearer of a suffering name" (p. 8). He is also the type of the artist of the self who uses his imagination to create a transformed self: a "surrogate / and avatar." The imagination's idealized vision of the questing self is brought out (by "making") into the object world, becomes a "self" that can embody the qualities its maker must suppress:

> aloof and bold
> with his raised foot poised
> for the oppressor's neck.

He is both disguised and straightforward in his presentation of self: the paradox of the art of the dramatized self that Kunitz expressed as "I stand within myself, myself my shield" ("The Guilty Man"). But here, the transformed self occupies an ambiguous public space as a cigar store Indian. Like the Indians,

the slave sculptor has good reason to dream strange dreams, to
cling to his integrity: "The cigars he offers / are not for sale." To
dream a future that revenges his present: "They [the cigars] fit
his hand / as though they were a gun."

The poet has common cause with this stance; he knows he
is a subverter and intruder in the social and economic world.
Kunitz shares the maker's dream of righteous revenge that creates an art which paradoxically destroys and nourishes: "The
triggered poem's no water-pistol toy / But shoots to kill, and is
a source of joy." ("A Choice of Weapons," *This Garland, Danger*).

The second poem, "Sacred to the Memory" (p. 9) takes as
its subject elegaic paintings commissioned by survivors that typically show a gravestone, a willow, and the mourning survivors.
This poem highlights another imaginative possibility of the folk
art subject that Kunitz explores and exploits: the very fact that
these paintings' motifs are limited and stylized creates a tension
between the personal ("Mourn for Polly Botsford, aged thirty-
nine") and the impersonal. More precisely the poem starts completely in the personal, even private world of the family, and
the specific family tragedies of death and mourning:

Mourn for Polly Botsford

Gradually it extends its sympathies outward from the precise
names of the dead to the survivors within the family, to the artist who eternalized this private grief only to succumb himself to
anonymous death, and on outward in concentric rings of sympathy until we are all included in the common fate of mortality.
The poem could be imaged as concentric circles with Polly
Botsford at the center and "all of us" as the outermost ring.

Is this not the precise movement of Kunitz' own imaginative growth? Instead of Polly Botsford, Kunitz typically places his dead father at the private personal center. He moves outward from there, struggling past his mother's stern grief, outward toward that impersonal, universal circle, where all humans are implicated and celebrated in their mortal condition and their longing for something more. The longing for something more makes use of the "gate/door/threshold" key image cluster:

> Mourn, too, for the nameless painter of the scene
> who, like them all, was born to walk a while
> beside the brook whose source is common tears,
> till suddenly it's time to unlatch the narrow gate
> and pass through the church that is not made with walls.

We see here Kunitz' ability to recognize that his personal longings for the unconditional (love, poetry, and eternal life) are akin to those offered by Christian faith, even while he rejects Christian orthodoxy. Or to recognize in himself the impulse to pray even as he repudiates or denies prayer in the line that immediately precedes a prayer's opening invocation:

> I've a long way to go
> Who never learned to pray
>
> O the night is coming on
> ("The Game")

To the extent that religious longing is a longing for the unconditional, Kunitz is in complete harmony with it. The longing itself is authentic; it is the social form he repudiates, just as he repudiates religion's architectural forms: "If I must build a church / Though I do not really want one" ("Revolving Meditation").

Like many of the best poems in this book, "Words for the Unknown Makers" is about the legend of being. Its drama has gone beyond, or, in the poem's process, goes beyond, Kunitz' personal identity. Yet it still has its sources in the personal. These sources can now be clearly articulated and identified.

The central, original mystery is death. Death, not birth, is at the source of Kunitz' poetry. At the very least death and birth are confused and conflated as in the climactic image of "Open the Gates." Death is at the origin, yet, oddly enough, it is not seen at the *end* of the life's journey. That which is at life's end is seen as a threshold ("on the threshold of the last mystery," "King of the River"), a place of transition ("it's time to unlatch the narrow gate / and pass through," "Sacred to the Memory"). Death is imagined as a moment of intensified possibility and a challenge to courage ("no doubt the next chapter / in my book of transformations / is already written. / I am not done with my changes," final lines of "The Layers.").

Death is at the center and source. It is the father's death. Corollaries or analogues of death are a sense of intense personal loss and trauma. Concrete images for this source are "the wound" and its variants that recur throughout the poems. At a more abstract level both "nostalgia" and "house/home" are frequent images of this absence at the source.

This curious phenomenon of Kunitz' imagination that places the mystery of death at the source or beginning is seen clearly in "Sacred to the Memory" where Polly Botsford's death—a private and precise one—*begins* a poem that ends by including all living humans in its story. This is the perfect type of the legend of being. It shows the crucial role of the painter/artist/poet in creating that transition from personal family drama to the story that includes "them all": the legend of being.

The motto of "Girl in the Sampler" (p. 10) ("A Soft Answer Turneth Away Wrath," taken from one of the embroidery samplers in the show) is very appropriate to the child–parent relationship that Kunitz and his mother enacted. The "soft answer" might be "forgive." We can well imagine the girl's mother (" 'Do it right, child!' said her mother,") as Kunitz' stern and rigid mother. But humor, so clearly missing in Kunitz' own relationship with his mother, is present here.

The poem is framed with mottos and an upsurge of ironic humor in the closing motto mocks the "gentle" wisdom of the opening one. Again, this story applies perfectly to its ostensible subject, yet its hidden subject (beleaguered child and stern mother) is paralleled in Kunitz' life. Even as late as *The Layers*, Kunitz feels great ambivalence toward his mother and is quite as capable of endorsing the final resentful motto remark as he is that which counsels forgiveness and docility. But by and large, "Words for the Unknown Makers" is a series of poems whose unambivalent task is to rescue mortals and mortal artists from the "second perishing" ("For The Word Is Flesh") that comes when the living no longer remember the names of the dead and their deeds.

In this sense, "Words for the Unknown Makers," and especially the poem entitled "A Blessing of Women," fuses two primary tasks of Kunitz' imaginative life: to restore names and identities to the nameless dead (of whom his father is the most significant) and to locate and celebrate an affirmative vision of the feminine principle, a principle that he experienced as a blighting force in relation to his boyhood experience of his mother. Kunitz has arrived at the point where a genuine forgiveness of his mother takes place in the surrogate forms of the women in "A Blessing of Women." We see the almost subliminal links between Kunitz' mother and the women in biographical details that echo: Zeruah Higley Guernsey's creation of a beautiful quilt "executed in the ardor of her long pre-nuptial flight, and accomplished in 1835 for her ill-starred wedding day." The "ill-starred" nature of the wedding day is an interpretation emphasizing fatality and echoing his own recurring dream of his mother in a wedding gown ("The Testing-Tree") and the "curious legend" of his parents' relationship. What is by far the most striking feature of "A Blessing of Women" is its vivid recreation and celebration of the lives of the women and the objects they made.

If it is possible for a celebratory feminist poem to be written by a man, then Kunitz has written a superb example of such a poem in "A Blessing of Women." The women are creative, proud, autonomous, energetic. When their lives end tragically, the cause is men: "she [Deborah Goldsmith, itinerant painter] limned in watercolors the likeness of one George Throop, who married her, therewith terminating her travels and leading to her premature decease, at twenty-seven." If we were to contrast the women of "A Blessing of Women" with the protagonist of "She Wept, She Railed," we would immediately notice that the heroic life is now found in the ordinary life. For Kunitz now, all that is necessary to convert life into legend is to simplify the story of the life so that the legendary quality of the life can be revealed after the obscuring details are removed. It is no longer necessary to elevate the central figure, either through the heightened rhetorical language or allusion to such tragic and noble heroines as Judith, Helen, Cressida, and St. Catherine.

Nor is there any sense that the women in "A Blessing of Women" are projections of the poet's self. The women of "A Blessing of Women" represent a new possibility for Kunitz. They are fully realized women who are not derived either from his mother or from the figure of the beloved. Yet they partake of the admiration Kunitz feels for the mother's character and deeds and the affection he feels for the beloved. They are the fullest positive evocation of what Kunitz meant when he addressed his daughter:

> Your nation gives me joy
> as it has always given.

If I could have my choice
on the way to exile
I think I'd rather sleep forever
than wake up cold
in a country without women.
("A Journal for My Daughter")

Here Kunitz is able to do what he must do in order to truly evoke and celebrate his heroines: step aside, remove himself from the story except as chronicler and evoker:

BLESS THEM AND GREET THEM as they pass from their long obscurity, through the gate that separates us from our history, a moving rainbow-cloud of witnesses in a rising hubbub, jubilantly turning to greet one another, this tumult of sisters. (p. 14)

"The Catch" makes use of the dragonfly, an extremely evocative object for Kunitz. The insect moves like thought: it is thing become thought: "less image than thought / and the thought come alive." It's motion in air is that of the poet's mind in a poem, or the poet's mind as a process that, when captured in language, becomes "a prize": the poem itself. "The Catch" appears, from its subject, to be related to "The Dragonfly" but its actual echo is of "The Reckoning" where an intimate dialogue, a question from the other, a third object (dragonfly/transformed heart) and the word "prize" are all elements of a drama. "The Reckoning" was specifically about a failure of the lived life and how that can nevertheless be transformed into an enduring object of art. The earlier poem was tragic and guilty; its third thing (the heart) was so intimately a part of the self (heart) that magic was called upon to establish its otherness. Its tone was almost claustrophobic.

"The Catch" by contrast locates its third thing in objective nature: the dragonfly—something which is other than human and yet capable of being imaginatively linked to human concerns. The speaker can now refer to a natural process by which the third thing, the poem, is brought into connection with human affairs:

> Swoosh went the net
> with a practiced hand.
>   (p. 15)

The gesture is natural yet the result of long practice; not the mysterious and tragical metamorphosis of "The Reckoning." The relationship of the artist's self to the poem is also far less proprietary:

> This prize belongs to no one.

Yet when the poem enters its final lines, it becomes clear that the human condition is still seen as fraught with risk. The last eight lines enact a drama where the repetition of words and phrases ("look," "all," and "all your life") create an undercurrent of meaning that is increasingly ominous:

> "Da-da, may I look too?"
> You may look, child,
> all you want.
> This prize belongs to no one.
> But you will pay all
> your life for the privilege,
> all your life.

The price of desire ("All you want") is high ("all your life") and, as the second repetition of the phrase in the final line reveals: the nature of the payment is not merely intensive (all) but extensive: "all your life." Here is a quiet, deep paradox of late

Kunitz, a paradox rooted in the human condition—the price of delight and desire is mortality.

"The Lincoln Relics" is among the most successful and convincing of Kunitz' political poems because it fuses both the personal and the political. In a less successful poem, like "The Mound Builders," we encounter earnest, moral intelligence, but not the personal connection between the poet and his theme that would be necessary to move us. In "Around Pastor Bonhoeffer"—although the poem is at a complete remove from the poet, we recognize in the pastor's character the individual values and experiences Kunitz' poems have espoused: moral courage, a noble separateness, intense dedication to an ideal, the process of questing itself. In "The Lincoln Relics" Kunitz' personal involvement is two-fold. His most obvious involvement is as a character in the drama of sections 1, 3, and 4. But the deeper source of his involvement, what makes it possible for him to be a character in the poem, is that Lincoln is an incarnated Spirit Father. One theme of the poem is a last flowering of the father-son legend.

The presence of the father-son legend in the poem does not reduce the poem; Lincoln is not a father surrogate. "The Lincoln Relics" bears the same relation to the father-son legend as "A Blessing of Women" bears to the mother/beloved legend. The legend has gone beyond its personal, psychological sources. The poet's self and identity are now sufficiently secure so that the creation of the identity through the encounter is no longer the poem's central drama. The son/self is now the perspective from which to explore deeper, impersonal themes present in the legends.

Father Spirit becomes here an "ideal," that which (potentially) incarnates a kind of human perfection (toward which one might questingly aspire) and a moral perfection that Kunitz has consistently called "noble." This idealizing was present in "Vita Nuova" where it called on the poet to leave the wrangling social world and embark on an ennobling quest. At that time, such a quest was also a quest for a kind of immortality ("on the quiet lanes of my eternal kind"). In early Kunitz, Platonic Kunitz, the human condition was tainted with mortality and one of the major enterprizes was to rescue the father from decay and dissolution and establish him beyond and above time as an ideal principle. What the later Kunitz poem does with this idealized father figure is to reconcile mortality and nobility—to locate the legend in the life. Two key words, "dissolving" and "noble" fuse in a description of Lincoln's "relics":

> these relics on display—
> watchfob and ivory pocket knife,
> a handkerchief of Irish linen,
> a button severed from his sleeve—
> make a noble, dissolving music
> out of homely fife and drum,
> and that's miraculous.
>   (p. 22, ll. 11–17)

"Dissolving" is a verb linked to early Kunitz' obsession with the dead father and decay:

> O ruined father dead, long sweetly rotten
> Under the dial, the time-dissolving urn,
> Beware a second perishing, forgotten . . .
>   ("For the Word Is Flesh")

In "The Lincoln Relics" "dissolving" is allowed to have its full resonance of impermanence without contradiction, yet Kunitz is able to *affirm* it and yoke it to "noble." When he sets Lincoln

against the Neapolitan saint, he is repudiating his earlier transcendental impulses—his impulses to reject this world in favor
of an ideal world beyond time and death. Now he sees the transcendent principle (the Spirit Father) incarnated in this world
and capable of *transforming* this world, capable of making a
"*noble*, dissolving music / out of *homely* fife and drum" (my italics).

The entire movement of the father legend in Kunitz has been
from the Platonic ideal back down toward earth. As the father
approaches earth ("For the Word Is Flesh"; "Father and Son"),
it becomes clear that death and decay are the terrifying mysteries that the son must face if he wishes to bring the father down
into this world. In "The Way Down" he locates the father not
on the earth, but *in* the earth—and yet the earth is not the confining grave, because the father has become transformed from
biological father to father-spirit to "magician." As magician and
nature spirit he makes his way to the surface, becomes the to-
temic testing-tree. But he also becomes humanized: he is the
"long-lipped stranger" of "The Portrait." When, in "Three Floors,"
the boy discovers "a red Masonic hat / and a walking stick" he
has discovered "relics" of an actual father who still has magical
powers ("that night / I saw my father flying"). Similar relics bring
us to the final version of the impersonal, humanized yet magical
Spirit Father of Lincoln. In section 3, the poet has a vision of
Lincoln very similar to that of "Three Floors":

> In the Great Hall of the Library,
> as in a glass aquarium,
> Abe Lincoln is swimming around
> (ll. 48–50)

The father figure is no longer a static, Platonic ideal, but an
incarnation of the *transformative* principle. As Lincoln, he has
the power to transform our social selves:

> His innocence was to trust
> the better angels of our nature
> (ll. 18–19)

We, as citizens, had aspects of the ideal in our nature, which could potentially respond to Lincoln, could be further lifted up or transformed by him. But, by incarnating his father-principle, Kunitz has brought him into the world of mortality and tragedy. Lincoln is a tragic father: his transformative, ennobling powers are not a match for the twin betrayals: of the human condition itself (mortality) and the social, political world (assassination). Lincoln is the ideal that we must betray. As such, he wears the ultimate emblem of the father—the wound:

> Has no one told you
> how the slow blood leaks
> from your secret wound?
> (ll. 79–81)

Section 1, by contrasting Kunitz' response to the saint's relics with those of Lincoln, establishes that the speaker is neither naive nor gullible ("Saint's bones are only bones / to me"). Dramatically, it establishes him as a skeptic and thus, when he reveals his intense, idealizing admiration of Lincoln, we are more prone to entertain his assertions.

Section 2 shifts the strategy of the story: the poet is no longer a character and the impersonal, inclusive pronoun "our" has taken his place ("His innocence was to trust / the better angels of our nature"). As with the final, extraordinary line of "Around Pastor Bonhoeffer," the image of the "brotherhood of men" or even the family of man has taken over. In lines in "The Lincoln Relics" like:

> even when the Union cracked
> and furious blood
> ran north and south
> (ll. 20–22)

the poem points simultaneously toward Lincoln's image of "a house divided against itself" and Kunitz' personal sources and associations with family strife:

> In the crack
> of a divided house
> grew the resentment-weed.
> It has white inconspicuous flowers.
> ("Journal for My Daughter")

Kunitz has successfully subsumed the personal in the collective, the "I" in the "we," without sacrificing the links that give the poem's publicness a necessary urgency.

Section 2 recapitulates in a few lines the breaking apart and healing of the country:

> furious blood
> ran north and south
> along the lines of pillage.
> Secession grieved him
> like the falling-out of brothers.
> After Appomattox he laid
> the white flower of forgiving
> on Lee's crisp sword.
> (ll. 21–28)

It is significant that the healing word "forgive" is that which transformed the personal crises of Kunitz' work ("The Magic Curtain"), and that the white flower is a reversal of the resent-

ment-weed in Kunitz' other great poem of the need for forgiveness in families.

In the next line there is a strong implication that leaders
and spiritual guides have a role that, if noble, is circumscribed:
"What was there left for him to do?" Like the play he watches,
Lincoln's life is scripted and cued: "It was time for him now."
We might think of Yeats' "Lapis Lazuli," where Lear and Cor-
delia strut upon the stage of life: characters who, "if worthy their
prominent part in the play/ Do not break up their lines to weep"
but rather transcend their human identities and look upon impending tragedy with "gay" eyes. Yeats' characters exhibit a tragic
gaiety in the face of impending disaster ("if nothing drastic is
done/ Aeroplane and Zeppelin will come out,/ Pitch like King
Billy bomb-balls in/ Until the town lie beaten flat"). A major
distinction is that Kunitz insists on Lincoln's paradoxical nature
as a noble figure and a humble figure—in Kunitz' terms the legend is within the life now and within the simple physical objects
that are named and celebrated:

> his gold-rimmed spectacles,
> the pair with the sliding temples
> mended with a loop of string
> (ll. 41–43)

Yeats' heroic ideal—compacted entirely of character—was com-
patible with Kunitz' early work. But later Kunitz is far more
reconciled to this world and to its objects. Character must com-
pound with the things of this world.

Indeed, the role of *things*, of humble objects, is central to
the theme and movement of "the Lincoln Relics." In section 1,
the things listed are "relics on display" and capable of producing
"miracles." In section 2, things (the contents of his wallet, his
spectacles, the play, the flower and sword) play as large a role

as people. Perhaps these things are Blake's "minute particulars" that make the spiritual and imaginative world vivid, but they are more than that. As we see in the vision of section 3, "things" are what anchor us in this world:

> He [Lincoln] is slipping away from us
> into his legend and his fame,
> having relinquished, piece by piece,
> what rocked to his angular stride,
> partook of his man-smell,
> shared the intimacy of his needs.
>
> (ll. 63–68)

For the first time in Kunitz' work, the word "legend" is ambiguous. Lincoln must be rescued from his "legend and fame," brought back to his sensuous existence, his physical embodiment of human goodness. Lincoln is a ghost-father who must be rescued—*he* is in danger: the opening vision of him swimming "as in a glass aquarium" makes him the logical victim of the "piranhas darting / between the rose-veined columns, / avid to strip the flesh / from the Republic's bones." Lincoln is ideal (in this case, the Republic) incarnated; he is "flesh and bones" (not simply the "bones" of the saint in section 1). We turn to him in anguish in our time of crisis, precisely because he *is* human and personal and yet, as incarnation of the Republic, an ideal capable of transforming us toward "our better nature."

The Republic is already transformed: now it is the Empire, and the Washington of Nixon and the Vietnam War is, like Rome, an "Imperial City." If this is so, then the battle is lost; the flesh has already been stripped from the Republic's bones and Lincoln, "lighter at each turn, / giddy with loss," must rise up hopelessly above us into his legend. In terms of the public context that the first three sections have established and explored, the poem seems destined to defeat and despair. The respectful

address of the last 12 lines of section 3 ("Mr. President") ends
by completing the implications of the last image of section 2
("waving a smoking pistol"):

> Has no one told you
> how the blood leaks
> from your secret wound?
> (ll. 79–81)

The poem renews itself in section 4 by returning to an intensely personal perspective. The opening lines of the section
are of paradoxical renewal: "To be old and to be young / again,"
and mark the beginning of a revery in which Kunitz returns to
an earlier time in his own life:

> inglorious private
> in the kitchens of the war
> that winter of blackout,
> walking by the Potomac
> in melancholy khaki,
> searching for the prairie star,
> westward scanning the horizon
> for its eloquent and magnanimous light,
> yearning to be touched by its fire
> (ll. 83–91)

Kunitz has returned in reverie to his own experiences in the
Second World War Washington. The poem is structured on a
layering of histories: public and personal, and the two mingling
as here when the syntax and imagery ("searching for the prairie
star / westward scanning the horizon") echo Whitman's style and
his elegaic addresses to Lincoln. The "prairie star" has the power
to renew. The mortality that was extolled when seen in the
humble objects in Lincoln's pockets is now confronted by Kunitz as his own mortality:

> yearning to be touched by its fire:
> to be touched again, with the years
> swirling at my feet, faces
> blowing in the wind
> around me where I stand,
> withered, in the Great Hall.
>
> (ll. 91–96)

It is his own mortality and his own unquenchable yearning to be transformed. The section moves from the present ("To be old") to the past ("and to be young again") through wish or memory; and then up to the present again. It moves also from the personal and mundane ("inglorious private"; "melancholy khaki") to the majestic, impersonal desolation of its final five lines.

Again, the poem threatens to end facing its insoluble dilemma: mortality. It is mortality that has claimed the Spirit Father Lincoln—both his life (assassination) and his spirit as it lives in the Republic (the piranha of section 3). The Spirit Father, like Kunitz' father, has undergone a "second perishing." In section 4 the Spirit Father exists only as "prairie star" and the son/speaker acknowledges his own mortality and the essential powerlessness of his yearning for renewal. The momentum of language that characterized section 4—all the verbs, all process (walking, searching, scanning, yearning, swirling, blowing)—is brought to a sombre halt by the single word "withered."

Again, the poem that so sought miracle, transformation, and renewal, shifts drastically and unexpectedly in its final section to seek its fulfillment in another place:

> He steps out from the crowd
> with his rawboned, warty look,
> a gangling fellow in jeans
> next to a plum-coloured sari,
> and just as suddenly he's gone.
>
> (ll. 97–101)

We have a vignette: a glimpse toward the future, toward a further generation—what (if section 4 is a "son" of the Lincoln Spirit Father) could be called the grandson generation. And yet this future contains the past: the figure of the youth physically resembles Lincoln, and *reincarnation* becomes the "miraculous" principle that can renew both the spirit and the flesh—the whole being of Lincoln. The old poet in section 4 yearned for rebirth, but it is a new birth that creates the poem's final affirmation. The "melancholy khaki" and the "buried" image of the old poet as a tree in section 4 is renewed and bears fruit in the "plum-colored sari" of section 5. It is only a glimpse of hope, or in the larger political terms the poem also encompasses, a glimmer of hope spied in the youthful protestors.

Especially in its final section, "The Lincoln Relics" echoes against "Journal for My Daughter"—where youthful demonstrators of his daughter's generation are identified with and even envied for their youth and exuberance. We can easily enough grasp the implications of the first five lines of the final section, can see how aptly their implication of Lincoln's reincarnation fulfills the "spirit, flesh, and bones" of the preceding sections. But the final two lines are cryptic, mysterious—hint, but don't say. In "Journal for My Daughter" Kunitz claimed kinship with the young radicals but said "I am there not there, / ever uneasy in a crowd." In these final two lines perhaps Kunitz is himself reincarnated, allows himself to be there and not there:

> But there's that other one
> who's tall and lonely.
> (ll. 102–3)

Kunitz' poetry has always been based on two beliefs: that what imagination reveals to be true is true, and that language in poetry is magical, that is the word *is* the object and language is creative of reality (in this case, the higher reality of imagination). In such earlier poems as "Revolving Meditation," these beliefs were an overt part of the poem's drama, albeit an abstract part:

> Imagination cries
> That in the grand accountancy
> What happens to us is false;
> Imagination makes,
> Out of what stuff it can,
> An action fit
> For a more heroic stage
> Than body ever walked on.

By the time of "The Testing-Tree" this hierarchical contrast of "heroic" to "body" is no longer the case.

The metaphysics of heroism is bodied forth in the mundane physical world of a Worcester meadow or the downtown Bijou. Imagination—that was originally responsible for elevating the poem, for "converting life into legend," now has a different task— to locate the visionary world within the world of ordinary reality. In order to incarnate the visionary without seeming stylistically discordant Kunitz must adopt a matter-of-fact tone toward the magical, a style like that of "The Knot" where the ordinary and supernatural are identical. The metaphysical dramas that reveal the deepest levels of life now can take place in a bedroom rather than "within the city of the burning cloud" ("Open the Gates"). The spoken voice in "The Quarrel" has sufficient authority, the authority of understatement, to subsume the magical in the mundane and establish both realms as equally true and capable of revealing reality:

> The word I spoke in anger
> weighs less than a parsley seed,

but a road runs through it
that leads to my grave,
that bought-and-paid for lot
on a salt-sprayed hill in Truro
where the scrub pines
overlook the bay.
Half-way I'm dead enough,
strayed from my own nature
and my fierce hold on life.

(p. 30)

The opening line of "The Quarrel" is a gesture or event from the real world that fuses with and flows into the following lines and their imagery from a visionary biblical world (the parables of the mustard seed and the camel through the needle's eye conflated) and then returns again effortlessly to a precisely described landscape in the world. Nor could any lines illustrate better than the first three how "magically" Kunitz regards language; a "word" has an absolute, if paradoxical, physical existence: it has weight and dimension: a word *is* a thing—a magical thing.

In saying that Kunitz' late style is less rhetorical, more a spoken voice, I am not saying its music has disappeared. The music of "The Quarrel" involves a thread of assonance and internal rhymes that winds through the first eleven lines (weighs, grave, paid, sprayed, bay, half-way, strayed) to be brought to an abrupt halt as the sentence completes itself:

and my fierce hold on life.

The second sentence (three lines) is dense with long "i" sounds and syntactical balances:

If I could cry, I'd cry
but I'm too old to be
anybody's child.

Long "o" sounds are woven through the first two sentences (spoke, road, Truro, overlook, own, hold, old). The final four lines are a question that structures its music on alliteration (whom, hiss, harsh) played against a great variety of vowel and consonant sounds that create a complexity of both pitch and cadence.

"The Quarrel," of course, is a "love poem." By the time of *The Layers*, it is accurate to say that the love poems have moved past the mother/beloved legend, at least as far as two distinct figures go. What we now have as the dramatic structure of "The Quarrel" is two words rather than two characters. The word spoken in anger is derived from the mother. The word "Liebchen" is derived from the beloved, and specifically from Frieda of "The Magic Curtain." The two contrary states are no longer isolated in two figures (the mother and beloved) who enact their drama with the son-lover. Now, Kunitz has taken both words and both emotions (wrath and tenderness) into himself so that the "irregular" flame is a physical equivalent of the uneasy duality of his love. In the drama of language that is the poem, "Liebchen" does not cancel out the word spoken in anger (though the penitent speaker wishes it could) and he must acknowledge the "harsh, irregular flame" as the final reality.

The beloved has been attained; the adult intimate relationship which was the goal of the beloved quest is clearly in evidence in such poems as "Indian Summer at Land's End," "Route Six," and "The Quarrel." But the price of this attainment has been a deepening psychological drama: complexities of ambivalence. In the long journey of the life's work by which Kunitz makes his way back toward the world, the solipsistic purity of the "single beam of all my life intense" ("Vita Nuova") has become "the hiss of love, / that harsh, irregular flame." The father and mother—who once seemed to embody such opposite and unreconcilable attitudes and principles—are at last, in "The Unquiet Ones," seen to be "dark emissaries / of the two-faced god."

One of the odd consequences of the persistence of the family drama in Kunitz' work is that he remains a "son" in imagination throughout his long life. "The Unquiet Ones" rings new changes on that old phenomenon: the speaker is still a son (though in his sixties or seventies), but his parents are infants:

> Father and mother lie
> in their neglected cribs.
> (p. 31)

But as the next lines reveal these cribs are also graves. The parents are "obscure as moles / unvisited" (lines 5–6). For all its quiet, matter-of-factness, the imagination at work here is macabre. The dead parents have a subterranean life after death:

> When I put out the light
> I hear them stir, dissatisfied,
> in their separate places,
> in death as in life
> remote from each other,
> having no conversation
> except in the common ground
> of their son's mind.

When the light goes out, the darkened space of the room blends with the interior of the poet's mind, expanded to become a suitable meeting place for the estranged ghosts. This interior space is mysterious and complex. It is physical: its "common ground" is the earth where graves are. The "mind" becomes a cave—an underground chamber, as if it was a hollow skull hugely expanded and half-filled with dirt—a suitably primitive place for an encounter between two ghosts. The dead are alive; the living (son's mind) has become a static, inanimate space. The

psychic and physical space of the poem becomes progressively
more primitive:

> They slip through narrow crevices
> and, suddenly blown tall,
> glide into my cave of phantoms,
> unwelcome guests, but not
> unloved, dark emissaries
> of the two-faced god.

Prior to the strife of the two who engendered him, Kunitz
finally discovers a primordial unity: the two-faced god.

The imagistic and dramatic simplicity of this discovery must
be expanded to do justice to the poem's workings. Kunitz is a
poet one of whose main themes is personal identity: how the
son grows up through the family dynamic of mother–father–son.
At a more impersonal level, his later work frequently explores
the legend of being: how the self experiences the human condition. The poem begins in disorder and estrangement: "Years
ago I lost / both my parents' addresses." It ends in a fusion of
two into one: the two-faced god, Janus. It begins with a son; it
ends by invoking a god. The border between life and death is
crossed casually, as if it had no psychic validity or relevance.

How do such vast movements between beginning and end
occur? The parents are the key—the bridge. They are two who,
extending forward in time, fused to become one in a child—the
son, Kunitz. Or we could say that each of them contributed a
part of him- or herself to create the new unity of their son, who
reconciles their separateness in the unity of his body. But this
son's mind cracks: these are the "narrow crevices" through which
great disunity and strife: his warring parents. Psychologically, the
son's mind cracks: there are the "narrow crevices" through which
the parents' spirits enter. To reconcile these disunities, to cope

with the cracks has been one of Kunitz' imaginative goals since his earliest work:

> If in my sleep
>
> The ape, the serpent, and the fox I find
> Shut with my soul in fortune's writhing sack,
> I tame them with the sections of my mind
> And teach my mind to love its thoughtless crack.
>
> ("Beyond Reason")

In "The Unquiet Ones" the son's unity-aware-of-its-disunity seeks out origins again: behind the strife that his parents enacted and symbolized there must be a primal unity. He discovers this unity, not in a cosmology, but in the mysterious god Janus: a god whose form is physical and human. The reconciled unity of the son reaches across and *through* (they are only emissaries) the parents' strife to the deep, primordial reconciliation of two-in-one that Janus represents.

Janus is a most curious god. Of Italian origin, he has no divine counterpart among the Greeks. Seyffert, in his *Dictionary of Classical Antiquities*, describes him as follows:

> Even the ancients were by no means clear as to his special significance; he was, however, regarded as one of the oldest, holiest, and most exalted of gods . . . At every sacrifice, he was remembered first; in every prayer he was the first invoked, being mentioned even before Jupiter. In the songs of the Salii he was called the good creator, and the god of gods.
>
> In Rome all doors and covered passages were suggestive of his name.[1]

For Kunitz, poet of gates and thresholds, there could be no more appropriate god to preside over the poem.

1. Oskar Seyffert, *Dictionary of Classical Antiquities* (New York: Meridian, 1956).

One further point concerning Janus: he is a god, both of whose faces are male. For Kunitz, the power that unifies and reconciles opposites must be masculine. It is Spirit; it is the father-principle writ large and projected *back* to the most primordial or origins, or outward onto Nature.

The guests are "unwelcome" but not "unloved." On the psychological level, the poem's truth is of emotional contradiction lived with, of the vital paradox we call ambivalence. His affirmation is hesitant, couched in a double negative: "not/unloved." Nevertheless, "The Unquiet Ones" represents the most inclusive dramatic resolution of identity Kunitz achieves. Unlike most of his imaginative solutions, from "Vita Nuova" to "Quinnapoxet," here he does not reject or ignore the mother in his struggle to conclude the poem with a gesture that affirms his identity. Here he is able to give equal weight to the mother and to the father. (One reason he can do this is because the poem, like the first three sections of "The Testing-Tree," seeks an origin of identity that is primordial and prepersonal: a source of identity that precedes the psychological source of identity in the family dynamic of father–mother–son.)

The final poem in *The Layers* (the title poem) is a companion poem to "The Knot." These two poems and "King of the River" are Kunitz' ultimate poems of the legend of being. In these three poems the legend of being *is* the drama and subject of the whole poem. Not, as in its earlier appearances, merely the final transcendent gesture of a poem dominated by one of the other, more personal legends.

"The Layers" is a poem of great severity of diction and physical detail. If "The Knot" presented us with an *intensive* concentration of sensuous detail in its central image ("obstinate bud, / sticky with life, / mad for the rain again"), then the setting of "The Layers" is *extensive* and bare of detail: a stark, late

autumn or winter vista as opposed to the early spring green-
house enclosure of "The Knot." The opening lines of the poem
establish its theme as the legend of being and, within that legend, the subcategory of the journeying self:

> I have walked through many lives,
> some of them my own,
> and I am not who I was,
> though some principle of being
> abides, from which I struggle
> not to stray.
>
> (p. 35)

In some sense "The Layers" is a culmination of Kunitz'
technique of using words and phrases that occur in other poems
as a way of echoing and deepening a theme. The verb "stray"
occurs in "The Quarrel"—where we see the dire consequences
of betraying the central principle of love:

> Half-way I'm dead enough,
> strayed from my own nature
> and my fierce hold on life.

The verb "abides" echoes a key passage in "King of the River":

> nothing
> at all abides,
> but nostalgia and desire

It is by now clear that "nostalgia and desire" are themselves quite
possibly Kunitz' "principle of being" and his "own nature" from
which he struggles not to stray.

When Kunitz writes a poem of the legend of being, his dramatic agent will be either the spiraling self or the journeying
self. Interestingly, it is possible for Kunitz to write a poem that

is almost purely based on the spiraling self (i.e., "The Knot" or "Revolving Meditation"), but when he writes a poem dominated by the journeying self, there is always some point in the poem where the power of the spiral is also acknowledged. In "King of the River" the spiral manifests itself in the swirling assertions and negations that open each stanza ("If the heart were pure enough / but it is not pure") and culminate in the poem's final paradox, and also in the vertical image of the ladder whose two ways are to heaven and hell (both destinations outside time and thus linked to the transcendent, spiraling self). In "The Layers," the power of the spiral is acknowledged in the vertical smoke and the movement of the angels:

> I see
> . . . .
>   the slow fires trailing
> from the abandoned camp-sites,
> over which scavenger angels
> wheel on heavy wings.

The image of the wheeling angels and the campfires tells *its* truth (closely related to that of the bleeding knot): that we cannot escape our past and that it constantly reasserts its primal power through key images. The image appears to be one of desolation, but it contains positive aspects of the spiral also: the angel can be seen as a vertical elevation on the scale of being (is the winged self an angel at the end of "The Knot?")—an escape from the human condition and its limits, and the adjective "scavenger" indicates that something of value, something nourishing to the spirit can be found by circling above a fixed point and seeking there.

Likewise the journeying self discloses *its* truth: that we move through time, and thus we have a beginning and implicitly an end. The positive aspects that the journey metaphor emphasizes are process and change, survival through time and the moral qualities it calls for: courage and desire, affirmation in the face of negation.

Lines 7 through 10:

> When I look behind,
> as I am compelled to look
> before I can gather strength
> to proceed on my journey.

echo crucial lines from "Revolving Meditation ("Preferring to hear, as I / am forced to hear") that show the marriage of *fate* and *will* so central to Kunitz' consciousness and work. The self cannot escape the power of the past, and must acknowledge its own backward longing (nostalgia) or the autonomous, haunting power of past trauma that reasserts itself (the knot/wound). Such a periodic weakness of the will, a longing for the lost house, is fated. When this inevitable turning back fuses with the self's power of will it is capable of transforming the circumstance from one that undermines the self to one that nourishes the self and gives it "strength to proceed on [its] journey." "The Approach to Thebes" presented an earlier form of this marriage of fate and will and of its transformative power in terms of the mother/beloved legend. In "The Layers," the journey is far closer to its end than it was in "The Approach to Thebes" and the crises it faces are different:

> Oh, I have made myself a tribe
> out of my true affections,
> and my tribe is scattered!
> How shall the heart be reconciled
> to its feast of losses?
> In a rising wind
> the manic dust of my friends,
> those who fell along the way,
> bitterly stings my face.

> Yet I turn, I turn,
> exulting somewhat,
> with my will intact to go
> wherever I need to go,
> and every stone on the road
> precious to me.

If there can be such a thing as an anguish that is crystalline, a poignancy stripped of all ornament, direct and absolute, then it is present in these lines where the art of the dramatic lyric is brought to bear with a pure simplicity on the deepest mysteries of love, loss, and survival.

It is possible to "exult somewhat" in spite of the deepest losses, to keep one's "fierce hold on life," but it is no longer possible to "dance for the joy of surviving."

In the next lines the imagery of desolation reasserts itself as the speaker returns in memory to the nadir of being, the dark night of the soul. This passage, by its imagery ("I roamed through wreckage") is linked to the earlier passage of scavenger angels and abandoned campsites and thus to the spiraling self: the self compelled by the gravitational power of past trauma. This version of the spiraling self is at first more negating than nourishing, more scavenger than angel, but out of this deepest darkness comes illumination, revelation, affirmation:

> In my darkest night,
> when the moon was covered
> and I roamed through the wreckage,
> a nimbus-clouded voice
> directed me:
> "Live in the layers,
> not on the litter."

The voice provides Kunitz with his ultimate motto or proverb: the one that will sustain him throughout his journey and that even provides him with a major aspect of his late style: the layering of language, the spare style whose riches of meaning are archeological. Again the poem (or the voice) discloses the potential wisdom of the spiral self. Presumably the angels of line 15 were in a *descending* spiral in order to scavenge. The speaker of line 34, who roams through wreckage and litter, is a scavenger at ground level. The voice says: "Go deeper." The spiral has simply not descended far enough, and in order to find what is nourishing, the speaker must go below the surface. When the poem (in ll. 32–38) seems to arrive at the final wisdom of the spiraling self, it concerns going beneath the surface of things— it discovers that, as Heraclitus says, "the way down is the way up." That one can "live" in the layers—below the surface—is a paradox that seeks to overcome the human condition of mortality by verbally locating life in something very like a grave.

In the next lines, the poem returns to the present and to the image of a book. The book is an analogous image to that of the journey: it has its beginnings and its end. And yet, this image of the book, which has so much implicit ending in it, can be transformed. Like "the layers" which might descend to infinite depths of meaning on their vertical scale, the "book" might extend infinitely in its own direction. Chapters are only geological layers turned 90°—from an intensive vertical scale to an extensive, horizontal scale that accomodates time, or they are if you hint slyly at infinity or continuity as Kunitz does when he says "no doubt the *next* chapter / in my book" (my italics). This is the kind of statement (and poem) that must be measured against the human life span to gain its true resonance. This is the great poetry of old age that Yeats wrote and that few others have written.

"The Layers" reconciles the two primary processes of the spiraling self and the journeying self. If we regard personal death as the great negation, it might be possible to say that the journeying self is the grander conception in that it acknowledges the end and moves toward it (as indeed it must). The poem of the journeying self can contain images of the spiral self; the converse is not true. In this light the transcendence of the spiraling self is seen as a partial truth. If the imaginative solution provided to and by the spiraling self is transcendence, then the imaginative solution provided to *or* by the journeying self is "transformation":

> Though I lack the art
> to decipher it,
> no doubt the next chapter
> in my book of transformations
> is already written.
> I am not done with my changes.

The implicit end (personal death) is itself transformed. The essential unknowableness of what comes after life is affirmed: we are "on the threshold / of the last mystery" ("King of the River"). The image of chapters, of the "next" chapter, is an open-ended gesture. We understand what all the gestures of going on and looking backward, of desire and nostalgia, were all about: the gathering of strength in order to give the self over to the "last mystery" of the human condition. The self at this point is simultaneously modest ("I lack the art"; nor has the self written the book of its own transformations) and yet capable of a final, quiet, assertive affirmation. The final word, "changes," is a noun derived from a verb: in itself it reconciles being and becoming.

Index